In Defense of Animals

In Defense of Animals

The Second Wave

Edited by Peter Singer

Blackwell
Publishing

BLACKWELL PUBLISHING
350 Main Street, Malden, MA 02148-5020, USA
9600 Garsington Road, Oxford OX4 2DQ, UK
550 Swanston Street, Carlton, Victoria 3053, Australia

First published 2006 by Blackwell Publishing Ltd

7   2010

Library of Congress Cataloging-in-Publication Data

In defense of animals : the second wave / edited by Peter Singer.
     p. cm.
Includes bibliographical references and index.
ISBN 978-1-4051-1940-5 (hard cover : alk. paper)—ISBN 978-1-4051-1941-2 (pbk. : alk. paper)
1. Animal welfare—Moral and ethical aspects. 2. Animal rights movement.
I. Singer, Peter, 1946–

HV4711.I6 2006
179'.3—dc22

                                                         2005009479

A catalogue record for this title is available from the British Library.

Set in 10.5/13pt Dante
by Graphicraft Ltd, Hong Kong
Printed and bound in Singapore
by Fabulous Printers Pte Ltd

The publisher's policy is to use permanent paper from mills that operate a sustainable
forestry policy, and which has been manufactured from pulp processed using acid-free and
elementary chlorine-free practices. Furthermore, the publisher ensures that the text paper
and cover board used have met acceptable environmental accreditation standards.

For further information on
Blackwell Publishing, visit our website:
www.blackwellpublishing.com

Contents

Contents

Notes on Contributors

Matt Ball is co-founder of Vegan Outreach, a U.S.-based organization on the cutting edge of animal advocacy since 1991. An engineer by training, he was a Department of Energy Global Change Fellow and a Research Associate in the Biology Department at the University of Pittsburgh before working full-time for Vegan Outreach. He met his wife, Anne Green, while head of Students for Animal Liberation at the University of Illinois, Urbana-Champaign. They currently live in Pittsburgh with their daughter, Ellen, one of the top leafleters for the Vegan Outreach Adopt a College program.

Martin Balluch was born in Vienna, Austria, where he studied mathematics and physics. He worked for twelve years as a research associate and lecturer at the Universities of Vienna, Austria, Heidelberg, Germany, and Cambridge, UK. He has been active for animal rights in Austria and other countries since 1985. In 1997, he dropped out of his academic career and has been a full-time activist in the Austrian animal rights movement since then. He co-founded the Austrian Vegan Society in 1999, and since 2002 has been president of the Austrian Association Against Animal Factories.

Paola Cavalieri, who lives in Milan, Italy, is the editor of the international philosophy journal *Etica & Animali*. She is the author of *The Animal Question* and the co-editor, with Peter Singer, of *The Great Ape Project*.

Marian Stamp Dawkins is Professor of Animal Behaviour at the University of Oxford and Fellow in Biological Sciences at Somerville College. She is the author of *Animal Suffering: The Science of Animal Welfare*, *Through Our Eyes Only? The Search for Animal Consciousness*, *Unravelling Animal Behaviour*, and, with Aubrey Manning, *An Introduction to Animal Behaviour*.

Karen Dawn has worked as a researcher and writer for various Australian publications and on ABC's *7:30 Report*. She has written for *The Los Angeles Times* and *The Guardian*, and is a contributor to *Terrorists or Freedom Fighters*, an anthology edited by Steve Best and Anthony Nocella. Her media monitoring service, DawnWatch.com, helps activists encourage animal-friendly coverage. Dawn hosts and co-produces the recurring series *Watchdog*, on Los Angeles' KPFK radio.

David DeGrazia is Professor of Philosophy at George Washington University in Washington, D.C. He is the author of *Taking Animals Seriously: Mental Life and Moral Status*, *Animal Rights: A Very Short Introduction*, and *Human Identity and Bioethics*. With Thomas Mappes, he has coedited *Biomedical Ethics* in its fourth and subsequent editions. DeGrazia's articles have appeared in such journals as *Philosophy and Public Affairs*, *Bioethics*, and *The Hastings Center Report*.

Clare Druce co-founded the pressure group Chickens' Lib (now the Farm Animal Welfare Network) in the early 1970s, to oppose the battery system for laying hens. Since then, she has campaigned against a range of restrictive and abusive forms of animal husbandry. Her book *Minny's Dream*, an adventure story for children that highlights the deprivation of hens imprisoned in cages, was published in 2004.

Mary Finelli is a farmed animal advocacy consultant with a degree in animal science. She has worked for numerous animal protection organizations since 1986, and initiated and wrote *Farmed Animal Watch*, a weekly news digest, from 2001 to 2004.

Bruce Friedrich joined People for the Ethical Treatment of Animals (PETA) in 1996, and is the director of their vegetarian and farmed animal campaigns. Before joining PETA, Bruce ran a shelter for homeless families and the largest soup kitchen in Washington, D.C. He has been a social justice advocate for more than twenty years.

Dale Jamieson is Professor of Environmental Studies and Philosophy at New York University, and the author of *Morality's Progress: Essays on Humans, Other Animals, and the Rest of Nature*.

Philip Lymbery spent a decade working for Compassion in World Farming (CIWF), a leading European farm animal welfare organization. As CIWF's Campaigns Director, he founded and coordinated the European Coalition for Farm Animals (ECFA). After two years as international animal welfare and campaigns consultant, Philip now works for the World Society for the Protection of Animals (WSPA) as Director of Communications.

Jim Mason grew up on a Missouri family farm. He is co-author with Peter Singer of *Animal Factories: What Agribusiness is Doing to the Family Farm, the Environment, and Your Health*. His book *An Unnatural Order* traces the roots of the dominant worldview of human supremacy over animals and nature.

Gaverick Matheny is a Fellow in Agricultural and Resource Economics at the University of Maryland. He also directs New Harvest, a nonprofit research organization developing new meat substitutes (*www.New-Harvest.org*).

Miyun Park directs the Farm Animals and Sustainable Agriculture program of The Humane Society of the United States, in Washington, D.C. She was previously president of Compassion Over Killing (COK), where she focused on ending cruelty to farmed animals and conducted investigations at slaughterhouses, live animal markets, and factory farms. Miyun's advocacy efforts were featured in *The New York Times, The Washington Post, The San Francisco Chronicle*, and *CosmoGirl!* magazine, and she was the subject of an hour-length documentary produced by the Korean Broadcasting System.

Dale Peterson's recent books include *Eating Apes, Chimpanzee Travels, The Deluge and the Ark*, and *Storyville, USA*. He has also co-authored (with Richard Wrangham) *Demonic Males: Apes and the Origins of Human Violence* and (with Jane Goodall) *Visions of Caliban: On Chimpanzees and People*.

Richard D. Ryder studied experimental psychology in animal laboratories at Cambridge University and at Columbia University, New York, before becoming a pioneer animal rights advocate in the 1960s. His *Victims of Science* provoked political debate when published in 1975 and led to new legislation on animal experimentation in the United Kingdom and the European Union in 1986. He has several times been Chairman of the Royal Society for the Prevention of Cruelty to Animals Council. In 1970 he coined the term "speciesism," now in many dictionaries.

Peter Singer is Ira W. De Camp Professor of Bioethics in the University Center for Human Values at Princeton University and Laureate Professor in the Centre for Applied Philosophy and Public Ethics at the University of Melbourne. He first became well known internationally after the publication of *Animal Liberation* in 1975. His other books include *Democracy and Disobedience, Practical Ethics, How Are We to Live?, Rethinking Life and Death,*

One World, Pushing Time Away, and *The President of Good and Evil*. He is also editor of four other titles for Blackwell: *A Companion to Ethics* (1991), *A Companion to Bioethics* (with Helga Kuhse, 1999), *The Moral of the Story: An Anthology of Ethics Through Literature* (with Renata Singer, 2005), and *Bioethics: An Anthology* (with Helga Kuhse, 2nd edn., 2006). He is president of Animal Rights International, and of the Great Ape Project.

Henry Spira (1927–98) was a merchant seaman, journalist, civil rights activist, union reformer, and high school teacher before becoming the most effective American campaigner for animals of the 1970s and 1980s.

Pelle Strindlund is a Swedish activist and writer. He is the author of *Djurrätt och socialism (Animal Rights and Socialism)* and *I vänliga rebellers sällskap: kristet ickevåld som konfrontation och ömhet (In the Company of Amicable Rebels: Christian Nonviolence as Confrontation and Tenderness)*.

Paul Waldau is the Director of the Center for Animals and Public Policy at Tufts University School of Veterinary Medicine. He holds a Doctor of Philosophy degree from the University of Oxford, a Juris Doctor degree from the University of California Law School, and a Master's degree from Stanford University in Religious Studies. He is the author of *The Specter of Speciesism: Buddhist and Christian Views of Animals*, and has taught "Animal Law" courses at Harvard, Yale, and Boston College law schools.

Introduction

Peter Singer

The book that follows is very different from the one that appeared under the same title twenty years ago. That work reflected the first generation of the modern animal movement – a movement that began, hesitatingly, in the 1960s, in the United Kingdom. The first sign of a new, more radical approach to combating the maltreatment of animals was the willingness of some members of the League Against Cruel Sports to engage in sabotage to stop hunting with hounds. They started using chemicals to dull the fox's scent, or they laid false scents to mislead the dogs. By 1963, the Hunt Saboteurs Association emerged as a separate organization, freed from the constraints of the more traditional League.

At first, this new radicalism was still focused only on putting an end to hunting with hounds. But just one year after the founding of the Hunt Saboteurs Association, Ruth Harrison's *Animal Machines* was published. For the first time, the British public became aware of the existence of factory farming. This system of animal production, Harrison persuasively argued, acknowledges cruelty only when profitability ceases. Unfortunately for the animals, the individual productivity of a laying hen is less significant for the profitability of egg producers than the number of hens the producers can cram inside their sheds. Thus profitability proved compatible with a vast amount of cruelty.

A dairy farmer named Peter Roberts tried to persuade the major British animal welfare organizations to take up the issue of factory farming. Getting little response, in 1967 he started Compassion in World Farming. It has now grown into an international organization and a major player in farm animal welfare issues in Europe.

Philosophy got involved in the animal question in the early 1970s, when three graduate students at Oxford – Roslind and Stanley Godlovitch, together with John Harris – edited *Animals, Men and Morals*, the first modern work in which philosophers – among others – discuss the ethics of our treatment of animals. The book attracted virtually no attention. I tried to remedy this situation by writing by a review essay in *The New York Review of Books* under the more dramatic title "Animal Liberation." That was followed by my own book with the same title, and after that, a number of other philosophers began to write about the topic from their own ethical perspectives. As James Jasper and Dorothy Nelkin observed in *The Animal Rights Crusade: The Growth of a Moral Protest*, "Philosophers served as midwives of the animal rights movement in the late 1970s" (1992: 90). The metaphor is apt: philosophers were not the mother of the movement, but they did ease its passage into the world and – who knows – may have prevented it being stillborn. In his essay below, Richard Ryder, who was present at the birth, speculates on the reasons why it happened at that particular time.

In 1970 the number of writings on the ethical status of animals was tiny. Sixteen years later, when the first edition of this book appeared, it was small. In a comprehensive bibliography of writings on this subject, Charles Magel (1989) lists only 94 works in the first 1970 years of the Christian era, and 240 works from 1970 to 1988, when the bibliography was completed. The tally now must be in the thousands. Nor is this debate simply a Western phenomenon. Leading works on animals and ethics have been translated into most of the world's major languages, including Japanese, Chinese, and Korean, and scholars, writers, and activists in many countries have contributed.

This new edition reflects the current state of the animal movement. In the last twenty years the movement has grown and matured. Hence I have not felt the need to reprint the work of well-known thinkers, like Tom Regan, Stephen Clark, and Mary Midgley, who contributed to the first edition. Their essays are now widely available in anthologies, and they have written their own books explaining their positions more fully. In this edition, I wanted to give a voice to a new generation of thinkers and activists. Only one essay, Marian Dawkins's discussion of the basis for assessing suffering in animals, has been reprinted unchanged. Three essays – describing the situation for animals in farms, laboratories, and zoos – are revised versions of essays that appeared in the first edition. The remaining fourteen essays appear here for the first time.

The structure of the book is unchanged. We begin with essays on the ideas behind the movement. To come to grips with the crux of the ethical debate, it helps to distinguish two questions. The first revolves around the idea of "speciesism," a term that is now in good dictionaries, but did not even exist thirty-five years ago. (It was coined by Richard Ryder, in a leaflet about experiments on animals.) Speciesism is, in brief, the idea that it is justifiable to give preference to beings simply on the grounds that they are members of the species *Homo sapiens*. The first issue, then, is whether speciesism itself can be defended. The second issue is whether, if speciesism cannot be defended, there are other characteristics about human beings that justify placing greater moral significance on what happens to them than on what happens to nonhuman animals.

The view that species is in itself a reason for treating some beings as morally more significant than others is often assumed but rarely defended. Some who write as if they are defending "speciesism" are in fact defending an affirmative answer to the second question, arguing that there are morally relevant differences between human beings and other animals that entitle us to give more weight to the interests of humans. The only argument I've come across that looks like a defense of speciesism itself is the claim that just as parents have a special obligation to care for their own children in preference to the children of strangers, so we have a special obligation to other members of our species in preference to members of other species. Advocates of this position usually pass in silence over the obvious case that lies between the family and the species. Thus in *Darwinian Dominion*, Lewis Petrinovich, an authority on ornithology and evolution, says that our biology turns certain boundaries into moral imperatives – and then lists "children, kin, neighbors, and species" (1999: 29). If the argument works for both the narrower circle of family and friends, and the wider sphere of the species, it should also work for the middle case: race. But an argument that supported preferring the interests of members of our own race over those of members of other races would receive a hostile reaction from most people, who are not racists. Yet if the argument doesn't lead to the conclusion that race is a morally relevant boundary, how can it show that species is?

The late Harvard philosopher Robert Nozick, writing in 1983, argued that we can't infer much from the fact that we do not yet have "a theory of the moral importance of species membership" – and, in particular, of the moral importance of the fact that a being is a member of the species *Homo sapiens* – because nobody thought that we needed such a theory, and so no one had spent much time trying to formulate one. But even as Nozick was writing this, the issue of the moral status of animals, and hence of the moral importance of species membership, had become a pressing one, both philosophically and with a broader public suddenly concerned about factory farming and experiments on animals. So over the last twenty years, many philosophers have spent a lot of time trying to formulate a theory of the moral importance of being a member of the species *Homo sapiens*. And yet we still do not have a satisfactory account of why membership of our species should matter so much, morally. Nozick's comment, therefore, takes on a quite different significance. The continuing failure of philosophers to produce a plausible theory of the moral importance of species member-ship indicates, with increasing probability, that there is no such plausible theory.

That takes us to the second question. If species is not morally important in itself, is there something else that happens to coincide with the species boundary, on the basis of which we can justify the inferior consideration we give to nonhuman animals? Those who think that morality is based on a social contract argue that it is the lack of a capacity to reciprocate. Ethics, they say, arises out of an agreement that if I do not harm you, you will not harm me. Since animals cannot take part in this agreement, we have no direct duties to them. The difficulty with this approach to ethics is that it also means that we have no direct duties to small children, or to future generations yet unborn. If we produce radioactive waste that will be deadly for thousands of years, is it unethical to put it into a container that will last 150 years and then drop it into a convenient lake? If it is, ethics cannot be based on reciprocity.

Many other ways of marking the special moral significance of human beings have been suggested: the ability to reason, self-awareness, possessing a sense of justice, language, autonomy, and so on. But the problem with all of these allegedly distinguishing marks is, as noted above, that some humans are entirely lacking in these characteristics and few want to consign these humans to the same moral category as nonhuman animals. Moreover, as David DeGrazia argues in his essay on personhood below, some nonhuman animals possess at least some of these more advanced cognitive character-istics. So – at best – these criteria do not mark the greater moral significance of *human* beings as such, but rather that of most humans and some non-humans over some humans and most nonhumans.

The animal movement is frequently parodied by those who either are wilfully misrepresenting it or do not understand its implications. So, to fore-stall misunderstandings, it is worth saying a little about what the rejection of speciesism does *not* imply. It does not mean that animals have all the same rights as you and I have. Opponents of speciesism are well aware of the existence of differences between members of our species and members of other species. Because of these differences, it would be meaningless to attribute to nonhuman animals such rights as the right to vote, to freedom of speech, or to freedom of religion. But then, it is equally meaningless to give such rights to two-year-old humans. That doesn't mean that we should give less weight to the interests that two-year-old humans do have, like the interests in being fed, in being warm and comfortable, and in being loved.

Similarly, something that harms normal adult humans may cause much less harm, or even no harm at all, to some nonhuman animals. If I were to confine a herd of cows within the boundaries of the state of New Jersey, I would not be doing them any harm at all. Cows are satisfied with lush pasture, contact with their offspring and other members of the group, and shelter from harsh weather – all things that New Jersey can provide. Cows have no desire to stroll down New York's Fifth Avenue, to hike in the Rockies, or to take a gondola ride in Venice. Some humans do. Hence, even if they are with their families and friends, and notwithstanding the many attractions of Newark and Trenton, confinement to New Jersey would be a hardship to those humans. The moral is: normal mature humans often have different interests from nonhuman animals.

Here is another example, more relevant to real problems about our treatment of animals. Suppose that, in order to advance medical research, we decide to perform lethal scientific experiments on normal adult humans, kidnapped at random for this purpose from public parks. Soon every adult would become fearful of being kidnapped if he or she entered a park. The resultant terror – and loss of the ability to enjoy visiting parks – would be a form of suffering additional to whatever pain was involved in the experiments themselves. The same experiments, carried out on nonhuman animals and causing a similar amount of pain during the course of the actual experiment, would cause less suffering overall, for the animals would not have the same anticipatory dread. This does not mean, I hasten to add, that it is all right to experiment on animals, but only that if the experiment is to be done at all, there is *some* reason, compatible with the principle of equal consideration of interests, for preferring to use nonhuman animals rather than normal adult humans.

In this example, the superior mental powers of normal adult humans would make them suffer more. In other circumstances, the nonhuman animal may suffer more because he or she cannot understand what is happening. If we capture wild animals, intending to release them later, we cannot convey to them that we do not intend to harm them. They will experience the general terror of being in a situation that is, to them, as threatening as any situation can possibly be.

The moral significance of taking life is more complex still. The traditional Judeo-Christian ethic teaches that the lives of human beings are sacred, but the lives of other beings are not. As I have argued at greater length in *Practical Ethics* and *Rethinking Life and Death*, we should not allow species to determine the wrongness of taking life. If it is wrong to take the life of a severely brain-damaged human infant, it must be at least as wrong to take the life of a dog or a pig at a comparable mental level. On the other hand, perhaps it is *not* wrong to take the life of a severely brain-damaged human infant, at least when the parents agree that it is better that their child should die. After all, such infants are commonly "allowed to die" in intensive-care units in major hospitals all over the world, and an infant who is "allowed to die" ends up just as dead as one who is killed. Indeed, one could argue that our readiness to put hopelessly ill nonhuman animals out of their misery is the one and only respect in which we treat animals better than we treat human beings.

We need to take a new approach to the wrongness of killing, one that considers the individual characteristics of the being whose life is at stake, rather than that being's species. Such a view may still consider killing beings with the mental capacities of normal human adults as more serious than killing beings who do not possess, and never have possessed, such mental capacities. When we see the lives of normal human beings tragically cut short – as happened, for example, in New York on September 11, 2001 – we are saddened by the thought that these people had hopes and plans that will now never be fulfilled. We think of the young woman who had been so excited about her new career in an investment bank with offices high up in the World Trade Center, or of the clerk who had finally saved enough to put a down payment on an apartment and set the date when he would marry his childhood sweetheart. We think, too, of the loved ones left behind to grieve. A being who lacks a clear conception of the past and the (possible) future cannot have these kinds of hopes and plans. Although nonhuman animals certainly can grieve for the loss of those to whom they are close, the nature of the grief must differ in accordance with the differing mental capacities of the beings. Hence it is not a bias in favor of our own species that leads us to think that different mental capacities make a difference in these circumstances, and that, accordingly, some deaths are more tragic than others.

The rejection of speciesism therefore does not require us to say that all lives are of equal worth, or that all interests of humans and animals must be given equal weight, no matter what those interests may be. It requires us to make only the more limited and defensible claim that where animals and humans have similar interests – we might take the interest in avoiding physical pain as an example – those interests are to be counted equally. We must not disregard or discount the interests of another being, merely because that being is not human.

Part I of the book, "The Ideas," starts with the most straightforward ethical case for a non-speciesist approach to the treatment of animals – a utilitarian argument. Gaverick Matheny sets this out clearly and succinctly, deals with some objections, and concludes by showing that even for those who would accept only a much weaker version of the principle of equal consideration of interests, there is a compelling ethical case for ceasing to treat animals as means to our ends. Marian Dawkins provides the scientific basis for one of the essential premises of Matheny's – or virtually any – argument about how we should treat animals. She shows how scientists can gain insight into what animals feel, and into their capacity to suffer. David DeGrazia takes up the idea of "personhood" beyond the human species. His essay is part of a growing literature that explores morally significant characteristics that cross species boundaries. This line of thinking is relevant not only to issues regarding nonhuman animals, but also to life-and-death decisions for human beings: for example, for critically ill newborn infants, or for those in a persistent vegetative state. But DeGrazia concludes by reminding us that personhood is not the only morally significant characteristic, and its importance may have been overestimated.

Paola Cavalieri puts the debate about animals into a sweeping historical perspective encompassing crucial moments in philosophic thought. She starts with ancient Greece, then moves to seventeenth-century Europe, and finally looks at the last fifty years. Her contrast between the human-centered approaches taken by Heidegger and Derrida and the more egalitarian approach taken by many contemporary English-language philosophers reveals the conventional self-interest that often lurks behind what appears to be deep metaphysics. Paul Waldau looks at the major religious traditions, another source of our attitudes to animals and how we should treat them. Here too, as Waldau suggests, although different religions offer contrasting views on the existence or otherwise of a yawning moral gulf between humans and animals, everyday practices towards animals may be more similar than these different views would lead one to expect.

Part II, entitled "The Problems," contains three revised and updated essays from the first edition, and two new essays. This section covers four areas in which animals need defense: in laboratories, in farms, in zoos, and in their own habitats. These four categories leave many others untouched: puppies and kittens bought for Christmas and then dumped when they grow into adults; circuses where animals are trained by threat and punishment to perform; and cruel sports like bull-fighting and fox-hunting. Nevertheless, each of the four topics covered here is significant in its own way. Most of the campaigning in the modern animal movement over the last thirty years has focused on animals used in laboratories and farms. In Europe both areas were targeted from the beginning of this period, with some, if still inadequate, progress. Richard Ryder's essay indicates both the progress and the continuing abuse of animals used in research. Clare Druce and Philip Lymbery set out the European Union reforms in how farm animals may be kept. These European reforms are far in advance of anything that is happening in America – perhaps because in the United States, until quite recently, the animal movement focused almost entirely on the use of animals in research. As Jim Mason and Mary Finelli show, agribusiness regards animals as cogs in a vast production machine. This trend started in America and is still more highly developed there than anywhere else, but it has now spread all over the world.

Dale Jamieson's essay on zoos covers an area that, because it obviously does not serve a critical human need, would seem to be more amenable to change through ethical argument. Indeed, the public will no longer accept, for public display, ways of caging animals that were common fifty years ago (although the public will continue to buy pork, chicken and veal from animals kept in much worse conditions). Some zoos have made significant efforts to improve their standards. But others have not, and Jamieson asks whether even those zoos that have improved the way they keep animals can justify their continued existence.

The final essay in this section describes a practice that will, it can safely be said, find few defenders among those who pick up this book, even those who eat meat. But I did not included Dale Peterson's essay simply in order to shock readers. What Peterson describes is nothing more than speciesism taken to the extreme. Chimpanzees, bonobos, and gorillas are not members of our species. If, as some have maintained, that is enough to exclude them from the circle of beings who may make moral claims against us, what is wrong with treating them as edibles? If, on the other hand, we cross the species boundary and admit the nonhuman great apes to the protected circle, where is the line to be drawn between eating great apes and eating pigs or calves? The moral gulf between humans and other animals appears, from our anthropocentric perspective, too wide to leap. Yet as our knowledge of the other great apes grows, they are proving to be a bridge species, not only in genetic, behavioral, and cognitive senses, but also morally.

All of the essays in Part III, "Activists and Their Strategies," are new and, with the exception of the final essay, which draws on the work of Henry Spira, they are all written by people who were not part of the animal movement when the first edition of this book appeared – either because they were too young, or because they were doing other things. The strategies described range from encouraging people to become vegans to committing civil disobedience, and from breaking into farms and rescuing hens to writing polite letters to newspapers. That the movement has been able to find new activists, with new ideas about how best to change the way we treat animals, is obviously an encouraging sign. So too is the fact that the authors of these essays are no longer all from English-speaking countries, as they were in the first edition. Whereas in the 1980s most people would have looked to the United Kingdom or to America for models of how to fight against the suffering of animals, now we can, with equal justification, turn to European nations like Austria and Sweden, which have in some respects become leaders in progressive reforms for animals. (To say this is not to deny the obvious fact that these nations too fall far short of the standards that a truly ethical, non-speciesist society would adopt towards animals.)

One viewpoint that is not represented in this book is the advocacy of violence in the cause of animals. The animal movement as a whole is overwhelmingly opposed to the use of violence against any sentient beings, including those who exploit animals. Considering the size of the movement, now numbering in the millions, violent incidents have been extremely rare – much more so than in the American anti-abortion movement (often misnamed the "pro-life movement"), some members of which have murdered doctors who carry out abortions. Nevertheless, threats of violence have been used, and some actual bodily assaults have occurred. The media, of course, give prominence to such events, and soon start talking about "animal rights terrorists," a phrase that rapidly tars the entire animal movement. In July 2004 even the liberal British *Guardian* ran an editorial that invoked "al-Qaida terrorists" in discussing the impact of animal activists on research.

Violence and intimidation may, in the short term, achieve goals that prevent the abuse of animals. In Britain, campaigns using intimidation have been credited with preventing the building of a proposed Cambridge University primate research center, and with disrupting the building of a new animal research laboratory at Oxford University. Nevertheless, the use of such means undermines the animal movement's ethical basis. In a democratic society, change should come about through education and persuasion, not by intimidation. Committing violent acts for political goals sets a dangerous precedent – or, to be more accurate, it follows dangerous precedents. The anti-abortion extremists who have fire-bombed abortion clinics and murdered doctors are no doubt just as sincere in their convictions as defenders of animals. It is difficult to find democratic principles that would allow one group to use intimidation and violence, and deny the same methods to the other.

Nonviolent responses to the frustrations of the democratic process carry less risk of doing damage to the fabric of civil society. Gandhi and Martin Luther King have shown that civil disobedience can be an effective means of demonstrating one's sincerity and commitment to a just cause. Those who break the law openly and nonviolently – as Pelle Strindlund, Miyun Park, and Martin Balluch describe doing, in different ways, in the essays that follow – are more likely to gain the respect and support of the public than those who strike secretly in the dark, and use fear, rather than persuasion, to change behavior. As the essays in the last section of this book show, there are many effective, nonviolent ways of reducing, and taking steps towards eliminating, the suffering that humans inflict on animals.

References

Jasper, James, and Nelkin, Dorothy (1992) *The Animal Rights Crusade: The Growth of a Moral Protest*, New York: Free Press.

Magel, Charles (1989) *Keyguide to Information Sources in Animal Rights*, Jefferson, N.C.: McFarland.

Nozick, Robert (1983) "About Mammals and People," *New York Times Book Review*, November 27, p. 11.

Petrinovich, Lewis (1999) *Darwinian Dominion: Animal Welfare and Human Interests*, Cambridge, MA: MIT Press.

Part I

The Ideas

1

Utilitarianism and Animals

Gaverick Matheny

In North America and Europe, around 17 billion land animals were raised and killed during 2001 to feed us. Somewhere between 50 and 100 million other animals were killed in laboratories, while another 30 million were killed in fur farms. The vast majority of these animals were forced to live and die in conditions most of us would find morally repugnant. Yet their use – and the use of comparable numbers of animals every year – has been justified by the belief that nonhuman animals do not deserve significant moral consideration. Several plausible ethical theories argue that this belief is mistaken. Utilitarianism is one such theory that condemns much of our present use of animals. If this theory is reasonable, then most of us should change the way we live.

Ethics

There is broad consensus within both religious and secular ethics that an ethical life respects virtues like fairness, justice, and benevolence. At the heart of these virtues lies a more basic principle: I cannot reasonably claim that my interests matter more than yours simply because my interests are *mine*. My interests may matter more *to me*, but I cannot claim they matter more in any objective sense. From the ethical point of view, everyone's interests deserve equal consideration.

In the Judeo-Christian tradition, this sentiment is embodied in "The Golden Rule" attributed to Moses: "Love your neighbor as you love yourself"

(Matthew 22:39) and in the Talmud, "What is hateful to you, do not to your fellow men" (Shabbat 31a). In the secular tradition, this sentiment is embodied in the "principle of equal consideration of interests": "Act in such a way that the like interests of everyone affected by your action are given equal weight." This phrase may lack the elegance of Scripture but conveys the same general idea. The principle of equal consideration of interests asks that we put ourselves in the shoes of each person affected by an action and compare the strengths of her or his interests to those of our own – regardless of *whose* interests they are. To be fair, just, and benevolent, any ethical rule we adopt should respect this principle.

Utilitarianism

Utilitarianism is an ethical theory with the rule, "act in such a way as to maximize the expected satisfaction of interests in the world, equally considered." This rule is a logical extension of the principle of equal consideration of interests in that it says I should sum up the interests of all the parties affected by all my possible actions and choose the action that results in the greatest net satisfaction of interests. Another way of thinking about this is to imagine which actions I would choose if I had to live the lives of all those affected by me. Because the rule of utilitarianism represents a simple operation upon a principle of equality, it is perhaps the most minimal ethical rule we could derive. Utilitarianism is said to be universalist, welfarist, consequentialist, and aggregative. Each of these properties needs some explanation.

Utilitarianism is *universalist* because it takes into account the interests of all those who are affected by an action, regardless of their nationality, gender, race, or other traits that we find, upon reflection, are not morally relevant. The rule "act in such a way as to maximize the expected satisfaction of interests" is one we would be willing to have everyone adopt. Some writers have even claimed, forcefully, this is the *only* such rule.

Utilitarianism is *welfarist* because it defines what is ethically "good" in terms of people's welfare, which we can understand as the satisfaction (or dissatisfaction) of people's interests. Most of us are interested in good health, a good job, and our friends and family, among other things. We could reduce many if not all of these interests to something more general, such as an interest in a happy, pleasurable, relatively painless life. I will use the word "interests" to describe whatever it is that we value here – all those things that matter to us. We can safely say we all have an interest, at a minimum, in a pleasurable life, relatively free of pain. And from experience, we know when our happiness is decreased, as when we suffer acute pain, any other interests we may have tend to recede into the background. That being so, utilitarianism promotes an ethical rule that seeks to satisfy our interests, particularly those in a pleasurable, relatively painless life.

Utilitarianism is *consequentialist* because it evaluates the rightness or wrongness of an action by that action's expected *consequences*: the degree to which an action satisfies interests. These consequences can often be predicted and compared accurately with little more than common sense.

Finally, utilitarianism is said to be *aggregative* because it *adds* up the interests of all those affected by an action. To make a decision, I need to weigh the intensity, duration, and number of interests affected by all of my possible actions. I choose the action that results in the greatest net satisfaction of interests – "the greatest good for the greatest number." Utilitarian decisions thus involve a kind of accounting ledger, with our like interests serving as a common currency. This is no easy exercise. But, as we'll see, in many of our most important moral judgments, even a rough comparison of interests is enough to make a wise decision.

The Advantages of Utilitarianism

Utlitarianism has several advantages over other ethical theories. First, its consequentialism encourages us to make full use of information about the world as it is. If you have access to the same information as I do, you can argue with me about how I ought to act. This lends utilitarianism a greater degree of empirical objectivity than most ethical theories enjoy.

Some ethical theories hold less regard for consequences than does utilitarianism and address their ethical rules either to actions themselves or to the motivations prompting them. These rules would often lead to misery if they were followed without exception. For instance, we would not have praised Miep Gies, the woman who hid Anne Frank and her family from the Nazis, had she followed the rule "never tell a lie" and turned the Franks over to the Nazis. Most of us believe the kind of deception Gies engaged in was justified, even heroic. So when should you tell a lie? When the consequences of not telling the lie are worse than the consequences of telling it. To decide otherwise would be to engage in a kind of rule worship at the expense of other people's interests. Because we are often forced to choose between the lesser of two evils, any rule about particular actions – lying, promising, killing, and so on – can lead to terrible results.

At the same time, it would be foolhardy to live without any general principles. I would not be an efficient utilitarian if, every time I approached a stoplight, I weighed the consequences of respecting traffic laws. This would waste time and regularly lead to poor results. It would be best if I adopted "rules of thumb" that, in general, promote the greatest satisfaction of interests by guiding my actions in ordinary situations. Such rules of thumb would likely include most of our common views about right and wrong. However, in extraordinary situations, these rules of thumb should be overridden, as in the case of Miep Gies. In this way, utilitarianism supports most of our common moral intuitions while, at the same time, overriding them in important cases where following them could be catastrophic.

Utilitarianism's aggregative properties offer additional advantages. Our moral decisions regularly benefit one individual at the expense or neglect of another. For instance, in North America and Europe, some citizens are taxed in order to provide financial support to the disabled, among others. Is it ethical to benefit one group with this tax while another suffers some expense? While such conflicts arise regularly in public policy, they also arise in our personal choices. In deciding to spend $1,000 on a piece of artwork instead of on a donation to a charity, I know a charity now has less money with which to help those in need than it would had I given it my $1,000. Is it ethical to have benefited myself while neglecting others? Utilitarianism, in allowing some exchange of costs and benefits, can help us answer questions like these, whereas many other ethical theories cannot.

Many of the moral stances implied by utilitarianism are familiar and widely accepted. Historically, utilitarians were among the most outspoken opponents of slavery and the strongest proponents of women's suffrage, public education, public health, and other social democratic institutions. In recent years, utilitarians have advanced some of the strongest moral arguments for charity to the poor and sick. At the same time, however, utilitarianism leads us to moral views many of us do not already accept. Prominent among these are moral views regarding nonhuman animals.

Do Any Nonhumans Have Interests?

By the principle of equal consideration of interests, interests matter, regardless of *whose* interests they are. We can agree that we all have an interest, at a minimum, in a pleasurable life, relatively free of pain. Pleasure and pain *matter* to all of us who feel them. As such, it follows that we are obliged to consider, at a minimum, the interests of all those who are capable of feeling pleasure and pain – that is, all those who are *sentient*. We can then say that sentience is a sufficient condition for having interests and having those interests considered equally.

Are any nonhuman animals sentient? That is, are any nonhumans biologically capable of feeling pleasure and pain? There are few people today, including biologists, who seriously doubt the answer is yes. For most of us, our common sense and experience with animals, especially dogs and cats, are sufficient to let us answer affirmatively. However, our common sense and experience cannot always be trusted, and so we should look for further evidence that animals other than ourselves are sentient.

How do we know that other *human beings* are sentient? We cannot know for certain. My friend who shrieks after burning himself on the stove could be a very sophisticated robot, programmed to respond to certain kinds of stimuli with a shriek. But, because my friend is biologically similar to me, his awareness of pain would offer a biological advantage, his behavior is similar to my own when I am in pain, and his behavior is associated with a stimulus that would be painful for me, I have good reason to believe my friend feels pain.

We have similar reasons for believing that many nonhuman animals feel pain. Human beings evolved from other species. Those parts of the brain involved in sensing pleasure and pain are older than human beings and common to mammals and birds, and probably also to fish, reptiles, and amphibians. For most of these animals, awareness of pain would serve important functions, including learning from past mistakes.

Like my potentially robotic friend, these animals also respond to noxious stimuli much the same way we do. They avoid these stimuli and shriek, cry, or jerk when they can't escape them. The stimuli that cause these behaviors are ones we associate with pain, such as extreme pressure, heat, and tissue damage. These biological and behavioral indications do not guarantee sentience, but they are about as good as those that we have for my human friend.

Whether invertebrates such as insects feel pain is far less certain, as these animals do not possess the same equipment to feel pain and pleasure that we have; and, by their having short life-cycles in stereotyped environments, the biological advantages of being sentient are less obvious.

That some nonhuman animals feel pain needn't imply that their *interests* in not feeling pain are as intense as our own. It's possible that ordinary, adult humans are capable of feeling more intense pain than some nonhumans because we are self-conscious and can anticipate or remember pain with greater fidelity than can other animals. It could also be argued, however, that our rationality allows us to distance ourselves from pain or give pain a purpose (at the dentist's office, for instance) in ways that are not available to other animals. Moreover, even if other animals' interests in not feeling pain are less intense than our own, the sum of a larger number of interests of lesser intensity (such as 100,000 people's interests in $1 each) can still outweigh the sum of a smaller number of interests of greater intensity (such as my interest in $100,000).

So it is possible, even in those cases where significant human interests are at stake, for the interests of animals, considered equally, to outweigh our own. As we will see, however, in most cases involving animals, there are no significant human interests at stake, and the right course of action is easy to judge.

Some Rebuttals

Philosophers have never been immune to the prejudices of their day. In the past, some advanced elaborate arguments against civil rights, religious tolerance, and the abolition of slavery. Similarly, some philosophers today seek to justify our current prejudices against nonhuman animals, typically not by challenging the claim that some nonhumans are sentient, but rather by arguing that sentience is not a sufficient condition for moral consideration. Common to their arguments is the notion that moral consideration should be extended only to those individuals who *also* possess certain levels of rationality, intelligence, or language, or to those capable of reciprocating moral agreements, which likewise implies a certain level of rationality, intelligence, or language.

It is not clear how these arguments could succeed. First, why would an animal's lack of normal human levels of rationality, intelligence, or language give us license to ignore her or his pain? Second, if rationality, intelligence, or language were necessary conditions for moral consideration, why could we not give moral preference to humans who are more rational, intelligent, or verbose than other humans? Third, many adult mammals and birds exhibit greater rationality and intelligence than do human infants. Some nonhuman animals, such as apes, possess language, while some humans do not. Should human infants, along with severely retarded and brain-damaged humans, be excluded from moral consideration, while apes, dolphins, dogs, pigs, parrots, and other nonhumans are included? Efforts to limit moral consideration to human beings based on the possession of certain traits succeed neither in including all humans nor in excluding all nonhuman animals.

The most obvious property shared among all human beings that excludes all nonhuman animals is our membership of a particular biological group: the species *Homo sapiens*. What is significant about species membership that could justify broad differences in moral consideration? Why is the line drawn at species, rather than genus, subspecies, or some other biological division? There have been no convincing answers to these questions. If species membership is a justification for excluding sentient animals from moral consideration, then why not race or gender? Why could one not argue that an individual's membership of the biological group "human female" excludes that individual from moral consideration? One of the triumphs of modern ethics has been recognizing that an individual's membership of a group, alone, is not morally relevant. The cases against racism and sexism depended upon this point, as the case against speciesism does now.

If a nonhuman animal can feel pleasure and pain, then that animal possesses interests. To think otherwise is to pervert the sense in which we understand pleasure and pain, feelings that matter to us and to others who experience them. At a minimum, a sentient animal has an interest in a painless, pleasurable life. And if he or she possesses this interest, then he or she deserves no less consideration of his or her interests than we give to our own. This view, while modern in its popularity, is not new. The utilitarian Jeremy Bentham held it at a time when black slaves were treated much as we now treat nonhuman animals:

> The day may come when the rest of the animal creation may acquire those rights which never could have been witholden from them but by the hand of tyranny. The French have already discovered that the blackness of the skin is no reason why a human being should be abandoned without redress to the caprice of a tormentor. It may one day come to be recognized that the number of the legs, the villosity of the skin, or the termination of the *os sacrum*, are reasons equally insufficient for abandoning a sensitive being to the same fate. What else is it that should trace the insuperable line? Is it the faculty of reason, or perhaps the faculty of discourse? But a full-grown horse or dog is beyond comparison a more rational, as well as a more conversable animal, than an infant of a day, or a week, or even a month, old. But suppose they were otherwise, what would it avail? The question is not, Can they reason? nor Can they talk? but, Can they suffer? (1988 [1823]: 1988: 310–11)

The principle of equal consideration of interests requires we count the interests of any individual equally with the like interests of any other. The racist violates this rule by giving greater weight to the interests of members of her own race. The sexist violates this rule by giving greater weight to the interests of members of his own sex. Similarly, the speciesist violates this rule by giving greater weight to the interests of members of his own species.

If an animal is sentient and if sentience is a sufficient condition for having interests, then we should consider that animal's interests equal to our own when making ethical decisions. The essays in this book by James Mason and Mary Finelli, by Richard Ryder, and by Miyun Park show that we fall far short. Animals are used in a wide range of human activities, including agriculture, product testing, medical and scientific research, entertainment, hunting and fishing, the manufacture of clothing, and as our pets. In most of these activities, we treat animals in ways that do not show proper regard for their interests and thereby are unethical. I will limit discussion here to our treatment of animals in agriculture, laboratories, and the wild.

Food

Other essays in this book discusses factory farming practices in detail. It is difficult, however, to convey these conditions in print, so I encourage you either to visit a factory farm or to watch video footage from these facilities at the website listed at the end of this essay. Factory farm conditions are believed by many to be so inhumane that it would be better if animals living in these facilities had not existed. Deciding what makes a life worth living is no simple matter, but we can think how we consider whether or not to euthanize a hopelessly sick dog or cat.

The pain experienced by animals in factory farms is likely greater than that experienced by many of those sick dogs and cats we choose to euthanize, as factory-farmed animals often experience an entire lifetime of pain, compared with a few weeks or months. If, for instance, we knew that our dog or cat would have no choice but to be confined in a cage so restrictive that turning around or freely stretching limbs is difficult if not impossible; live in his own excrement; be castrated or have her teeth, tail, or toes sliced off without anesthesia, I suspect most of us would believe that euthanizing the animal is the humane choice. It would be better, then, if farmed animals who endure these conditions did not exist.

One is hard-pressed to find, even among philosophers, any attempt to justify these conditions or the practice of eating factory-farmed animals. We have no nutritional need for animal products. In fact, vegetarians are, on average, healthier than those who eat meat. The overriding interest we have in eating animals is the pleasure we get from the taste of their flesh. However, there are a variety of vegetarian foods available, including ones that taste like animal products, from meat to eggs to milk, cheese, and yogurt. So, in order to justify eating animals, we would have to show that the pleasure gained from consuming them *minus* the pleasure gained from eating a vegetarian meal is greater than the pain caused by eating animals.

Whatever pleasure we gain from eating animals cannot be discounted. However, equal consideration of interests requires that we put ourselves in the place of a farmed animal as well as in the place of a meat-eater. Does the pleasure we enjoy from eating a chicken outweigh the pain we would endure were we to be raised and killed for that meal? We would probably conclude that our substantial interest in not being raised in a factory farm and slaughtered is stronger than our trivial interest in eating a chicken instead of chickpeas. There is, after all, no shortage of foods that we can eat that don't require an animal to suffer in a factory farm or slaughterhouse. That our trivial interest in the taste of meat now trumps the pain endured by 17 *billion* farmed animals may be some measure of how far we are from considering their interests equally.

Accordingly, equal consideration of interests requires that we abstain, at a minimum, from eating factory-farmed products – particularly poultry and eggs, products that seem to cause the most pain per unit of food. Ideally, we should not consume products from any animal that we believe is sentient. This is the least we can do to have any real regard for the pain felt by other animals. Eating animals is a habit for most of us and, like other habits, can be challenging to break. But millions of people have made the switch to a vegetarian diet and, as a result, have enjoyed better health and a clearer conscience.

The use of animals for food is by far the largest direct cause of animal abuse in North America and Europe; and our consumption of animal flesh, eggs, and milk probably causes more pain than any other action for which each of us is responsible. The average North American or European eats somewhere between 1,500 and 2,500 factory-farmed animals in his or her lifetime. If we ended our discussion here and all became vegans, we would effectively abolish 99 percent of the present use of animals. Still, there are other ways in which animals are abused that deserve discussion. The use of animals in laboratories, in particular, provides a testing ground for the principle of equal consideration of interests.

Laboratories

Somewhere between 50 and 100 million animals are killed each year in North American and European laboratories. As Richard Ryder describes in his essay in this book, these include animals used in testing new products, formulations, and drugs as well as those used in medical and scientific research. U.S. law does not require research or testing facilities to report numbers of most of these animals – primarily rats, mice, and birds – so there is considerable uncertainty about the statistics.

There are potentially non-trivial benefits to human beings and other animals in using nonhuman animals for testing and in medical and veterinary research. That being so, utilitarianism cannot provide as simple an objection to the use of animals in experiments as it did to the use of animals for food. It can, however, provide a yardstick by which to judge whether a particular experiment is ethical.

We should first ask whether the experiment is worth conducting. Most product tests on animals involve household or personal care products that are only superficially different from existing products. How many different formulations of laundry detergent or shampoo does the world need? And much basic research involving animals may answer intellectually interesting questions but promise few benefits to either human or nonhuman animals. Do we need to know what happens to kittens after their eyes are removed at birth, or to monkeys when deprived of all maternal contact from infancy? In every case, we should ask if the pain prevented by an experiment is greater than the pain caused by that experiment. As experiments routinely involve thousands of animals with an uncertain benefit to any human or nonhuman animal, in most cases these experiments are not justified. It is difficult to imagine that the pain experienced by 100 million animals each year is *averting* an equivalent amount of pain.

However, if we believe that an experiment is justified on utilitarian grounds, there is another question we should ask to check our prejudices. Most adult mammals used in lab research – dogs, cats, mice, rabbits, rats, and primates – are more aware of what is happening to them than and at least as sensitive to pain as any human infant. Would researchers contemplating an animal experiment be willing, then, to place an orphaned human infant in the animal's place? If they are not, then their use of an animal is simple discrimination on the basis of species, which, as we found above, is morally unjustifiable. If the researchers are willing to place an infant in the animal's place, then they are at least morally consistent. Perhaps there are cases in which researchers believe an experiment is so valuable as to be worth an infant's life, but I doubt that many would make this claim.

Wildlife

Except for those hunted and fished, wild animals are often ignored in discussions of animal protection and seen as the domain of environmental protection. Part of this neglect is probably justified. I would certainly choose to be an animal in the wild over being an animal in a factory farm. Nevertheless, animals in the wild deserve as much moral consideration as do those animals in farms or laboratories. Likewise, wild animals raise important questions for those interested, as we are, in the proper moral consideration of animals' interests.

There are few human activities that do not affect the welfare of wild animals. Particularly in developed countries, humans consume a tremendous amount of energy, water, land, timber, minerals, and other resources whose extraction or use damages natural habitats – killing or preventing from existing untold billions of wild animals. Many of these activities may well be justified. Nevertheless, most of us can take steps to reduce the impact we have on wild animals without sacrificing anything of comparable moral significance.

Most of these steps are familiar ones encouraged by environmental protection groups. We should drive less, use public transit more, adopt a vegetarian or preferably vegan diet, reduce our purchases of luxury goods, buy used rather than new items, and so on. For decades, environmentalists in Europe and North America have also encouraged couples to have smaller families. In Europe, it is not uncommon to find one-child families, and the same is beginning to be true in North America. Smaller families not only carry many social and economic advantages to parents and nations, they also significantly reduce the resources used and the number of animals threatened by human consumption. Of course, most of these measures help humans, too. Investments in family planning, for instance, are probably the most cost-effective measures to reduce global warming.

Conclusions

I have argued that utilitarianism is a reasonable ethical theory, that this theory includes animals in its moral consideration, and that it obliges us to make dramatic changes in our institutions and habits – most immediately, that we become vegetarian or preferably vegan. While my aim here has been to present a *utilitarian* argument, similar arguments regarding our mistreatment of animals have been put forward on the basis of all of the major secular and religious ethical theories (cited below). But even less ambitious ethical arguments should convince us that much of our present treatment of animals is unethical.

Take, for instance, what I will call the "weak principle" of equal consideration of interests. Under the weak principle, we will consider the interests of nonhuman animals to be equal *only* to the like interests of other nonhuman animals. I don't believe there is any good reason to adopt the weak principle in place of the strong one discussed earlier. But, even if we were to adopt the weak principle, we would reach many of the same conclusions.

Almost all of us agree that we should treat dogs and cats humanely. There are few opponents, for instance, of current anti-cruelty laws aimed at protecting pets from abuse, neglect, or sport fighting. And therein lies a bizarre contradiction. For if these anti-cruelty laws applied to animals in factory farms or laboratories, the ways in which these animals are treated would be illegal throughout North America and Europe. Do we believe dogs and cats are so different from apes, pigs, cows, chickens, and rabbits that one group of animals – pets – deserve legal protection from human abuse, while the other group – animals in factory farms and in labs – deserve to have their abuse institutionalized? We cannot justify this contradiction by claiming that the abuse of farmed animals, for example, serves a purpose, whereas the abuse of pets does not. Arguably, the satisfaction enjoyed by someone who fights or otherwise abuses dogs and cats is just as great as that enjoyed by someone who eats meat.

What separates pets from the animals we abuse in factory farms and in labs is physical proximity. Our disregard for "food" or "lab" animals persists because we don't see them. Few people are aware of the ways in which they are mistreated and even fewer actually see the abuse. When people become aware, they are typically appalled – not because they have adopted a new ethical theory, but because they believe animals feel pain and they believe morally decent people should want to prevent pain whenever possible. The utilitarian argument for considering animals helps us to return to this common-sense view.

There are remarkably few contemporary defenses of our traditional treatment of animals. This may suggest that the principal obstacles to improving the treatment of animals are not philosophical uncertainties about their proper treatment but, rather, our ignorance about their current abuse and our reluctance to change deeply ingrained habits. Even the most reasonable among us is not invulnerable to the pressures of habit. Many moral philosophers who believe that eating animals is unethical continue to eat meat. This reflects the limits of reasoned argument in changing behavior. While I can't overcome those limits here, I encourage you, as you read this book, to replace in your mind the animals being discussed with an animal familiar to you, such as a dog or cat, or, better yet, a human infant. If you do this, you are taking to heart the principle of equal consideration of interests and giving animals the consideration they deserve.

Reference

Bentham, Jeremy (1988 [1828]) *The Principles of Morals and Legislation*, Amherst, N.Y.: Prometheus.

Further Reading

William Shaw's *Contemporary Ethics: Taking Account of Utilitarianism* (Oxford: Blackwell, 1999) provides an excellent introduction to utilitarian theory. Arguments for the moral consideration of animals have been advanced from a wide range of ethical perspectives, including utilitarianism (Peter Singer, *Practical Ethics*, 2nd edn, New York: Cambridge University Press, 1993), rights-based deontology (Tom Regan, *The Case for Animal Rights*, Berkeley: University of California Press, 1983), contractarianism (Mark Rowlands, *Animal Rights: A Philosophical Defence*, New York: St Martin's Press, 1998), common-sense morality (Peter Singer, *Animal Liberation*, New York: HarperCollins, 2001; David DeGrazia, *Taking Animals Seriously: Mental Life and Moral Status*, Cambridge: Cambridge University Press, 1996; Mylan Engel, "The Immorality of Eating Meat," in L. Pojman (ed.), *The Moral Life: An Introductory Reader in Ethics and Literature*, New York: Oxford University Press, 2000), and religious moralities (Andrew Linzey and Tom Regan (eds), *Animals and Christianity: A Book of Readings*, New York: Crossroads, 1988). The reader is encouraged to watch video footage from factory farms such as *Meet Your Meat*. *www.goveg.com/meetmeat.html*.

2

The Scientific Basis
for Assessing Suffering
in Animals

Marian Stamp Dawkins

"As far as our feelings are concerned, we are locked within our own skins."
I have always found B. F. Skinner's words to be a particularly succinct
and dramatic statement of the problem of attributing feelings to anyone
but ourselves. I have also been impressed by the fact that although almost
everyone acknowledges that this difficulty exists, we go about our daily
lives, and particularly our interactions with other people, as though it did
not. We all pay lip service to the idea that subjective feelings are private
but respond to the people around us as though experiences of pain and
pleasure were as public as the fact that it is raining. Thank goodness that we
do. Someone who stuck rigidly to the idea that all subjective experiences
were essentially private and that there was not, and never could be, evidence that other people experienced anything at all would be frightening
indeed. He or she would be without what is, for most of us, perhaps the
most important curb on inflicting damage on another person: the belief that
the damage would cause pain or suffering and that it is morally wrong to
cause those experiences in other people. This is one of the cornerstones of
our ideas about what is right and what is wrong. And yet this suffering we
are so concerned to avoid is, if we are strictly logical about it, essentially

This chapter was first published in the original edition of *In Defense of Animals* (Oxford: Basil Blackwell,
1985). Reproduced here by permission.

private, an unpleasant subjective state that only we ourselves can know about, experienced by the particular person who inhabits our own skin.

Much of our behavior towards other people is thus based on the unverifiable belief that they have subjective experiences at least somewhat like our own. It seems a reasonable belief to hold. There is enough common ground between people, despite their obvious differences of taste and upbringing, that we can attempt to put ourselves in other people's shoes and to empathize with their feelings. The fact that we can then often successfully predict what they will do or say next, and above all the fact that they may tell us that we have been successful in understanding them, suggests that the empathy has not been entirely inaccurate. We can begin to unlock them from their skins. We assume that they suffer, and decide, largely on this basis, that it is "wrong" to do certain things to them and "right" to do other things.

Then we come to the boundary of our own species. No longer do we have words. No longer do we have the high degree of similarity of anatomy, physiology, and behavior. But that is no reason to assume that they are any more locked inside their skins than are members of our species. Even in the case of other people, understanding feelings is not always easy. Different people find pleasure or lack of it in many different ways. It takes an effort to listen and understand and to see the world from their point of view. With other species, we certainly have additional difficulties, such as the fact that some animals live all their lives submerged in water or in the intestines of bigger animals. But those difficulties are not insuperable – merely greater. We know what most humans like to eat, what makes them comfortable, what is frightening, from our own experience. With other species we may have to make an effort to find out. The purpose of this essay is to set down the sorts of things we should be finding out if we really want to know whether other animals are suffering or not. I shall argue that it is possible to build up a reasonably convincing picture of what animals experience if the right facts about them are accumulated. This is not in any sense to deny the essentially private nature of subjective feelings, or to make any claims about the nature of mental events. It is simply to say that, just as we think we can understand other people's experiences of pleasure, pain, suffering, and happiness, so, in some of the same ways, we may begin to understand the feelings of animals – if, that is, we are prepared to make an effort to study their biology. Of course, we cannot *know* what they are feeling, but then nor can we *know* with other people. That lack of absolute certainty does not stop us from making assumptions about feelings in other people. And, suitably equipped with certain biological facts about the particular species we are concerned with, nor should it with other animals either.

A word, first, about what the term "suffering" actually means. It clearly refers to some kinds of subjective experience which have two distinguishing characteristics. First, they are unpleasant. They are mental states we would rather not experience. Secondly, they carry connotations of being extreme. A mild itch may be unpleasant, but it does not constitute "suffering" in the way that prolonged, intense electric shocks would do. One of the problems about suffering is that it is not a unique state. We talk about suffering from lack of food, but also about suffering from overeating, as well as from cold, heat, lack of water, lack of exercise, frustration, grief, and so on. Each of these states is subjectively different as an experience and has different physiological and behavioral consequences. Suffering from thirst is quite different from suffering from a bereavement, yet the same blanket term ["suffering"] is used to cover them both. About the only thing they have in common, in fact, is that they can both be extremely unpleasant, and someone experiencing either of them might feel a desire to be in a different state. For this reason, a definition of suffering as "experiencing one of a wide range of extremely unpleasant subjective (mental) states" is about as precise as we are going to be able to devise. If we were dealing with just one sort of experience – that resulting from food deprivation, for example – we would be on much firmer ground. We could study the physiological effects and what the particular species did about them. We could measure hormone levels and brain activity and perhaps come to a precise definition. But no such simplicity exists. Animals in intensive farms have plenty to eat and yet we still worry that they may be suffering from something other than lack of food. Some species may suffer in states that no human has ever dreamed of or experienced. To be on the safe side, we will, for the moment, leave the definition deliberately broad, although we will later be in a position to be a bit more precise.

Our task, therefore, is to discover methods of finding out whether and in what circumstances animals of species other than our own experience unpleasant emotional states strong enough to warrant the term "suffering." It is the very unpleasant nature of these states that forms the core of the problem. This is what we must look for evidence of – not (to stress the point made earlier) that we can expect direct evidence of unpleasant experiences in another being, but we can expect to gather indirect evidence from various sources and put it together to make a reasonably coherent case that an animal is suffering. There are three main sources of such evidence: the animal's physical health, its physiological signs, and its behavior.

Physical Health

The first and most obvious symptom of suffering is an animal's state of physical health. If an animal is injured or diseased, then there are very strong grounds for suspecting that it is suffering. All guidebooks and codes on animal care agree on how important it is to see that an animal is kept healthy and to treat any signs of injury or disease at once. For many species the signs of health (bright eyes, sleek coat or feathers) as well as those of illness (listlessness, loss of appetite, etc.) have been listed and in any case are well known to experienced animal keepers. There may be slight problems sometimes. Mammals that are hibernating or birds that are incubating their eggs may refuse food and show considerable loss of weight. These are normally signs of ill-health but in these particular cases seem to be perfectly natural events from which the animals subsequently emerge well and healthy. This simply illustrates that even the "obvious" signs of suffering, such as physical ill-health, are not infallible and have to be taken in conjunction with other evidence, a point we will return to later.

Another difficulty with using physical health (or the lack of it) to decide whether or not an animal is suffering is that it is not, of course, the disease or injury itself which constitutes the suffering: it is the accompanying mental state. An animal may be injured in the sense of being physically damaged, yet show no apparent signs of pain. The experiences of other people are very revealing here. Soldiers can be wounded in battle but, at the time, report little or no pain. Conversely, people complaining of severe and constant pain can sometimes baffle their doctors because they have no signs of tissue damage or abnormality at all. Damage to the body does not always accompany the highly unpleasant experiences we call "suffering from pain." Physiology is less help than one might expect in trying to decide when injury gives rise to pain. Although many physiologists believe that the mechanisms of pain perception are roughly similar in humans and other mammals, the physiological basis of the perception of pain is not well understood for any species. It is impossible to say with any certainty that whenever such-and-such a physiological event occurs people always report "That hurts!"

It is known that there are small nerve fibers all over the body which respond to painful stimuli, but it is difficult to interpret the messages they carry. The situation is further complicated by the existence of other nerve fibers which come out from the brain and affect the extent to which the messages in the pain fibers are allowed to travel up the spinal cord into the brain. Sometimes the messages get through and sometimes they do not, and this affects the extent to which pain is actually felt.

While pain continues to be a puzzle to physiologists, it would, however, be a mistake to use this an excuse for ignoring the effect which injury often has on animals. Mild pain may be difficult to pin down, but signs of intense pain in both human and nonhuman animals are unmistakable (they include squealing, struggling, convulsions, etc.). Uncertainty about whether disease, injury, or loss of condition does lead to "suffering" in a few cases should not be used to dismiss this valuable source of evidence about unpleasant mental states in animals. If animals show gross disturbances of health or injuries with symptoms of pain, it is reasonable to say that they suffer. Experiments or other tests conducted with animals which involve deliberately making them ill, inducing deformities, or maiming them in some way can therefore be suspected of causing suffering, unless there are good reasons (such as the fact that an animal uses a deformed limb in an apparently normal fashion) for thinking that it is not experiencing anything unpleasant.

Sometimes the capture and transport of farm animals causes weight loss, injury, and physiological deterioration so severe as to lead to death. In such circumstances the case that the animals suffered during the journey becomes very difficult to refute. In fact, the main difficulty with the physical ill-health criterion of suffering lies less with the (somewhat remote) possibility that animals may not suffer despite being injured or diseased and more with the opposite possibility: that they may appear to be physically healthy and still be undergoing intensely unpleasant mental experiences, perhaps arising from being constantly confined in a small cage. It is this possibility – that not all mental suffering may show itself in gross and obvious disturbance of physical health – that has led people to look for other ways of trying to decide when an animal is suffering.

Physiological Signs

One of the most important of these methods, which has been gaining ground recently because of advances in the technology now available to it, involves monitoring the physiological processes going on inside an animal's body. As already mentioned, some of the things which are done to animals, such as transporting cattle in certain sorts of trucks, do have such traumatic effects that injury and even death may result. But even before such gross signs of suffering set in, it may be possible to detect physiological changes within the animal – changes in hormone level, for example, or in the ammonia content of muscles. Changes take place within the animal even when, on the surface, all still appears to be well. Changes in brain activity, heart rate, and body temperature can also be picked up.

"Stress" is the name given to the whole group of physiological changes (which may also include activation of the sympathetic nervous system and enlargement of the adrenal glands) that take place whenever animals are subjected to a wide range of conditions and situations, such as overcrowding, repeated attacks by a member of their own species, and so on. One way of viewing these physiological symptoms of stress is as part of an animal's normal and perfectly adaptive way of responding to conditions which are likely, if they persist, to lead to actual physical damage or death. Thus the heart rate goes up in preparation for an animal's escape from danger, when it will need more oxygen for its muscles in order to do this effectively. The change in heart rate suggests that the animal has recognized possible danger in the form, say, of potential injury caused by the attack of a predator. This leads to a serious difficulty in the interpretation of physiological measurements of stress. It may be perfectly possible to pick up a change in the level of a particular hormone or in heart rate, but what exactly do these changes mean for the animal? There is no justification for concluding that it "suffers" every time there is a bit more hormone in its blood or its heart rate goes up slightly. On the contrary, these signs may simply indicate that the animal is coping with its environment in an adaptive way. Changes in brain activity may signify nothing more than that the animal is exploring a new object in its environment. We would certainly not want to describe an alert and inquiring animal as "suffering." On the other hand, when physiological disturbances become severe (when the adrenal glands are very enlarged, for instance), then they become the precursors of overt disease, and we probably would want to say the animal was suffering.

The problem is to know at precisely what stage physiological changes in the animal stop being part of its usual adaptive response to its environment and start indicating a prolonged or intensely unpleasant state of suffering. The problem lies not so much in detecting the changes as in their interpretation and in relating them to possible mental state. At the moment this remains a major drawback. Physiological measures, although a valuable indication of what is going on beneath the animal's skin, do not tell us everything we want to know about mental states.

Behavior

A third, and very important, source of information about suffering in animals is their behavior. Behavior has the great advantage that it can be studied without interfering with the animal in any way. (Even with today's technology, making physiological measurements may itself impose some sort of hardship on the animal.) Many animals display particular signs which can, with care, be used to infer something about their mental states. Charles Darwin recognized this when he entitled his book about animal communication *The Expression of the Emotions in Man and Animals*. The problem, of course, is to crack the code and to work out which behavior an animal uses to signal which emotional state.

Various different approaches have been tried. The most direct involves putting an animal in a situation in which it is thought to "suffer" (usually mildly) and then observing its behavior. For instance, if we wanted to know how a pig behaved when it was "suffering from fear" or "suffering from frustration," we might deliberately expose it briefly to one of its predators (to frighten it) or give it a dish of food covered with glass (to frustrate it). Its behavior in these circumstances would give some indication of what it does when it is afraid or frustrated. We could then go on to an intensive pig farm and watch the pigs there to see if they showed similar behavior. If they did, this would give us some grounds for inferring that they too were afraid or frustrated.

This method does have rather severe limitations, however. For one thing, the way a pig expresses frustration at not being able to get at food covered with glass may be quite different from the way it expresses frustration at not having any nest material, so we may simply overlook evidence of frustration through being unfamiliar with its various forms of expression. More seriously, even if we had correctly identified the way in which a pig expressed "frustration" or "fear," we would still be left with the same problem of calibration that we encountered with other methods such as the measurement of physiological variables. We would still not know, in other words, *how much* behavior associated with fear or frustration has to be shown before we are justified in saying that the animal is "suffering." A fox temporarily caught in a thicket or unable to get into a henhouse may show agitated movements which are evidence of mild frustration, but we would hardly want to say that it is "suffering." But the same animal, confined for long periods of time in a small, bare cage from which there is no way out and performing the same backwards-and-forwards movements over and over again, might justifiably be described as suffering. Somewhere we want to draw the line, but it is difficult, without some further evidence, to know where.

What this method fails to do – indeed, what all the methods we have described so far fail to do – is to come to grips with the really essential issue of what we mean by suffering, to give an indication of how much what is being done to the animal really matters to the animal itself. We may see injury, measure physiological changes, or watch behavior, but what we really want to know is whether the animal is subjectively experiencing a state sufficiently unpleasant to it to deserve the emotive label "suffering." Does its injury cause pain? We need, in other words, the animal's opinion of what is being done to it – not just whether it finds it pleasant or unpleasant but *how* unpleasant it finds it.

"Asking" the Animals

At first sight it may seem quite impossible even to think of trying to obtain any sensible, scientifically based evidence on this point. We cannot ask animals to tell us in so many words what it feels like to be inside their skins. But even with other human beings words are not always our most powerful source of information. We say things like, "Actions speak louder than words" or "He put his money where his mouth is." The word "mouthing" actually carries an implicit suspicion of "mere words." We are, in fact, particularly impressed by someone who does not just say that he dislikes or disapproves of something but shows it by taking some action and "voting with his feet." For all our human reliance on words and the complexity of our languages, we are often more impressed by what other human beings do than by what they say. And the things that impress us most about what they do – making choices between difficult alternatives, moving from one place to another, forgoing a desirable commodity for a later, larger reward – are things that many nonhuman animals do too.

Other animals besides humans can make choices and express their preferences by moving away from or towards one environment or another. They can be taught to operate a mechanism which in some way changes their environment for better or worse. A rat that repeatedly presses a lever to get food or to gain access to a female is certainly "telling" us something about the desirability, for him, of these things. The rat which crosses an electric grid to get at a female is telling us even more. Silverman (1978) describes an experiment in which rats and hamsters were certainly making their views plain enough. These animals were being used in an experiment to study the effects of cigarette smoke. They were kept in glass cylinders into which a steady stream of smoke was delivered down a small tube. Many of the animals quickly learned to use their own feces to bung up the tubes and block the smoke stream. It was not completely clear whether it was the smoke itself or the draft of air that they objected to, but it was quite clear that they disliked what was being done to them. Words here would simply have been superfluous.

This "asking without words" approach has now been used in a wide variety of situations. It is a direct way of finding out, from the animal's point of view, what it finds pleasant or unpleasant. Choice tests, in which animals are offered two or more alternatives, enable them to "vote with their feet." For example, as I have described elsewhere (Dawkins 1977), chickens which have been kept in battery cages have shown clearly that they prefer an outside run to a cage. These two very different environments were presented to hens at the opposite ends of a corridor from the center of which they could see both simultaneously. They were then free to walk into either one. Most of the hens chose to go into the outside run, not the battery cage, the first time they were given the choice. A few of the hens chose the battery cage at first, probably because that was what they were used to – the run was such a novel experience for them that they did not seem to know what it was. But all they needed was a few minutes' experience of the run, and by the second or third time that they were faced with the choice, they too chose the run. This seems to be a fairly objective way of saying that the hens liked the experience of being outside in a run more than they liked being in a battery cage.

While this result is perhaps not particularly unexpected, animals' own preferences do sometimes produce surprises. The Brambell Committee (1965), which produced an important report on intensive farming in the UK, recommended that fine hexagonal wire should not be used for the floors of battery cages on the grounds that it was thought (by well-meaning humans) to be uncomfortable for the hens' feet. When allowed to choose between different floor types, however, the hens actually preferred the fine mesh to the coarser one which had been recommended by the Committee, as Hughes and Black (1973) reported. Other animals that have been "asked" their opinion of their surroundings are laboratory mice and rats, which have shown preferences for certain sorts of nest box and cage size; and Baldwin and Ingram (1967) allowed pigs to choose their own temperature and light levels by providing them with switches they could operate with their snouts to alter the amount of heat and light. Sometimes animals' preferences result in an actual saving for the farmer. Curtis (1983) reported a study on a group of young pigs which actually turned their heating down at night, below the level that humans thought should be maintained all the time, which resulted in a considerable saving in fuel. Such a happy coincidence between what animals like and what is best for commercial profit does not, however, always occur.

In any case, just because an animal prefers one set of conditions to another, that does not necessarily mean that it suffers if kept in the less preferred ones. In order to establish the link – that is, to make the connection between preference (or lack of it) and suffering – it is necessary to find out how strong the animal's aversion to the less attractive situation is, or how powerfully it is attracted to preferred conditions. If a male rat will cross a live electric grid to get a female or a hen goes without food in order to obtain somewhere to dustbathe, they are demonstrating that these things are not just "liked" but are very important to them indeed. Many people would agree that animals suffer if kept without food or if given electric shocks. If the animals tell us that other things are as important as or more important to them than food or the avoidance of shock, then we might want to say that they suffer if deprived of these other things as well.

We have, therefore, to get animals to put a "price" on their preferences. Now, it is obviously something of a problem to decide how to ask animals how they rate one commodity, such as food, against something that may be quite different, such as the opportunity to dustbathe, wallow in mud, or fight a rival. But the problem is not insuperable, and one of the easiest ways to determine this is through what psychologists call "operant conditioning," which simply means giving an animal the chance to learn that by pressing a lever, say, it gets something it likes, such as a piece of food (a reward), or can avoid something it doesn't like (a punishment). Depending on the animal, what it has to do can vary. Birds often find it easier to peck a disk than to operate a lever, which a rat would do readily, and fish, of course, would have difficulties with either and would have to be given, say, a hoop to swim through. Once the animal has learned to do whatever has been devised for it, the experimenter can then begin to raise the "price" by making the animal peck the key or press the lever not just once but many times before it gets anything at all. In the Netherlands van Rooijen (1983) reports that he has used this method to measure the strength of the preference of pigs for earth floors by forcing them to make a larger number of responses in order to be allowed access to the earth.

When food is being used as the reward, animals usually appear to be prepared to work harder and harder for the same reward, indicating, not surprisingly, that food is very important to them. Other commodities, however, seem to be less important. Male Siamese fighting fish can readily be trained to do things for the reward of being able to see and display at a rival fish of the same species. But if the number of responses the fish has to make for each opportunity to display at a rival is increased, the fish do not work any harder and so obtain a smaller number of views of their rival, according to Hogan, Kleist, and L. Hutchings (1970). A similar result has been reported for cocks pecking at keys for food and for the sight of another cock. When the number of pecks required for each presentation (bit of food or sight of a rival) was increased, the birds would work much harder for food than to see their rival. Access to a rival seemed in both these examples to be less important to the animals than food.

An Objective Measure of Suffering

There are, then, ways of obtaining measures of how much an animal prefers or dislikes something. Here is the key to discovering the circumstances in which an animal finds things so unpleasant that we want to say that it is suffering. If it will work hard to obtain or to escape from something – as hard as or harder than it will work to obtain food, which most people would agree is an essential to health and welfare – then we can begin to compile a list of situations which cause suffering and, indeed, can arrive at a tentative further definition of suffering itself: animals suffer if kept in conditions in which they are without something that they will work hard to obtain, given the opportunity, or in conditions that they will work hard to get away from, also given the opportunity. "Working hard" can be given precise meaning, as explained earler, by raising the "price" of a commodity and seeing how much it is worth to the animal. We then have the animal's view of its environment.

Of course, we have to make one important assumption: that if animals are prepared to work hard in this way, they do experience a mental state which is "pleasant" if something is rewarding and "unpleasant" if they are trying to avoid that something. We have, in other words, to make a leap from inside our own skins to the inside of theirs. But this leap is a very bare minimum. It does not assume that other animals find the *same* things pleasant or unpleasant as we do, only that working to obtain or working to avoid something is an indication of the presence of these mental states and that working hard is an indication that they are very pleasant or very unpleasant. Exactly what other animals find very pleasant or very unpleasant is left to experimental tests. In other words, the leap that we have to make from our skins to theirs takes into account the possibility that their suffering or their pleasure may be brought about by events quite different from those that cause them in us. We are not imagining ourselves shut up in a battery cage or dressed up in a bat suit when we try to find out what it is like to be a hen or a bat; we are trying to find out what it is like to *be* them. There is a lot of difference between the two. In the first case we would see animals as just like us, only with fur or feathers. In the second case we acknowledge that their view of the world may be very different from our own, that their requirements and what makes them comfortable or uncomfortable may be nothing like what we ourselves would require. We then have to get down to the business of finding out what their view of the world really is. Operant conditioning may be the key, the window on to their world, but it takes quite a lot of effort to get all the answers we need.

Even then we are not completely home and dry. Preference tests and operant conditioning, though immensely valuable tools, do not provide all the answers. A dog might show very strongly, if "asked" in this way, that he would rather not go to the vet. One could make out a strong case for saying that he "suffers" if forced to do so. Cattle, given a free choice, do not always eat what is good for them and may even poison themselves. It would therefore be a mistake to use these methods in isolation from other measures of suffering. A synthetic approach (one, that is, that takes into account all the measures that we have discussed) is probably the safest bet in the long run. Since each of these measures has something to be said against it, some limits to its usefulness, the safest approach is therefore to make as many different sorts of measurement as we can and then to put them together to see what sort of conglomerate picture we get. For example, suppose some hypothetical animals were kept in small cages, in conditions that were very different from those of their wild ancestors. Suppose people had expressed considerable worry that they were suffering. How might we go about evaluating this claim?

We might look first at the physical health of the animals. If we found them to be very healthy, with bright eyes and sleek, glossy coats and no signs of injury or parasites, we might then want to proceed to other measures. If we noticed that the animal showed a number of unusual behavior patterns not shown by freer animals of the same species, the next step would be to investigate what caused them to behave in this way. In the first case it might be that the unusual behavior was solely the result of the animals showing positive reactions to their keepers. We might also find that the animals appeared to "like" their cages and that they would choose them in preference to other conditions which well-meaning humans thought they would prefer. In such circumstances our verdict might be that although the animals were kept in highly unnatural conditions, they did not, on any criteria, appear to be suffering as a result. On the other hand, the conclusions might be very different even for physically healthy animals. If the animals showed evidence of a high degree of frustration, prolonged over much of their lives, with evidence of a build-up of physiological symptoms that were known to be precursors of disease, we might begin to think they were suffering. If, in addition, they showed every sign of trying to escape from their cages, and indeed did so when given the opportunity, our evidence on this point would become even stronger.

The point of these hypothetical examples is to show how, given different sorts of evidence, different conclusions can be reached about whether or not animals are suffering. We have still not observed their mental states directly. Nor have we escaped altogether from some use of analogy with our own feelings to tell us what a member of another species might be experiencing. In the last analysis, we have to rely on analogy with ourselves to decide that any other being (including another human) experiences anything at all, since our own skin is the only one we have any direct experience of being inside. But analogy with ourselves that relies on seeing animals as just like human beings with fur or feathers is quite different and much more prone to error than analogy which makes full use of our biological knowledge of the animal concerned – the conditions in which it is healthy, what it chooses, its behavior and its physiology. This second kind of analogy, the piece-by-piece construction of a picture (What does the animal like? What makes it healthy? What are its signs of fear or frustration?), is hard work to construct, as it needs a lot of basic research on each kind of animal with which we might come into contact. But it is the only kind of analogy which, in the end, will give us any real hope of being able to unlock other species from their skins and of beginning to see the world through not just our eyes but theirs as well.

References

Baldwin, B. A., and Ingram, D. I. (1967) "Behavioural Thermoregulation in Pigs," *Physiology and Behaviour* 10, 267–72.

Brambell, F. W. R. (1965) *Report of the Technical Committee to Enquire into the Welfare of Animals Kept under Intensive Livestock Husbandry System*, London: HMSO.

Curtis, S. E. (1983) "Perception of Thermal Comfort by Farm Animals," in S. H. Baxter, M. R. Baxter, and J. A. C. MacCormack (eds), *Farm Animal Welfare and Housing*, The Hague: Martinus Nijhoff, pp. 3–7.

Dawkins, M. S. (1977) "Do Hens Suffer in Battery Cages? Environmental Preferences and Welfare," *Animal Behaviour* 25, 1034–46.

Hogan, J. A., Kleist, S., and Hutchings, C. S. L. (1970) "Display and Food as Reinforcers in the Siamese Fighting Fish (*Betta splendens*)," *Journal of Comparative and Physiological Psychology* 70, 351–7.

Hughes, B. O., and Black, A. J. (1973) "The Preference of Domestic Hens for Different Types of Battery Cage Floor," *British Poultry Science* 14, 615–19.

Silverman, A. P. (1978) "Rodents' Defence Against Cigarette Smoke," *Animal Behaviour* 26, 1279–81.

Van Rooijen, J. (1983) "Improverished Environments and Welfare," *Applied Animal Behavioural Science* 12, 3–13.

3

On the Question
of Personhood beyond
Homo sapiens

David DeGrazia

What is a person? Are any nonhuman beings persons? This essay will address these and several related questions.

The Concept of Personhood

The word "person" traces back at least to the Latin *persona*: a mask, especially as worn by an actor, or a character or social role. The concept evolved into the Roman idea of a *bearer of legal rights* – so that, notably, slaves did not qualify as persons – before broadening into the Stoic and Christian idea of a *bearer of moral value*; perhaps this transition involved broadening the relevant conception of law from human legal systems to "natural" (moral) law. The modern concept, as exemplified in John Locke's writings (Locke 1694: Bk 2, ch. 27), understands persons as beings with certain complex forms of consciousness. I will take this modern concept as our shared concept of personhood.

In ordinary life, when we refer to persons we are usually referring to particular human beings. The term refers paradigmatically to normal human beings who have advanced beyond infancy and toddler years. As paradigm persons, normal human children, adolescents, and adults are psychologically complex, highly social, and linguistically competent. What about human babies and fetuses, or those individuals, such as the severely retarded or severely demented, whose psychological and social capabilities are dramatically impaired – are they persons? Are any nonhuman animals?

Addressing such questions requires a more detailed account of personhood. Importantly, the concept applies to some beings beyond *Homo sapiens*. For we often categorize as persons certain imaginary nonhuman beings and some nonhuman beings whose existence is debatable. Thus Spock from *Star Trek*, E.T. the extraterrestrial, and the speaking, encultured apes of *The Planet of the Apes* impress us as being persons. Moreover, if God and angels exist, they too are persons. This demonstrates that "person" does not simply mean "human being" or even "human being [with certain capabilities]." The term refers to a kind of being defined by certain psychological traits or capacities: beings with particular complex forms of consciousness, such as self-awareness over time, rationality, and sociabililty. So, in principle, there could be nonhuman persons, for it is imaginable – and perhaps true – that certain nonhumans have the relevant properties.

It is sometimes suggested that, in addition to referring *descriptively* to beings with certain psychological properties, as just discussed, the term "person" conveys *someone with moral status* (or perhaps *full moral status*). But whether or not "person" combines descriptive content with such a moral content, it clearly has descriptive content.[1] And, because the assumption that moral status requires personhood is increasingly challenged today – for example, by those who hold that many animals also have moral status – it will be advantageous to focus on the term's descriptive meaning, which is less controversial.

How should we elucidate personhood in greater detail? Although many fairly specific analyses have been offered, it is not difficult to expose their inadequacies. Consider Harry Frankfurt's thesis that persons are beings capable of autonomy – in his terminology, "freedom of the will" – roughly, the capacity to examine critically the motivations that move one to act in a particular way, and either identify with these motivations or reject and work to change them (Frankfurt 1971; cf. Dennett 1978: ch. 14). Thus an autonomous being, or person, may have an incessant desire to drink, due to alcoholism, but may fight this desire and seek to extinguish it. Yet to require so much cognitive development for personhood is to require too much. No one really doubts that normal two- or three-year-olds and moderately retarded individuals are persons, yet they may lack the critical reflection needed for autonomy in this sense. Another view, suggested by Peter

Strawson (1959: 104), is that to be a person is to have both mental and bodily characteristics. But this is far too inclusive, as many nonhuman animals we would not call persons have both types of characteristics.

It will be instructive to consider another definition that may strike one as plausible: persons as rational, self-aware beings (Singer 1993: 110–11). The problem here is that neither rationality nor self-awareness is an all-or-nothing trait. Many creatures we would not call persons display some degree of rationality, which comes in degrees. For example, a dog who wants to go outside believes that heading to the dog door will get him there, and then intentionally heads to the dog door as a means to getting outside displays simple instrumental rationality.[2] Meanwhile, self-awareness admits of different kinds as well as degrees. For example, presumably all animals capable of intentional action, such as dogs, have some degree of *bodily* self-awareness, an awareness of their own bodies as distinct from the rest of the environment. Relatively social mammals also have *social* self-awareness: an awareness of how they fit into group structures, the expectations that come with their positions in the group, what may happen if they act against those expectations, and so on. Vervet monkeys are socially self-aware to an impressive degree (Cheney and Seyfarth 1990). A third kind of self-awareness is *introspective* awareness, consciousness of one's own mental states. Whether any nonhuman animals have this capacity is uncertain. In any case, owing to the diversity of kinds of self-awareness, each of which comes in degrees, it illuminates little to say simply that personhood requires self-awareness. Which type? If one responds that introspective awareness, say, is necessary and sufficient for being a person, it would be appropriate to reply that this trait is only one of a cluster of traits that seem about equally implicated in the concept of a person. To identify it alone as definitive would be arbitrary.

Thus I suggest that personhood is associated with a cluster of properties without being precisely definable in terms of any specific subset: autonomy, rationality, self-awareness, linguistic competence, sociability, the capacity for intentional action, and moral agency. One doesn't need all these traits, however specified, to be a person, as demonstrated by nonautonomous persons. Nor is it sufficient to have just one of them, as suggested by the fact that a vast range of animals are capable of intentional action. Rather, a person is someone who has enough of these properties. Moreover, the concept is fairly vague in that we cannot draw a precise, nonarbitrary line that specifies what counts as enough. Like many or most concepts, personhood has blurred boundaries. Still, "person" means something, permitting us to identify paradigm persons and, beyond these easy cases, other individuals who are sufficiently similar to warrant inclusion under the concept.

Do we know of any persons, extinct or currently living, beyond *Homo sapiens*?

Other Hominid Persons

Normal children of our species, *Homo sapiens*, are among the paradigm persons. Surely, then, at least some members of other hominid species were also persons, for there is no reason to think they were all vastly less endowed with personhood-relevant properties than human children are. Let me explain.

Although ours is the only surviving hominid species, hominid evolution featured various others, including *Homo erectus*, *Homo habilis*, *Homo rudolfensis*, *Australopithecus africanus*, *Australopithecus robustus*, and others. Interestingly, two of the great ape species, chimpanzees and bonobos, and the various hominid species, including ours, had a common ancestor who lived only 5 to 7 million years ago (Dawkins 1993: 82; see also Hecht 2003).

Now consider whichever hominid species we evolved from. Typical members of that species were genetically a bit different from us. Yet it is hardly plausible that *no* members of that species were sufficiently like our (normal) human children – who are clearly persons – to qualify as persons. Indeed, there is no natural marker that could separate the two species in the course of evolution; it is not as if some decisive mutation created a massive gulf dividing us from our immediate predecessors. Any dividing line in hominid evolution would be something to draw in an arbitrarily chosen place at least as much as a biological reality to find. So, because normal human children are clearly persons, at least some hominids who were not *Homo sapiens* were persons as well. Therefore, in actual fact and not just science fiction and speculative religion, there have been persons beyond *Homo sapiens*.

One might object that, since our concept of personhood is relatively modern, it makes no sense to attribute it to prehistoric hominids. But the objection is confused. While our *concept* of personhood is modern, the concept designates a *kind of being* with certain complex forms of consciousness. Such beings existed long before any arrived at the modern concept, just as plutonium and dinosaurs existed long before anyone employed the concepts of plutonium and dinosaurs.

Ordinary Great Apes and Dolphins as Borderline Persons

Even if hominid evolution featured some persons beyond our species, one might argue, there are no known cases of *living* nonhuman persons. But as the only candidates we know are terrestrial beings, this contention begs the question of whether any nonhuman animals are persons. I will argue that normal representatives of the great ape and certain cetacean species are *borderline persons*, lying in an ambiguous gray area between paradigm persons and those who are clearly not persons.

To which animals are we referring? The great apes include ("common") chimpanzees, bonobos (sometimes called "pygmy chimpanzees"), gorillas, and orangutans. Sometimes for convenience I will refer to great apes simply as "apes" – although there are also "lesser apes," gibbons and siamangs, to whom I will not be referring. Cetaceans include all whales, including the smaller whales known as dolphins (of the family *Delphinidae*) and porpoises (of the family *Phocoenidae*). Sometimes the term "dolphin" is used broadly to include both of these families of smaller whales, and for convenience I will adopt this broader usage. Available evidence suggests that apes and dolphins are the most cognitively, emotionally, and socially advanced nonhuman animals, making them the best known candidates for presently living nonhuman persons.

Let's briefly review some of this evidence, beginning with the great apes. Although their capacity for intentional action is evident in virtually every-thing they do, it is especially apparent in certain activities that express un-usual deliberateness, reasoning, or planning. For example, chimpanzees regularly use tools such as moss for a sponge, stems as probes for insects, and rocks as nut-crackers (see, e.g., McGrew 1992: 44–6). Meanwhile, all of the apes engage in social manipulation, including deception, of their fellows (see, e.g., Byrne 1996; de Waal 1997: 39–40; Tomasello and Call 1997: 235–59). Further, apes are self-aware in more than one way. Bodily self-awareness, which is manifested in all intentional action, is more im-pressively revealed in apes' imitation of bodily gestures,[3] use of mirrors to investigate otherwise inaccessible markings on their own bodies,[4] and use of televised images of their out-of-view arms to reach hidden objects (see Tomasello and Call 1997: 52). Social self-awareness, meanwhile, is evident in apes' natural social structures, which feature dominance hierarchies, long-term relationships, and shifting allegiances; individuals need to know their positions, and the associated expectations, within these complex social dynamics in order to thrive (see Byrne 1996; Goodall 1986: chs 7, 8, 18, 19; Maple 1980: chs 2, 3, 6). Naturally, evidence for their social self-awareness is also evidence for their sociability more generally. An especially striking manifestation of sociability is found in rudimentary culture: the transmission from one generation to the next of novel behaviors such as building nests, using leaves for medicinal purposes, or fashioning certain types of tools. Differing behaviors across populations within the same species are attributed to culture where there are no plausible genetic or environmental explanations for the differences (see, e.g., McGrew 1992; Vendantam 2003). Finally, there is some evidence of moral agency among apes. The most convincing is observation of apparently altruistic actions that seem neither instinctual nor conditioned – for example, chimps' adopting and raising an abandoned, disabled infant boy.[5] More controversial is whether everyday displays of what appear to be courage, compassion, and other qualities that count as virtues in humans – but may have a biological basis – should count as genuinely moral in apes, whose capacity for *full-fledged* moral agency (including deliberation and moral judgment) is itself uncertain.[6]

Like apes, dolphins act intentionally. Moreover, a high degree of deliberateness and/or rationality is suggested by innovative behaviors such as cooperative hunting that appears responsive to immediate circumstances (Mann et al. 2000). Some dolphins routinely wear cone-shaped sponges over their beaks, possibly a protective measure (tool use) as they nose along the bottom in search of food (Connor and Peterson 1994: 195–6). And captive dolphins have been known to demonstrate exceptional intelligence, as when one mastered the subtle rule, "Do something novel" (Connor and Peterson 1994: 187–8). As mentioned, bodily self-awareness is manifested in intentional action. But it is more graphically evident when dolphins exhibit their extraordinary capacity to imitate the actions and postures of others (including seals, penguins, and humans) as well as human speech (see, e.g., Connor and Peterson 1994: 188–91); there have even been reports of spontaneously learning complex routines simply by observing others.[7] And dolphins have now demonstrated the capacity to recognize themselves in mirrors (Reiss and Marino 2001). Meanwhile, both great sociability and social self-awareness are strongly suggested by their highly complex social life, which features all of the following: dominance hierarchies and long-term relationships, including intense mother–calf bonding (Norris and Dohl 1980); recognition of one another's signature whistles and possibly the calling of each other by imitating their whistles (see, e.g., Caldwell and Caldwell 1971;

Connor and Peterson 1994: 191); and "social" sex (Connor and Peterson 1994: 112–14). (Another intriguing phenomenon is the voluntary, temporary beaching of healthy whales in the company of a dying, beached group member, which may express solidarity or friendship [Connor and Peterson 1994: 102–3], but I do not know whether dolphins have been observed engaging in this behavior.) Whether dolphins are capable of moral agency is debatable. Surely, they exhibit traits considered virtues in humans, such as courage and tenderness towards close relations, but the possible biological basis of these traits leaves their status as virtues uncertain. As dolphins and other cetaceans have apparently assisted not only species members in distress, but also sharks and humans, the attribution of genuine altruism is common (see, e.g., Norris and Dohl 1980). Considering the overall social and cognitive complexity of these animals, I find this interpretation plausible. But another possible explanation is that they were simply exhibiting their natural habit of pushing unusual objects to the surface; only those human beings who made it to shore lived to report the experience.

On the whole, great apes and dolphins are fairly well endowed with personhood-relevant properties. Yet, with a few exceptions discussed in the next section, they are not so well endowed with these traits to qualify clearly as persons. Normal human children, by comparison, are robustly competent in language, clearly capable of introspective awareness – having knowledge of their own feelings, desires, and beliefs – and more likely to show signs of autonomy. My suggestion, then, is that normal, post-infancy great apes and dolphins are *borderline persons*. Given the vagueness of the concept of personhood, that is, there is no definite yes-or-no answer to the question of whether they are persons.

The Personhood of Certain Language-Trained Animals

So far we have not refuted the common assumption that known cases of presently existing nonhuman persons are lacking. I challenge that assumption in this section.

The results of several rigorous ape-language studies are impressive.[8] I will focus on three test subjects. First, the bonobo Kanzi learned, by observation without explicit training, to use the keyboard on which his mother was being trained, quickly becoming more proficient than the intended pupil. Although Kanzi's comprehension exceeds his productive language skills, he produces strings of two or three words that have clear meaning in their context. Most astonishing, however, is his comprehension of spoken English – which he understands even when using headphones that prevent trainers from giving bodily cues to the correct answers. Not only does he demonstrate his grasp of novel utterances (e.g., "Take the vacuum cleaner outdoors") by performing the action requested; he also shows mastery of rudimentary syntax by distinguishing word sequences whose meanings differ only due to word order (e.g., "Pour the coke into the milk" and "Pour the milk into the coke") (see, e.g., PBS 1995; Savage-Rumbaugh 1986; Savage-Rumbaugh and Brakke 1990).

Meanwhile, the gorilla Koko lives in an environment of American Sign Language and spoken English. She combines a vocabulary of hundreds of signs into strings of three or more signs. The English vocabulary she understands is considerably larger. Interestingly, she signs to other language-trained gorillas and has signed very slowly when working with humans who are less familiar with the language. Among Koko's novel definitions are these. "What's an insult?" "THINK DEVIL DIRTY." "When do people say darn?" "WORK. OBNOXIOUS." "What's a smart gorilla?" "ME." She has called a mask "EYE HAT" and a lighter "BOTTLE MATCH." Referring to an event in the past, when asked what happened on her birthday, she signed "OLD GORILLA." Koko has even provided hints of introspective awareness, for example by signing "RED MAD GORILLA" when angry, and some evidence of significant moral agency when apologizing for having bitten a companion the day before ("SORRY BITE SCRATCH" and "WRONG BITE") and explaining the act by saying she was mad (see, e.g., Patterson 1978; Patterson and Gordon 1993).

The orangutan Chantek has learned over 150 signs of sign language and has learned, without training, how to understand much spoken English. He signs for objects that are not present – for instance, asking to go places in the backyard to look for a favorite cat. Chantek also apparently signs for manipulative purposes, for example signing "DIRTY" as a pretense to go to the bathroom to play with the washing machine. Also creative are certain original combinations of signs such as "EYE DRINK" for contact lens solution and "DAVE MISSING FINGER" for someone who had lost a finger (see, e.g., Miles 1993).

Cetaceans may have the most complex natural communication systems among nonhuman animals. Their vocal repertoires of whistles, squeaks, pops, groans, and clicks have been observed to elicit distinct yet consistent responses (Connor and Peterson 1994: ch. 4). Nevertheless, I would not claim that these natural systems have sufficient complexity to constitute languages. However, two bottlenose dolphins, Phoenix and Akeakamai, have received training in both an acoustic language and a visual language featuring hand signals. Signs refer to objects, actions, properties, and relationships; word sequences are constructed according to word-order rules permitting more than 2,000 combinations with distinct meanings. The dolphins have shown a mastery of syntax with their distinct responses to such imperatives as "person surfboard fetch" (bring the person to the surfboard) and "surfboard person fetch" (bring the surfboard to the person). Further achievements include executing two orders simultaneously without being trained to do so, grasping four-word strings the first time they were presented, and coordinating responses with the other dolphin (Herman 1991; Herman and Morrel-Samuels 1990).

I contend that the five animals just described (and perhaps others) are persons. Each demonstrates not only the personhood-relevant properties attributed to normal apes and dolphins in the previous section, but also enough linguistic competence to count as possessing language. Some probably have other relevant properties beyond what is species-typical. For example, Koko provides strong hints of introspective awareness and significant moral agency. Human children who are as cognitively, emotionally, and socially complex as these apes and dolphins qualify as persons. For the same reasons, these rather extraordinary animals are persons.

One might wonder, however, why I have attributed personhood to certain linguistically trained apes and dolphins, but only borderline personhood to other members of their species. Perhaps the successful linguistic instruction of the former group merely reveals preexisting, complex forms of consciousness that all normal apes and dolphins should be presumed to possess. Such an inference would be reckless, however, for two reasons. First, it is possible that Kanzi, Koko, Chantek, Phoenix, and Akeakamai are exceptionally talented for their species, helping to explain why they have achieved a high level of linguistic competence while other trainees have done less well (although an alternative explanation is that the more successful pupils were subject to superior training methods – see DeGrazia 1996: 183–98). Second, I find it very plausible to believe that the acquisition of language greatly increases the complexity of thought of which one is capable (DeGrazia 1996: 154–8). If so, then even if normal apes and dolphins have the capacity – with suitable training – to acquire language, the undeveloped capacity would not entail mental life whose complexity rivals that of linguistically competent animals.

The Significance or Insignificance of Personhood

Some members of hominid species other than *Homo sapiens* were persons. So are a few living nonhuman animals. And ordinary great apes and dolphins are borderline persons inasmuch as there is no uniquely correct answer to the question of whether they are persons. Do these facts have any significance beyond their possible conceptual interest to the philosophically minded? That depends on whether, and to what extent, personhood itself matters.

Moral tradition, especially in the West, has maintained the following: (1) persons have exclusive or at least radically superior moral status; (2) nonpersons have radically inferior moral status; (3) there are no beings in between these two categories; and (4) no nonhuman animals are persons. If the arguments of this essay are correct, this traditional picture is at least partly distorted, because claim (3) is undermined by the large class of borderline persons while claim (4) is refuted by the most linguistically competent nonhuman animals. Consequently, the still influential image of a wide, unbridgeable gulf dividing humans from all other creatures proves to have no basis in reality.

I believe the traditional picture is even more distorted than these points suggest. While I cannot defend my assertion here (but see DeGrazia 1996: ch. 3), I contend that claims (1) and (2) are also false. Even if there are some morally important differences between persons and nonpersons, the claim that persons have exclusive or *radically* superior moral status is indefensible. Sentient animals have significant moral status in virtue of having a welfare; they are not merely, or even primarily, tools for our use or playthings for our amusement. Even if personhood proves to have some moral significance, sentience is far more fundamental and important. Or so I have argued elsewhere – and other contributors to this volume concur.

So does personhood matter morally? I will discuss two possible bases for thinking so. While I find the first more plausible than the second, I believe both are reasonable theses that merit our careful attention.

A bit of theoretical background is needed to explain the first thesis about personhood's importance. Despite differences, the moral frameworks affording the strongest protections for animals agree that animals deserve *equal consideration*. More precisely, these frameworks agree that where humans and animals have a comparable interest – say, avoiding suffering – the animal's interest deserves as much moral weight as the human's comparable interest.

(Animals and humans have a comparable interest where they have roughly the same thing at stake.) So equal consideration implies that the moral presumption against causing animals to suffer is about as strong as the presumption against causing humans to suffer.

Most champions of equal consideration for animals acknowledge some morally important differences between normal humans – persons – and most or all nonhuman animals. The point of greatest convergence is that the presumption against killing persons is stronger than the presumption against killing nonpersons. This claim is consistent with equal consideration if your life-interest, your interest in remaining alive, is *not* comparable to your cat's life-interest – if, that is, different things are at stake for you and your cat because you (ordinarily) stand to lose much more from death. Although providing a fully coherent justification for this claim of non-comparability is very difficult, here I simply note that many defenders of animals accept it. Thus, one possible source of importance for personhood is this: *personhood is necessary and sufficient for life-interests of full strength.*[9]

This thesis implies that animal persons such as Kanzi and Koko have rights to life comparable to ours. It would therefore be morally outrageous to use them in lethal experimentation even if their interest as language users diminished. What about borderline persons? I believe we should regard human and nonhuman borderline persons as having rights to life like ours, though I cannot defend this claim here.[10] If this is correct, then to the extent that similar points can be made about liberty – freedom from harmful confinement – another implication is that dolphins should be confined only when the conditions of confinement represent a net benefit for them. I suspect that this would mean banning dolphin exhibits. More generally, it would call for extending to apes and dolphins legal rights to life and liberty.[11]

A second possible thesis about the importance of personhood is this: *personhood is necessary and sufficient for deserving full (equal) consideration.* On this view, the interests of persons deserve full moral protection while the interests of sentient nonpersons deserve serious, but less than full, consideration.

This unequal-consideration framework can be developed in different ways. One possible picture is a sliding scale of moral status, determined by the possession of personhood-relevant properties and culminating in the plane of persons. Accordingly, while we should never cavalierly cause anyone to suffer, the presumption against causing persons to suffer is stronger than the presumption against causing dogs to suffer (justifying, for example, some experimentation we would not permit on persons), which is stronger than the presumption against causing a reptile to suffer, and so on. An alternative specification of this framework posits not a sliding scale among nonpersons, but simply two tiers: that of persons, whose interests are generally not to be sacrificed in the name of utility; and the tier of sentient nonpersons, whose interests are subject to consequentialist tradeoffs.[12]

Naturally, the two assertions about the importance of personhood face theoretical and moral challenges. Both, for example, face the problem of human nonpersons: can we really accept the apparent implication that their lives are less morally protectable than ours, or that their interests across the board deserve less weight than ours? If not, how can we afford them adequate protection without contradicting our thesis about the importance of personhood?

Even if both major theses about personhood's importance are correct (something I doubt), personhood is less important than moral tradition has assumed. The world does not divide neatly into persons and nonpersons, some individuals beyond *Homo sapiens* are persons, and many are borderline persons. These facts have practical implications – which we should clarify, disseminate to the broader public, and employ as a basis for reforming attitudes and practices.

Notes

Thanks to Peter Singer for several useful suggestions.

1. I develop this argument in DeGrazia (1997: 312–14).
2. I argue that many animals can act intentionally and to some degree rationally in DeGrazia (1996: 129–72).
3. For a summary of relevant evidence, see Wise (2000: 204–5).
4. Gordon Gallup (1977) demonstrated such mirror use in chimpanzees and orangutans. See also Patterson and Gordon (1993: 71).
5. "Boy Adopted by Chimps," article on *news.com.au*, March 15, 2002.
6. I explore this issue in DeGrazia (1996: 199–200).
7. For a review, see Herman (1980: 406–7).
8. For an overview of the debate over animal language, see DeGrazia (1996: 183–98).
9. Similar points can be defended regarding humans' and animals' interests in liberty and functioning (DeGrazia 1996: ch. 8), although they raise special complications.
10. My arguments appear elsewhere (see DeGrazia 1996: 264–8).

11. Thus I largely support the calls for reform outlined in Singer and Cavalieri (1993) and, although I believe his definitions of "person" and "autonomy" are problematic, Wise (2000). I also salute Martha Nussbaum's (2003) call for constitutional rights for animals.
12. For a theoretically powerful effort to develop this account, see McMahan (2002).

References

Byrne, Richard (1996) "The Misunderstood Ape: Cognitive Skills of the Gorilla," in Anne Russon, Kim A. Bard, and Sue Taylor Parker (eds), *Reaching into Thought*, Cambridge: Cambridge University Press, pp. 111–30.

Caldwell, M. C., and Caldwell, D. K. (1971) "Statistical Evidence for Individual Signature Whistles in Pacific Whitesided Dolphins, *Lagenorhynchus obliquidens*," *Cetology* 10, 1–9.

Cavalieri, Paola, and Singer, Peter (eds) (1993) *The Great Ape Project*, New York: St Martin's Press.

Cheney, Dorothy, and Seyfarth, Robert (1990) *How Monkeys See the World*, Chicago: University of Chicago Press.

Connor, Richard, and Peterson, Dawn (1994) *The Lives of Whales and Dolphins*, New York: Holt and Co.

Dawkins, Richard (1993) "Gaps in the Mind," in Paola Cavalieri and Peter Singer (eds), *The Great Ape Project*, New York: St Martin's Press, pp. 80–7.

DeGrazia, David (1996) *Taking Animals Seriously: Mental Life and Moral Status*, Cambridge: Cambridge University Press.

—— (1997) "Great Apes, Dolphins, and the Concept of Personhood," *Southern Journal of Philosophy* 35, 301–20.

Dennett, Daniel (1978) *Brainstorms*, Hassocks, England: Harvester.

de Waal, Frans (1997) *Bonobo*, Berkeley: University of California Press.

Frankfurt, Harry (1971) "Freedom of the Will and the Concept of a Person," *Journal of Philosophy* 68, 829–39.

Gallup, Gordon (1977) "Self-Recognition in Primates," *American Psychologist* 32, 329–38.

Goodall, Jane (1986) *The Chimpanzees of Gombe*, Cambridge, MA: Harvard University Press.

Hecht, Jeff (2003) "People and Chimps Belong Together on the Family Tree," *New Scientist*, May 24, p. 15.

Herman, Louis (1980) "Cognitive Characteristics of Dolphins," in Louis Herman (ed.), *Cetacean Behavior*, New York: Wiley & Sons, pp. 364–430.

—— (1994) "What the Dolphin Knows, or Might Know, in Its Natural World," in Karen Pryor and Kenneth Norris (eds), *Dolphin Societies*, Berkeley: University of California Press, pp. 349–64.

Herman, Louis, and Morrel-Samuels, Palmer (1990) "Knowledge Acquisition and Asymmetry between Language Comprehension and Production," in Marc Bekoff and Dale Jamieson (eds), *Interpretation and Explanation in the Study of Animal Behavior*, Vol. I, Boulder, CO: Westview, pp. 283–312.

Locke, John (1694) *An Essay Concerning Human Understanding*, 2nd edn.

McGrew, W. C. (1992) *Chimpanzee Material Culture*, Cambridge: Cambridge University Press.

McMahan, Jeff (2002) *The Ethics of Killing*, New York: Oxford University Press.

Mann, Janet, Connor, Richard C., Tyack, Peter L., and Whitehead, Hal (2000) *Cetacean Societies*, Chicago: University of Chicago Press.

Maple, Terry (1980) *Orang-utan Behavior*, New York: Van Nostrand Reinhold.

Miles, Lyn White (1993) "Language and the Orang-utan," in Paolo Cavalieri and Peter Singer (eds), *The Great Ape Project*, New York: St Martin's Press, pp. 42–57.

Norris, Kenneth, and Dohl, Thomas (1980) "The Structure and Function of Cetacean Schools," in Louis Herman (ed.), *Cetacean Behavior*, New York: Wiley & Sons, pp. 211–61.

Nussbaum, Martha (2003) "Beyond 'Compassion and Humanity': Justice for Non-Human Animals," third Tanner Lecture, delivered at Cambridge University, March 6.

Patterson, Francine (1978) "Linguistic Capabilities of a Lowland Gorilla," in Fred Peng (ed.), *Sign Language Acquisition in Man and Ape*, Boulder, CO: Westview, pp. 160–200.

Patterson, Francine, and Gordon, Wendy (1993) "The Case for the Personhood of Gorillas," in Paola Cavalieri and Peter Singer (eds), *The Great Ape Project*, New York: St Martin's Press, pp. 58–77.

PBS (1995) *Monkey in the Mirror* (documentary on primate cognition).

Reiss, Diana, and Marino, Lori (2001) "Mirror Self-Recognition in the Bottlenose Dolphin: A Case of Cognitive Convergence," *PNAS* 98 (May 8), 5937–42.

Savage-Rumbaugh, Sue (1986) *Ape Language*, New York: Columbia University Press.

Savage-Rumbaugh, Sue, and Brakke, Karen (1990) "Animal Language: Methodological and Interpretive Issues," in Marc Bekoff and Dale Jamieson (eds), *Interpretation and Explanation in the Study of Animal Behavior*, Vol. I, Boulder, CO: Westview, pp. 313–43.

Singer, Peter (1993) *Practical Ethics*, 2nd edn, Cambridge: Cambridge University Press.

Strawson, Peter (1959) *Individuals*, London: Methuen.

Tomasello, Michael, and Call, Josep (1997) *Primate Cognition*, New York: Oxford University Press.

Vedantam, Shankar (2003) "From Orangutans, A Cultural Display," *The Washington Post*, March 1, p. A3.

Wise, Steven (2000) *Rattling the Cage*, Cambridge, MA: Perseus.

4

The Animal Debate

A Reexamination

Paola Cavalieri

Accustomed to centuries of mean discussions about how much animals can actually suffer, and how much suffering we may impose on them for human benefit, we may tend to think that nonhumans are indeed second-class beings. True, their condition deserves to be improved, but in the end, they will always belong in a different moral category. It can be argued, though, that the inferior status to which animals are relegated is, like many other historical phenomena, really accidental. A different perception of animals could have prevailed had it not been defeated in some specific clashes of views.

Such clashes, I will suggest, occurred at critical moments in the history of our dominion over the other animals. This claim rests on the more general methodological view that our ideology partially results from our concrete problems and ways of life. Many approaches to the history of ideas defend this general view, so I will not justify it here. What I will do instead is to apply it to the history of our conceptions of animals. In doing this, however, I shall pay special attention to the role played in the handling of the crisis by the different theoretical tools available on any specific occasion.

On a preliminary reconstruction, Western debate on the treatment of animals can be assembled around three key moments, two of which were followed by long periods of stagnation. The first moment saw a struggle within the Classical Greek world between the idea of an original bond among all conscious beings and a contrasting global plan of rationalization of human and nonhuman exploitation. The latter prevailed, and the situation remained unaltered for the many centuries of Christianized Europe. Then, the scientific revolution of the seventeenth century generated a novel round of controversy by setting a new agenda for animals, one which required the removal of the only constraint left on their treatment – the prohibition of cruelty. This agenda, while not entirely successful, forced the advocates of animals into a defensive position. Accordingly, the overall level of discussion declined, and the reinstatement of some form of concern for animal suffering long remained the only ethical issue at stake. In the last few decades, a third critical moment has arrived with a new turn of the screw in animal exploitation. The rapid process of industrialization and mechanization of farming practices has altered the traditional landscape, and has generated a new wave of debate, characterized by the fact that reactions have preceded attempts at rationalization, and that different voices have been raised against the new kind of exploitation. In considering these voices, I will claim that two different strands of thought are clearly distinguishable, and that while one of them is still conditioned by past distortions, the other has overcome them.

Framing the Question:
The Prevalence of Rationalization

A different view of animals existed at the dawn of our civilization. There was a time and a place in which nonhumans were perceived by some among the intellectual masters of the age as cognate and allied beings. The time was the fifth century BC, and the place was Greece. Keeping in mind that, if it is impossible to deal with history without criticism, this holds even more in the case of documentary sources from classical antiquity, we shall try to draw a concise picture of what was utterly original in the Greek debate.

It is related that, around the middle of the fifth century, the naturalist philosopher Empedocles of Agrigentum, after a victory at the Olympic games, rejected the customary procedure of slaughtering an ox. Instead, he built an ox out of aromatic plants and shrubs, and he ritually shared it with all those who were present. In doing this, he made a gesture that called into question the entire practice of the bloody sacrifice around which revolved the life of the political community – the *polis* – and the covenant between the Greeks and their gods. How could this happen? We can infer from one of the surviving fragments of his work that Empedocles considered the killing of animals for food as criminal. More important perhaps, we know that he was a follower of Pythagoras of Samos.

Pythagoras was not a philosopher in the subsequently accepted sense of the word. Naturally associated with Apollo – the god lying at the source of Greek wisdom – he was one of the archaic sages whose teachings were mainly oral and esoteric, and whose lives shaded into legend. Accordingly, what has reached us of his thinking – a large and often contradictory body of information coming from late biographies and mentions by other authors – has had to be subjected to a complex work of interpretation. Renowned for his speculations in mathematics and music, as well as for his endeavor to reform the political life of the Greek colonies in Magna Graecia, Pythagoras taught that we should respect the rules of justice, not only in our dealings with human beings, but also in our dealings with nonhuman animals. In line with such teaching, as it is clear from Empedocles' gesture, he urged the replacement of bloody sacrifices by offers of frankincense and herbs on bloodless altars. Moreover, a vegetarian himself, he forbade the eating of animal flesh.

Vegetarianism is important since it directly points to the value of animal life. Challenging the most widespread practice in which animal lives are routinely taken prevents the question of the status of nonhumans from being relegated to a secondary ethical concern. Possibly because of this, Pythagoras' vegetarianism tends to be dismissed by many critics as inconsequential, or as a mere "superstition." It is inconsequential, it is claimed, because it is merely a part of a *bios*, a virtuous existence aiming at the self-interested goal of purification and contemplation. What the critics overlook, however, is that the elaboration of an ideal form of life is a constant feature of Greek thought, and self-interest is a natural part of it. The virtuous life is also the good life. So, the actual problem is, what is the "way" to such a life? And, for Pythagoras, an important part of the way is being just toward animals. As for the charge of superstition, it is tied to the doctrine of metempsychosis, or of the transmigration of souls. On this view, Pythagoras was not really interested in animals. Human beings were still the object of his concern, and this concern extended to animals only because of an eccentric belief. But Pythagoras was not alone in accepting the doctrine of metempsychosis. In different versions, the idea of a general transmigration of souls was a component of ancestral Greek thought still present in Plato. The fact that it matched respect for nonhumans only in some authors clearly suggests that there is no strict relation of cause and effect between the two.

The truth, then, seems to lie elsewhere. Pythagoras' philosophy expressed an integrated worldview based on the notion of harmony. Mathematics was the instrument to decode the universal harmony of the cosmos, music was the art that could best express harmony, and, at a normative level, politics and ethics should heighten harmony both among humans and between humans and the other "ensouled" beings – nonhuman animals. Already present in the form of similarity and kinship, harmony ought to be implemented through the virtue of friendship. That is the reason why Pythagoras used to commend this virtue, and also the reason why, when he so preached, he did not fail to extend it to animals, as similar and related beings.

From a more general perspective, on the other hand, Pythagorism is perhaps the highest expression of a deep current in Greek thought about animals whose origins can be traced back to the great tradition of the agricultural mystery cults of Orphism – an ideologically alternative tradition to the existent system of the *polis*. Traces of such a view can be detected in both Plato's Academy and Aristotle's Lyceum. Indeed, Plato himself suggested that human beings and animals once lived a life in common, and even conversed on philosophical questions. But perhaps the clearest evidence of the continued existence of this view comes from Plato's second successor in his school, the philosopher and mathematician Xenocrates of Chalcedon. Before the end of the fourth century BC – two centuries after Pythagoras' death – when the Athenians punished a man for flaying a living ram, Xenocrates declared that torturing is no worse than killing; that what is really criminal is taking the life of a being who is of one's own kind, *homogenés*. If one thinks of the sacral significance which was attached to blood relationships in the initial stages of Western civilization, one can grasp the radicality of the tradition which emerged in Xenocrates' claim.

How, and when, did this strand of thinking disappear from the main philosophical scene? To give even a brief answer to this question, we should widen our perspective. Around the middle of the fourth century BC, the system of the *polis* wavered. New, huge political and economic realities were about to replace it, undermining with their multi-ethnicity the ancient distinction between Greeks and Barbarians, and with their autocratic structures the traditional civic institutions. Prominent among the reactions caused by such changes was the need to rationally systematize and sanction the old order. The author who took up this task was Aristotle – no longer a sage, but the philosopher *par excellence*, the great systematizer. Aristotle built a hierarchical, teleological worldview focusing on differences in essence rather than similarities. Within this framework, on the one hand, he defended the old practice of discriminatory slavery, arguing that some human beings are by nature slaves; on the other, he replied to the challenge that vegetarian thought and practice had long represented for the *polis* dependence on animal sacrifice and consumption, arguing that all nonhuman beings are slaves in an even deeper sense, insofar as they exist merely for our use. Central to both claims was the alleged inability, due to their lack of rationality, of "natural" slaves or animals to plan and direct their lives.

It was a fateful verdict. If, in the human case, it led to slavery ceasing to be a philosophical problem for centuries, except for inconsequential moralizing considerations about the universal "brotherhood" of humankind, as far as nonhumans were concerned it produced a lasting justificatory framework for their complete subjugation. The alternative view of animals did not disappear, and the third century AD still produced a philosopher like Porphyry – the Neo-Platonic thinker who, in his *De abstinentia*, summarized past debates, advocated vegetarianism, and acutely criticized most rationalizations for animal exploitation. But it was Aristotle, not Porphyry, who, because of the obvious advantages that his view offered, as well as of his later "adoption" by Christianity, set the tone for the entire Western world till the beginning of the modern era.

An Ideological Resumption: Proposing Further Demotion

The view that René Descartes put forward in the seventeenth century is so contrary both to common sense and to empirical findings that one wonders how it could have been formulated at all. Animals do not suffer. Not possessing language, they do not possess reason. Not possessing reason, they are not feeling beings, but mere automata. In the face of such a counterintuitive claim, some authors have attempted to amend the perspective, claiming that, if not in his main works, at least in some private letters, Descartes granted animals some sensations, thereby showing that he did not himself believe his theory.

This is enlightening, but in a sense opposite to the one suggested. Why, in fact, did Descartes argue for a stance he could not really accept? Why did so many of his contemporaries blindly take it at its face value? At least part of the explanation lies not at the level of philosophical thinking, but rather at the level of felt social needs. Through late antiquity and medieval times, when hierarchy and subjection were the rule even among human beings, the status of animals as mere means had never been challenged. They had been exploited in whatever ways humans saw fit – except for an injunction against cruelty. Though usually justified in terms of an ethics of virtue, or of the possible consequences of cruel habits for human beings, this injunction withstood the centuries. But something was changing in Descartes's era.

This era saw the establishment of the experimental method in science and, concomitant with it, the spreading of a new area of inquiry, empirical physiology, which embodied a practice requiring the plain abandonment of any qualms about cruelty. The practice was called "vivisection," and consisted in studying physiological processes by literally cutting living animals. Occasionally present in antiquity – instances of it are mentioned in the Hellenistic age and during the Roman Empire – "vivisection" had been abandoned in the periods when the appeal to influential authors of the past, rather than autonomous research, dominated even empirical fields of study. But the methodological revolution of the seventeenth century caused a resumption, and a real outburst, of the practice – so much so that public sessions of vivisection were common among experimentalists and the "educated public."

The notion of cruelty has much to do with the intentions of the perpetrator, and with the "gratuitousness" of the infliction of suffering. However, it is also connected with the level of suffering involved. Vivisection did imply extraordinary levels of suffering, inflicted knowingly and openly by some of the most respected members of society. The problem was so evident that something was needed to counteract the budding criticisms, and to allow the unimpeded continuation of the practice. In this light, to advance, or to adhere to, the view that vivisected animals did not suffer offered a good escape route. True, such a view – the beast-machine theory – entailed the implausible idea of a radical discontinuity between humans and animals. Descartes's endeavor, however, was favored by his ability to draw upon two different theoretical sources – classical metaphysics, with its rational, immortal souls for humans, and the new mechanistic view of nature as mere matter for animals. The resulting doctrine allowed investigators to perform vivisection in an even more ruthless manner.

To accept this reconstruction means to accept the idea that the first significant revival of the debate on animals did not stem from a critical reflection on past biases, but from an intensification of human exploitation. In this light, it is no surprise that the new discussion, far from challenging conventional premises, narrowed the focus. Instead of starting from the question, "How much do animals count?" it started from the question, "How much can animals suffer, if at all?" This led to a dispute about animals' mental capacities, with the main normative problem – "Are we entitled to inflict suffering on animals at all?" – disappearing into the background.

Descriptive disputes about the mental capacities of the members of other species were not new. But when, for example, some Greek philosophers denied reason to animals, what was at stake was their inclusion in the human community and in the fundamental covenants on which that community was thought to be based. In contrast, what characterized the later debate was merely the problem of how much restraint animals' sentience should impose on our exploitative behavior. Thus, authors advocating the view that animals can indeed suffer concluded, at most, that it was "barbarous" to ignore this. And even those Enlightenment thinkers who developed a critique of Descartes's doctrine, far from advocating reform, merely plunged into a controversy on animal souls – a controversy devoid of any actual moral implications.

That Descartes, although he could not settle the problem of vivisection once and for ever, cast a long shadow on subsequent reflection is shown by an author who still influences the endeavor to develop a new ethic for our relationship with animals – the nineteenth-century German philosopher Arthur Schopenhauer. Schopenhauer grants a central ethical role to the feeling of compassion, and naturally extends compassion to members of other species. Strongly attacking Descartes because of the gulf he created between ourselves and animals, Schopenhauer nevertheless accepts the idea that nonhumans are means to our ends. They can be used for work, he states, and only "the excess of the imposed exertion becomes cruelty" (Schopenhauer 1965: 182). Cruelty is thus once again the key ethical concept, and suffering the only ethical concern. What, then, about inflicting death? The possibility of not killing animals for food, though considered, is quickly set aside. For, Schopenhauer states, the pain animals suffer through death is not so great as humans would suffer by denying themselves their flesh. Like Jeremy Bentham's grounds for excluding vegetarianism from his plea for animals – if we kill animals for food in a painless way "we are the better for it, and they are never the worse" (1948: 311) – this stance is a good example of what we might call the post-Cartesian attitude. For Descartes's complacent humanism set the stakes so low that the best its critics managed to do was to go back to a (softened) version of Aristotle's doctrine of animal slavery.

Confronting Reification:
False Tracks and a New Perspective

Modern technology is often described as the social outcome of a theoretical approach which, privileging an instrumental reason that aims at the domination of objects, achieves at the same time a domination of subjects through reification. Perhaps in no instance is this more evident than in the case of our treatment of nonhumans. Around the middle of the past century, when, despite lingering opposition, science had hugely extended the use of animals in research, the technological explosion put a new twist on the practice of raising and killing animals for food. The introduction of factory farming marks a momentous step in the overall process of our subjugation of animals, both because of the number of the individuals exposed to its dreadful mechanized procedures and because it affects the whole of society.

We have seen that the perturbation of an equilibrium tends to reopen discussions. If, in the case of vivisection, the prevailing aspect was the devising of a new theory aimed at justifying the status quo, in the case of intensive farming philosophical criticism preceded any defenses of the practice. A possible reason for this is that while vivisection mainly involved scientists, that is, a category interested in ideologically vindicating its choices, the driving forces behind the industrialization of agriculture were farmers and manufacturers neither able, nor inclined, to attempt a justification of the ways in which they sought profit. In contrast, theoretical opposition to the new practice was favored by the strong current of ontological revulsion for the manipulation of "nature" running through most continental philosophy. It was therefore from this side, and in particular from German philosophy, that, a few years after the end of World War II, the first reaction developed.

Without doubt, the most influential voice was that of Martin Heidegger, the dissenting heir to Western metaphysical tradition who was involved in Nazi cultural programs and whose life-long reflection produced in the end rather mystical outcomes. In connection with his critique of the technological essence of modernity, Heidegger defended a "primal ethics" based on a non-invasive policy of letting-be – a sort of detachment, or "releasement," allowing living and non-living things to be what they are. Against the background of this account of being-in-the-world, he censured the "horrifying" transformation of agriculture into modern agribusiness, arguing that if formerly to cultivate meant to take care, what had superseded this was a callous industrial enterprise. All the more so, he stated that "agriculture is now a mechanized food industry, in essence the same as the manufacture of corpses in the gas chambers and death camps. . . ." (text of a conference held in Bremen, 1949, cited in Schirmacher 1983: 25).

Did these striking judgments presage a challenge to the paradigm of human superiority? The answer is in the negative. For what Heidegger had in mind when comparing modern farming practices to Nazi extermination policies was not the mass killing of nonhumans, but agriculture as a whole, including the cultivation of the land and the building of dams to provide hydroelectricity. This lack of discrimination tallies well with the fact that, in spite of his criticism of conventional metaphysical humanism, Heidegger's treatment of nonhumans sounds like a repetition of the traditional derogatory attitudes. "Only man dies. The animal perishes," he states for example (Heidegger 1971: 78), referring to an alleged qualitative alterity of nonhumans, and famously arguing that, while humans are *world-forming*, animals are *world-poor*. On the other hand, when one realizes that the statement on agriculture is the only one in which Heidegger overtly criticized Nazi crimes, the fact that the question of harm to others is overshadowed by the defense of a specific account of being-in-the-world reveals a further, significant problem with his position – that disregard for individual interests as the primary source of moral obligations which marks the traditional view of ethics as derived from global worldviews.

It is just this traditional view which has been questioned by that recent revival of French thought that challenged the supremacy of German philosophy within the continental scene. Undeniably, an important aspect of what has come to be known as postmodern reflection is the critique of great meta-narratives – overarching theories that make sense of everything. Could this new attitude generate a different approach to the animal issue? An indication in this regard might seem to come from the deconstructionist approach of Jacques Derrida. Though presenting himself as a scholar of Heidegger, and devoting much time and energy to glossing and interpreting his work, Derrida has repeatedly stated that, if there is a question on which he disagreees with Heidegger, it is the "discourse of animality." When it comes to animals, Derrida claims, Heidegger's revolution in thinking comes to a halt, and the deep currents of humanism reemerge. In contrast with this, and in the context of his deconstruction of the Cartesian subject and categories, Derrida imputes to Western philosophy a "sacrificial structure" which not only licenses countless ways of negating the other, but also allows the noncriminal putting to death of animals. Then, carefully dismantling the binary opposition between human and animal mind, he questions the idea that every transgression of the commandment "Thou shalt not kill" must concern only humans.

From this, one might expect an approach directly pointing to the issue of the value of nonhuman life. The inference, however, is unwarranted. For, despite his avowed intention, Derrida retains the human subject as central, and, with a shift from the perspective of the sacrificed to the perspective of the sacrificer which is a clear mark of the humanistic tradition of virtue ethics, construes vegetarianism not as the sparing of animal lives, but as a shorthand to good conscience. Furthermore, when going beyond merely speculative questions like, "In which sense is the other not only a human other?" he openly defends the existence of an "abyssal gap" between humans and nonhumans. What, then, is Derrida actually criticizing in the present treatment of animals? Apparently, nothing but the specific features of technological manipulation – the organization and exploitation of an artificial survival in conditions that once would have been judged monstrous, the "genocidal torture that we often inflict . . . by raising *en masse*, in an industrialized manner, the herds to be exterminated" (Derrida and Roudinesco 2001: 112). In view of all this, it is difficult not to agree with the judgment of English philosopher David Wood (1999), according to which Derrida's charges against Heidegger are true of Derrida's own discussion of "animality."

Thus, neither of the two most representative continental criticisms of industrial animal factories issued in a general questioning of the status quo. And if part of the reason for this might lie with the pressures to conformity in a society ideologically and economically based on animal exploitation, arguably another part has to do with theoretical problems with the continental approach itself – an approach hardly equipped for the task of framing different questions from the ones that have been asked for centuries.

There is, however, a different sort of tradition in moral philosophy which gradually developed the potential to overcome ingrained perspectives. Flourishing in the British world, this tradition recognized in ethics an independent inquiry endowed with its standards of justification, and rapidly adopted that analytic method marked by clarity and explicit argumentation that substantiated attacks on metaphysics in other branches of philosophy. In the late 1960s, authors working in this area removed two significant obstacles standing in the way of a larger reappraisal of the animal issue. On the one hand, by arguing that, when what is at stake is basic moral treatment, there is no room for the arbitrariness of general belief-systems, they made it impossible to justify the status of beings on the basis of the undemonstrable metaphysical claims so often advanced in the case of animals, such as the idea that they differ in essence from human beings, or that they do not possess immortal souls. On the other, by clarifying that the class of beings who can deserve moral protection does not logically coincide with the class of beings who can act morally, they cleared away the conventional intellectual bias of Western thought, throwing the moral community's doors open to non-rational beings.

With the elimination of these obstacles, it became increasingly difficult to keep humans and nonhumans in the traditional, separate moral categories. In contrast with most of our past, we live in egalitarian times. Owing to growing social pressures from groups previously discriminated against, and to a long period of rational criticism, the principle of equality according to which like cases are to be treated alike was gradually freed from the ideological encrustations which prevented it from actually taking effect. Could this process be limited to human beings? Or was it possible instead that the driving force behind human egalitarianism could push toward a further extention of equality? When, at the beginning of the 1970s – in a period in which concern for the individual suffering, rather than for the unnatural treatment, of factory-farmed animals was spreading among the English-speaking public – the consequentialist philosopher Peter Singer first confronted the issue, he began with just these questions.

Equipped with an anti-metaphysical and egalitarian doctrine like classical utilitarianism, Singer challenged the two main claims supporting current exploitative practices. The first one is the common, straightforward allegation that animals "are not human." We have long assumed that we are the only (at best, the most) morally important beings in the world. When, however, neither the introduction of general belief-systems, nor the (allegedly) exclusive capacity for moral action can support this assumption, the idea that being human is ethically relevant amounts to the attribution of moral weight to membership in the species *Homo sapiens*. Confronted with this latter perspective, Singer appealed to the requirement of consistency. Stressing that discriminatory forms of biologism like racism and sexism have been rejected by human egalitarianism, he argued that, if our morality is to be coherent, speciesism – that is, discrimination based on species membership – should also be discredited.

But forms of biologism are not the only hindrances to equality. There still is the possibility of hierarchical classifications based on mental level – the more complex the mental level of beings, the higher their moral status. Though this sort of "perfectionism" – a nice word for an ugly thing – also long dominated ethical outlooks relating to human beings, contemporary egalitarian authors rejected it. Faced with the fact that humans are different in their capacities, they argued that the satisfaction of our interests is important for us irrespective of any other capacities we may possess, and translated the principle of human equality into the principle of equal consideration of interests. Yet the appeal to the (alleged) lower mental level of animals still plays a central role in the attempt to justify nonhuman unequal status. In questioning this second, and more philosophical, argument, Singer reiterated his charge of inconsistency. We should, he stated, either reject perfectionism, or accept it – if we reject it in the case of humans, and accept it when it comes to animals, our position is untenable. Then, in light of the fact that this charge can lead both to the equalization of animals and to a stratification of the value of humans, Singer made a further move. If we link our pursuit of equality to interests, he argued, equality cannot stop except at the point where interests disappear. Since interests go as far as sentience goes, it is logic itself which requires that we extend equal consideration to nonhuman sentient beings. His conclusion, which pushed utilitarian radicalism well beyond Bentham's views, was that we should stop treating animals as means to our ends, and should liberate them from human dominion.

With Singer, the problem of the industrial manipulation of animals finally met a response questioning not its details, but its entire foundation. While philosophical vegetarianism reappeared on the scene, a new round of the debate began.

Rationalizations of exploitation are often intertwined, and when some arguments are found faulty, often others are affected too. Thus, in the context of the renewed discussion, assumptions taken for granted within various ethical traditions came under challenge, and many conventional views were undermined. The claim that abstract reasoning is essential for moral action was countered by the idea that beings can be virtuous even when their conduct is merely guided by an immediate perception of the interests of others. To contract theorists it was pointed out that their doctrine has a dark side: whereas the idea that one's behavior towards others should be influenced by their capacity for retaliation and/or reciprocation may be defensible in the case of roughly similar beings, this same idea becomes a mockery when it comes to weaker or less endowed beings. Even the complacently accepted Kantian claim that human life has absolute worth while animal life is expendable lost any appeal after the exposition of its surreptitious derivation from a metaphysical (if not religious) worldview. Finally, against this background, it became possible to claim that even the protection afforded by the main contemporary moral theory – human rights doctrine – can be extended to nonhuman beings. For if the will to secure equal rights to all humans, whatever their cognitive level, implied that the criterion for their ascription should not be the possession of any exacting mental characteristic, but the mere capacity to enjoy freedom and welfare, and life as a precondition for them, then consistency requires that the same rights should be granted to (most) animals. According to such argument, all contemporary discriminatory practices – not only raising for food, but also scientific experimentation and the most varied forms of exploitative use – should be prohibited, and the nonhuman beings involved should be granted that institutionalized protection of vital interests that we have till now confined to ourselves.

Conclusion

In the light of all this, it seems plausible to conclude that the post-Cartesian era has finally been brought to an end, and that, stepping beyond Aristotle, we have today returned, after more than twenty centuries, to the original Greek appraisal of the worth of other animals. Not only has the status of nonhumans as slaves been challenged, but, beyond appeals to compassion and mere focus on the cruelties involved in animal exploitation, it is now possible to defend the idea that animal lives have value – that it is wrong not merely to inflict suffering on them, but also to kill them. In a sense, a circle has been completed. That basic equality in moral status that, in a wholly different context, was abstractly perceived – so to speak, known by intuition – by the first sources of Western wisdom has now been filled in with the concrete results of a rigorous philosophical analysis. Though this is not the same as implementing social reform, it is at least a necessary condition for it.

Essential References

Aristotle (1973) *Politics*, Oxford: Oxford University Press.

Bentham, Jeremy (1948) *An Introduction to the Principles of Morals and Legislation*, New York: Hafner Press.

Calarco, Matthew (2004) "Deconstruction Is Not Vegetarianism: Humanism, Subjectivity, and Animal Ethics," *Continental Philosophy Review* XXX, 1–27.

Cavalieri, Paola (2001) *The Animal Question: Why Nonhuman Animals Deserve Human Rights*, New York: Oxford University Press.

—— (in press) "A Missed Opportunity: Humanism, Anti-Humanism and the Animal Question," in Jodey Castricano (ed.), *Animal Subjects: An Ethical Reader*, Waterloo, Ont.: Wilfrid Laurier University Press.

Derrida, Jacques (1989) *Of Spirit: Heidegger and the Question*, Chicago: University of Chicago Press.

—— (1991) "'Eating Well,' or the Calculation of the Subject: An Interview with Jacques Derrida," in Eduardo Cadava et al. (eds), *Who Comes After the Subject?*, New York: Routledge.

—— (2002) "The Animal That Therefore I Am (More to Follow)," *Critical Inquiry* 28 (Winter), 369–418.

Derrida, Jacques, and Roudinesco, Elisabeth (2001) *De quoi demain . . . : Dialogue*, Paris: Fayard/Galilée.

Descartes, René (1970) *Philosophical Letters*, Oxford: Clarendon Press.

—— (1996) *Discourse on the Method and Meditations on First Philosophy*, New Haven and London: Yale University Press.

Detienne, Marcel (1994) *The Gardens of Adonis*, Princeton: Princeton University Press.

Dombrowski, Daniel A. (1984) *The Philosophy of Vegetarianism*, Amherst: University of Massachusetts Press.

Heidegger, Martin (1971) "The Thing," in *Poetry, Language, Thought*, New York: Harper & Row.

—— (1977) "The Question Concerning Technology," in *The Question Concerning Technology and Other Essays*, New York: Harper & Row.

—— (1995) *The Fundamental Concepts of Metaphysics: World, Finitude, Solitude*, Bloomington: Indiana University Press.

—— (1996) *Being and Time*, Albany, N.Y.: SUNY Press.

—— (1998) "Letter on Humanism," in *Pathmarks*, Cambridge: Cambridge University Press.

Iamblichus (1986) *De vita Pythagorica: Imablichus' Life of Pythagorus*, Rochester, N.Y.: Inner Traditions.

Miller, Harlan B. (1994) "Science, Ethics, and Moral Status," *Between the Species* 10, 10–18.

Nagel, Thomas (1978) "Ethics as an Autonomous Theoretical Subject," in G. S. Stent (ed.), *Morality as a Biological Phenomenon*, Berkeley: University of California Press.

Plato (1953) *Timaeus*, in *The Dialogues of Plato*, 4th edn, Oxford: Oxford University Press.

—— (1995) *The Statesman*, Cambridge: Cambridge University Press.

Plutarch (1984) *De esu carnium: Plutarch's Moralia*, Vol. XII, Cambridge, MA: Loeb Classical Library.

Porphyry (1977, 1979, 1995) *De abstinentia: De l'abstinence*, Paris: Les Belles Lettres.

Regan, Tom (1983) *The Case for Animal Rights*, Berkeley: University of California Press.

Rupke, Nicolaas A. (ed.) (1987) *Vivisection in Historical Perspective*, London: Croom Helm.

Sapontzis, Steve F. (1987) *Morals, Reason and Animals*, Philadelphia: Temple University Press.

Schirmacher, Wolfgang (1983) *Technik und Gelassenheit: Zeitkritik nach Heidegger*, Freiburg: Karl Alber.

Schopenhauer, Arthur (1965) *On the Basis of Morality*, Indianapolis: Bobbs-Merrill.

—— (1969) *The World as Will and Representation*, New York: Dover Publications.

Singer, Peter (1990) *Animal Liberation*, 2nd edn, New York: New York Review of Books.

—— (1993) *Practical Ethics*, 2nd edn, Cambridge: Cambridge University Press.

—— (1995) *Rethinking Life and Death*, Oxford: Oxford University Press.

—— (2003) "Animal Liberation at 30," *The New York Review of Books*, 15 May.

Sorabji, Richard (1993) *Animal Minds and Human Morals*, London: Duckworth.

Warnock, Geoffrey J. (1971) *The Object of Morality*, London: Methuen.

Wolfe, Cary (2003) *Animal Rites*, Chicago: University of Chicago Press.

Wood, David (1999) *"Comment ne pas manger:* Deconstruction and Humanism," in H. Peter Steeves (ed.), *Animal Others: On Ethics, Ontology, and Animal Life*, Albany, N.Y.: SUNY Press.

5

Religion and Animals

Paul Waldau

The possibilities and problems of "religion and animals" can be seen in the following comparison. In its revised Catechism, issued in 1994, the Catholic Church proclaimed, "Animals, like plants and inanimate things, are by nature destined for the common good of past, present and future humanity." Contrast this assertion with the following from the popular *Metta Sutta* recited by millions of Buddhists every day: "Just as a mother would protect with her life her own son, her only son, so one should cultivate an unbounded mind towards all beings, and loving kindness towards all the world." Religion is a notoriously complex area of human existence. Nevertheless, it can be said, quite simply, that the record of some religious institutions in defending animals is one of abject failure, often driven by extraordinary arrogance and ignorance. Yet at other times religious believers have lived out their faith in ways that have been fully in defense of nonhuman lives.

This more positive view has, across place and time, been common. Engagement with lives outside our species has produced for some religious believers an understanding that other animals are the bringers of blessings into the world. Some believers have also held that some nonhuman animals are persons in every sense that humans are persons, and even ancestors, family, clan members, or separate nations. Life forms outside the human species have regularly engaged humans' imagination at multiple levels, and thus often energized religious sensibilities dramatically.

Because of this, one does not have to look far to uncover positive connections between some forms of religion and concerns for nonhuman animals. The links between these two are, in fact, unfathomably ancient. Our remote ancestors were fascinated with nonhuman lives, and the origins of human dance, musical instruments, art, and even a sense of the sacred have been tied directly to the fascination that our ancestors exhibited regarding the neighboring, nonhuman members of the earth community.

But the prevalence of dismissive views in religious circles cannot be denied. Views like that of the Catholic Catechism which are anchored in a radical subordination of nonhumans to humans – what Mary Midgley (1984) called the "absolute dismissal" of nonhuman animals now tragically prevalent in most modern industrialized countries – remain very common in religious circles today. Historically, there has been a link between religious traditions' willingness to demean nonhuman animals and the totality of modern secular societies' subordination of nonhuman animals' lives to human profits, leisure, and "progress" (see Sorabji 1993; Waldau 2001).

So fairness and balance in approaching this subject will require any explorer of "religion and animals" to acknowledge that, even if a preoccupation with other animals is an ancient theme in religious traditions, it has not been a prominent part of ethical discussion in modern religious institutions or in academic circles where religion is studied. Those who have championed the cause of nonhuman animals around the world since the resurgence of protective intentions and actions in the 1970s have only rarely consulted religious authorities when seeking communal support for increased animal protection. And religious authorities haven't often sought to participate in debates over how to defend wildlife, ensure that food animals are not mistreated, minimize harm to research animals, or honor the special place of companion (nonhuman) animals in humans' lives. The reluctance of animal advocates to seek the help of religious institutions and authorities alone says much about how "in defense of animals" modern religious traditions have been, or might be, in the world today.

I shall begin by considering what various religions have claimed about other animals. To what extent have religious traditions been guilty of what Richard Ryder (1970) called "speciesism" – the view that any and all human animals, but *no nonhuman* animals, should get fundamental moral protections? Speciesism makes membership in the human species the criterion of belonging within our moral circle. And to what extent do religious traditions provide resources and support for those seeking to defend animals?

If we consider what five major religious traditions (these are sometimes referred to as the "world religions") have claimed about "animals," it becomes clear that some religious positions serve well to defend nonhuman animals, while others offend profoundly.

Hinduism, which is best understood as a complex of diverse subtraditions, offers an immense range of views about the living beings who share our ecological community. Two general beliefs dominate how these Hindu subtraditions think of humans' relationship to the earth's other animals. First, humans are clearly recognized to be in a continuum with other life; second, humans are nonetheless considered to be the paradigm of what biological life *should* be. One thus commonly finds within Hindu sources claims that the status "human" is above the status of any other animal.

Both the continuum notion and the separation emphasis are part of the Hindus' belief in reincarnation, which asserts that any living being's current position in the cycle of life is a deserved position determined by the strict law of *karma*. This famous notion, which Hindus understand to reflect the eternal law of the universe, claims that all living beings, human and nonhuman alike, are born and reborn into stations in life determined by their past deeds. This view, which clearly implies that the universe has a fundamental moral structure, works out in ways that subordinate and otherwise demean nonhuman animals. Nonhuman animals, which by definition haven't acted in prior lives in ways that surmount their inferior nonhuman status, are denizens of a corrupt, lesser realm. Achieving human status means one has in past lives acted well. Humans who in this life act immorally are, according to Hindu thinking, destined to be reborn as a nonhuman animal, a demeaned status thought of as particularly unhappy compared to human life.

These two beliefs – humans' connection, humans' superiority – have resulted in tensions in Hindu views of other animals. A negative set of views, often used to justify dominance or harsh treatment, flows from the claims that earth's numerous nonhuman animals are inferior to any human. A competing, positive set of views flows from the continuum belief, for other animals, like humans, have souls and thus are worthy of ethical considerations (for example, the notion of non-harming, or *ahimsa*, applies to them).

On the positive side of attitudes toward nonhuman animals is the tradition's remarkable claim that other animals should not be killed. Many passages in the Hindu scriptures exhort believers to treat other animals as they would their own children. And central religious texts hold that the earth was created for both humans and nonhumans. These texts allow many contemporary Hindus to argue that all lives have their own interests, their own value, and thus a right to existence. Hence, daily life in India, especially at the village level, provides many examples of coexistence with other animals, the best-known example of which is the sacred cow.

The special treatment of some nonhuman animals suggests that Hinduism is not classically speciesist, for not all nonhumans are excluded from the moral circle. Relatedly, not all humans were necessarily included, for the inequalities existing within human society (often referred to as the caste system) were also justified as the direct result of good or bad deeds performed in former lives.

Beyond the special obligations to all living beings found in the Hindu tradition, one finds close associations of many Hindu deities with specific animal forms. The deities Rama and Krishna are believed to have reincarnated as, respectively, a monkey and a cow. Ganesh, an elephant-headed god, and Hanuman, the monkey god, have long been worshipped widely in India. These close associations provide another basis on which Hindu believers can act in defense of certain nonhuman animals.

Hinduism's earliest forms were intimately associated with animal sacrifice, which dominated the ritual life of the nascent tradition. Around 500 BC, this practice was challenged by Buddhists and Jains as cruel and unethical. This challenge had a great effect on the later Hindu views of the morality of intentionally sacrificing other animals, and *ahimsa*, the historically important emphasis on nonviolence, has now become a central feature of the tradition.

Buddhist views of nonhuman animals are not unlike Hindu views because both share the background cultural assumptions that characterize religions born in the Indian subcontinent. Buddhists thus also believe that all animals, human and otherwise, are fellow voyagers in the same process of lives interconnected by reincarnation. In Buddhist scriptures and practices, the teaching of compassion has often led to expressions of unequivocal concern for other living beings. This is one reason why both Buddhists and literature purporting to describe religious traditions generally often have claimed that Buddhism takes a kind, sympathetic view toward nonhuman lives. This is an important half-truth, for concern for other animals is often a very visible feature of the Buddhist tradition.

Such concerns are matched, however, by a complicating feature. The tradition also carries an overall negative view of other animals' existence and abilities relative to those of members of the human species. For example, a consistent disparagement of other animals appears in documents from the earliest stages of the tradition. Buddhist denunciations of other forms of life are closely allied with the coarse grouping of all nonhuman animals into a single realm. Under the hierarchical assumptions that dominated the Indian subcontinent, this realm was thought of as below the human realm. Hence, if a being is born as *any* kind of animal other than a human it is, in a very important sense, thought of negatively, for such a low birth means that the being in earlier lives did not meet the lofty goals that would allow that being to be born a human. Not unexpectedly, other animals' worlds are dismissed as unhappy places – as the Buddha says, "so many are the anguishes of animal birth."

Birth at a "subhuman" level in the Buddhist hierarchy, then, is a direct result of less than ideal conduct in earlier lives. And a corollary of this dismissal of nonhuman animals as lower is that such lives are regularly described by Buddhists as so simple relative to humans that their lives are easily understood by the qualitatively superior human capacity for moral and intellectual thinking. In other words, we can understand their lives, and thereby know that they would be happier if they were human. Another feature of Buddhist scriptures is that other animals are often viewed as pests in competition with elevated humans. These factors and others produce negative descriptions of other animals in the Buddhist scriptures.

As with Hinduism, negative views of other animals are moderated by central ethical commitments that, by any measure (modern or ancient), provide important defenses to other animals. The special commitment known in Buddhist scriptures as the First Precept commits each Buddhist to refrain from killing any life form. A vegetarian ideal is recognized in some portions of the tradition as well. There is also a special commitment in the Mahayana tradition known as the bodhisattva's vow, by which a Buddha-to-be refrains from entering *nirvana* until all beings are saved. This special vow reflects the prominence of the tradition's deep concern for beings outside the human species.

This strong ethical commitment to the value of other animals' lives keeps the Buddhist engagement with other animals from being classically speciesist, even though one finds in Buddhism a pervasive dismissal of other animals that is related to the tradition's heavy investment in hierarchical thinking. What makes this seem peculiar to modern activists who have developed their own defenses of animals is that, despite Buddhism's interest in individual animals as valued beings who should not be killed, the tradition has never emphasized seeing other animals in terms of *their* realities. The upshot is that many Buddhist claims about other animals exhibit the features of misleading caricature because they are premised on a dismissive prejudgment about possibilities of nonhuman animals' lives. In a scientific or analytical sense, Buddhists' views of nonhuman lives are under-determined by careful engagement with observable realities of the animals' actual lives, and over-determined by an ideology of human superiority.

The Abrahamic traditions – Judaism, Christianity, and Islam – also share common assumptions about nonhuman animals, although these are in important respects very different from the assumptions that undergird Hindu and Buddhist views of nonhuman animals. On the whole, the views of this family of religious traditions are, on issues involving nonhuman lives, dominated by a speciesist approach to deciding just which lives should be seen as within our moral circle. These Abrahamic traditions thus are, particularly in their mainline interpretations, characterized by a recurring assertion that the divine creator specially elected humans and designed the earth primarily for our benefit rather than for the benefit of all forms of life. This human-centeredness has manifested itself regularly in a tendency to justify practices that harm other animals.

But just as religion in general isn't easy to pin down with a simple judgment of either "pro-animal" or "anti-animal," so individual religious traditions are typically characterized by coexisting contradictory attitudes. The human-centeredness of the Abrahamic traditions is moderated at critical points by fundamental insights about the relevance of nonhuman lives to our ethical abilities. Thus, at least some part of each of these traditions asserts that there are moral dimensions to other animals' lives such that there should be limits on humans' instrumental uses of other animals.

In **Judaism**, views of nonhuman animals are subject to further complicating factors, including the fact that the Hebrew Bible contains several different ways of thinking about the earth's other animals in relation to the human community. One strain of the Hebrew scriptures, which has been called its realistic, this-worldly version, focuses on victory over other animals, while another, more idealized approach envisions peace with and between wild animals. Of these two visions, the first is more prominent in that humans' interests are characteristically seen in Judaism as far more important than the interests of any nonhuman animals. Philo, the first-century Jewish historian, employed an image of a continuous war by nonhuman animals against humankind. This image reflects a negative view of the animals not under humans' control, which is matched by a positive view of domesticated animals. There is some irony in this view, for valuing domesticated animals alone is, of course, merely a form of covert human-centeredness. There is further irony as well in the notion that wild animals are evil, since a common biblical theme is that the disorder in God's creation stems from wrongs committed not by nonhuman animals but by Adam and Eve and, later, an unfaithful Israel.

More positive is the competing notion that other animals were created by a God who is proud of them and feeds them each day. Other animals, then, can be seen quite positively as examples of right order living under God's reign in great contrast to sinful humans whom God must constantly discipline. This more positive notion is often symbolized by the idea that creation has a genuine and abiding goodness because God created it, a belief that underlies the recurring claim in the opening chapter of Genesis that God saw creation as "good."

Early Judaism features many protections of the welfare of some nonhuman animals (for example, Exodus 22–3 and 34, Leviticus 22 and 25, and Deuteronomy between 14 and 26). These undeniable protections are limited, however, to primarily (1) the welfare of humans' own domesticated animals, and (2) restrictions on the killing of the few animals which could be sacrificed. Some have also argued that the practice of animal sacrifice benefited nonhuman animals in general (limiting, for example, the total number of animals that could be killed). But, as with all religious sacrifice of nonhuman animals, the Jewish tradition's practice of animal sacrifice raises complex issues. Such sacrificial rituals were thought to relieve humans of impurity generated by their violations of moral rules or purity taboos. The obvious question arises, of course, as to why any *nonhumans* suffered on the basis of *human* wrongs. Religious traditions that permit sacrifice of individual animals for such purposes rely on the reasoning that human purity is more important than the nonhuman lives of the sacrificial victims. The question of why only animals useful and pleasing to humans were chosen for sacrifice also begs further inquiry.

The Jewish tradition, particularly by virtue of the body of traditional Jewish law that concerns itself with the suffering of other animals and animal welfare in general (known as *tsa'ar ba'alei chayim*, literally, sympathy for life), can claim that, like the best of the Hindu and Buddhist traditions, it clearly recognized the ethical aspects of defending nonhuman animals' interests, and that such care is mandated by the core values and insights of the tradition. So even when humans are conceived in the Jewish tradition as separate from the rest of life, there remains an important recognition of a sense of connection. The human-centeredness remains, of course, and subjects the tradition to criticisms along the line of speciesism, but the breadth of positive generalizations about living beings and the number of specific animals mentioned suggest that the early Hebrews noticed and appreciated the extraordinary diversity and interconnectedness of human and nonhuman beings.

Christianity inherited the Hebrew vision that all humans are made in the image of God and have been given dominion over the earth. Early

Christians in the formative stages of the tradition also borrowed from the Greek cultural tradition. In important ways the mainline Christian tradition narrowed the Hebrew side of its heritage by playing down the animal-friendly features of the Hebrews' attitudes while at the same time foregrounding the anti-animal aspects of the Greeks' vision that were tied to a special evaluation of humans' rationality. Some early proponents of Christianity, including Origen and Augustine of Hippo, exaggerated humans' distance from other animals. The result over time was a Christian amalgam in which certain obvious connections to nonhuman animals were radically subordinated, as when the mainline Christian tradition claimed that humans are so superior to the rest of creation that humans' morality rightfully excludes other animals' interests when they are in conflict with even minor human interests.

A consequence of this emphasis has been that prominent subtraditions within Christianity have exhibited the persistent refusal to examine the relevance of other animals' actual realities so characteristic of speciesism. An example of this is Pope Pius IX's refusal in the nineteenth century to allow establishment of a society for the protection of animals in Rome, when he said to the English anti-vivisectionist Anna Kingsford, "Madame, humankind has no duties to the animals" (Kalechofsky 199: 78; see also Gaffney 1986: 149).

There are, of course, voices within the Christian tradition that have sounded the inherently ethical themes of compassion for and coexistence with other animals. St Francis and Albert Schweitzer are well-known examples, but many others exist. In recent years, the theologian Andrew Linzey has claimed that it is the essence of Christian spirituality to carry out duties of care toward other animals.

While **Islam** also reflects the Abrahamic traditions' emphasis on humans as the centerpiece of the created universe, this influential tradition in various ways nurtures the competing moral insight that nonhuman animals' lives demand recognition by humans. Thus, in Islam tension exists between mainline claims that other animals have been placed on earth solely for the benefit of humans (see, for example, Qur'an 5:4; 16:5–8; 22:28; 22:36; 23:21; 36:71–3; and 40:79), and those claims that reflect various ways in which Muslims have recognized that other animals have their own importance as Allah's creatures. For example, Muslims clearly understand nonhuman animals to have souls. Qur'an 6:38 also admonishes that other animals have their own communities, and Muhammad himself commented, "Whoever is kind to the creatures of Allah, is kind to himself." Muhammad also compared the doing of good or bad deeds to other animals to similar acts done to humans. Qur'an 17:44 notes that nonhuman animals and the rest of nature are in continuous praise of Allah, although humans may not be able to understand this. The commentator Ibn Taymiyah argued regarding the Qur'an verses which state that Allah created the world to serve humanity, "In considering all these verses it must be remembered that Allah in His wisdom created these creatures for reasons other than serving man, for in these verses He only explains the benefits of these creatures [to man]" (cited in Deen (Samarrai) 1990: 190). There are, then, important traditions within Islam by which possible arrogance by humans – and speciesism – can be checked.

As in the past with Judaism and Hinduism, the practice of ritualized slaughter of animals for food had a central place early in the tradition's development. Unlike in Judaism and most of Hinduism, however, animal sacrifice is still a major part of Islamic practice. A principal example occurs at the end of Ramadan, the traditional month of fasting, when animals are slaughtered for a celebratory feast (the meat is often distributed to the poor). This practice reflects the basic belief that humans are the steward of Allah, which is one version of the claim that other animals, even if not on earth solely for human use, are subordinate to humans and in special instances ordained for humans' use. But even if it remains the case that humans are, in the Islamic vision, the living beings that most truly matter, ethical sensibilities regarding other animals are still given a place of respect. For example, the sacrificial practice includes rules that were originally intended to make the killing as humane as possible. Thus, the tradition provides recognition of the view that other animals have an integrity or inherent value of their own, even when the standard Abrahamic interpretation of humans as the centerpiece of creation is maintained.

Pervasiveness of the Animal Presence Outside the World Religions

The views mentioned above only begin to touch upon the range of possibilities that one finds within religious traditions on the place of nonhuman living beings in humans' lives. The lifeways or totality of daily life and practices as impacted by rituals and beliefs of many kinds of various indigenous peoples contain examples of humans' ability to develop respectful relationships with many kinds of nonhuman living beings. Neihardt begins his famous *Black Elk Speaks: Being the Life Story of a Holy Man of the Oglala*

Sioux with observations about sharing and kinship with other animals: "It is the story of all life that is holy and is good to tell, and of us two-leggeds sharing in it with the four-leggeds and the wings of the air and all green things; for these are children of one mother and their father is one Spirit" (Neihardt 1972 [1932]: 1).

Many diverse forms of contemporary nature-oriented spirituality, which tend to be decentralized and to give primacy to individual experience, emphasize nonhuman animals. Communications with specific kinds of animals (often mammals or birds known to be highly social and intelligent, such as dolphins or ravens) are frequently found in these nature-oriented spiritualities, all of which reflect deep concerns for and connections with nonhuman animals as fellow beings and even persons not unlike humans. Some respected members of contemporary science communities (for example, the primatologist Jane Goodall and the cognitive ethologist Marc Bekoff) emphasize the relevance of rigorous empirical study of animals to humans' spiritual quests.

Making Religion More Animal-Friendly

The story of religion and animals is thus a mixed one. But even if careful study of religion and animals can offer prospective defenses of nonhuman animals, the existing literature remains surprisingly one-dimensional. For example, entire books that purport to address a religious tradition's views of "animals" fail to refer in any way to the realities of the animals allegedly being discussed. This is increasingly untenable given that much more accurate information has been developed about our nonhuman cousins in the last four decades. These shortcomings reveal that ethical anthropocentrism continues to dominate much of our culture, as when mere images of other animals or those nonhuman animals which have been domesticated animals remain the principal focus because they are, misleadingly, held out as representative or the paradigm of *all* nonhuman lives. Since ethical anthropocentrism in the form of speciesism is also a defining feature of contemporary legal systems, business values, mainline economic theory, government policy decisions, and educational philosophies and curricula, it will surprise no one that major religious institutions continue to promote this narrow view.

Some special challenges for supporters and critics of religion on the issue of nonhuman animals include the role of customary views and symbols, the special place of ethical claims in religion, and prevailing practices regarding nonhuman animals.

Identifying the Role of Inherited Perspectives

The influence of inherited conceptions causes many religious believers' perspectives on nonhuman animals to be over-determined by something other than a careful engagement with the animals themselves. Inherited preconceptions commonly take the form of dismissive generalizations found in those documents held to be "revealed." Too often, one-dimensional sketches of a few local animals have operated as a definitive assessment of *all* nonhuman animals' abilities and moral significance. At other times, inaccurate stories, even when positive, obscure the actual realities of the local nonhuman animals. Custom and tradition have all too frequently underwritten inflexible claims about other animals, frustrating believers who wish to engage readily available, empirically based evidence that contradicts, in letter or spirit, their religion's inherited views.

Animal images that work as symbols in religious art, writing, dance, and oral traditions are only sometimes connected to the animals portrayed. Western scholars have often failed to comprehend other cultures' animal symbols because they have assumed that other cultures read nonhuman animals in the dismissive manner of the Western intellectual tradition. Such coarse analytic methods have resulted in serious underestimation of earlier cultures' sophistication regarding nonhuman animals. Caution, then, is critically important in studying animal images, which sometimes work primarily, even exclusively, to convey some feature of human complexity rather than any information about the nonhuman beings whose images are being employed.

Ethical concerns have long been central to religious traditions. As the brief review of religious belief above suggests, humans' ability to exercise concerns for "others" has historically included both humans and nonhumans.

Treatment of nonhuman animals is a critical element in assessing any religious tradition's views of other animals. Accounts of the actual, day-to-day treatment of other living beings reveal much about the deepest values in a religious tradition. Brutal treatment of cattle in the daily world outside a temple where worshippers pay homage to an idol in the shape of a bull or cow would suggest that, on the whole, the religion involved does not respect the harmed animals. And kind treatment of bulls and cows in daily matters, even when there are no images of these animals in the local people's rituals, would suggest something more positive. Which of these two religious communities would we say truly valued the cattle?

As carriers of views of the world around us, religious traditions are ancient educators. They profoundly affect the formation of cultural, ethical, social, ecological, intellectual, and political ideas. In this regard, religious traditions quite naturally have had a major role in transmitting views of nonhuman animals from generation to generation. This transmission role affects virtually everyone's basic ideas about these beings' natures, as well as their place in, or exclusion from, our communities of concern. An essential task in the study of religion and animals is to find the special roles that religious traditions play in developing or retarding views of the life around us.

Since the death of Augustine of Hippo almost 1,600 years ago, the vast majority of scholarship in the Western intellectual tradition has been premised on the assumption that humans are the only animals with intellectual ability, emotions, social complexity, and personality development. This dismissal of nonhuman animals, which remains a centerpiece in today's educational institutions, has been challenged by the rich information developed in modern life sciences. The vibrant debates in modern science regarding the specific abilities of nonhuman animals can be used to frame a peculiar irony. We still talk in our schools of "humans and animals," rather than using the far more scientific "humans and nonhumans" or "humans and other animals." But outside academia and even within some religious traditions, many believers have not adhered to the broad dismissal of nonhuman animals characteristic of the Western cultural and intellectual traditions. The best-known examples are the Jains, Buddhists, and many indigenous tradition believers who clearly treat other living beings as morally and religiously significant beings.

Thus even as mainline religious institutions have participated in dismissals of nonhuman animals from the agenda of "religious ethics," ethical concerns for nonhuman animals' welfare have continued to have a place in many religious believers' lives. This fact makes it misleading to suggest that all religious believers have dismissed nonhuman animals in the manner of the mainline Western intellectual and theological traditions that remain dominant today. Even if anthropocentric biases continue to dominate many modern religious institutions' official pronouncements, then, there remains vast potential for emergence of more informed and open-minded treatment of nonhuman animals in the doctrines, rituals, experiences, ethics, myths, social realities, and ecological perspectives of religious believers. It is quite possible that when a clearer picture of religion and animals is drawn, it will be a rich tapestry of alternatives for interacting with the earth's nonhuman lives.

This potential remains largely unrealized, of course, for it remains overwhelmingly true today that mainline religious institutions have left unchallenged virtually all practices of modern industrialized societies that are harmful to nonhuman animals. This failure arguably violates the ancient consensus which originated in all religious traditions that cruelty to other beings by humans is to be avoided whenever possible.

Religions, especially as they are ancient and enduring cultural and ethical traditions, have often been individual believers' primary source for answers to fundamental questions like, "Which living beings really should matter to me?" and "Who and what should be within my community of concern?" As such, religion has had profound impacts on countless humans' actions affecting the other, nonhuman living beings that live within and without our communities. Since religions so characteristically govern day-to-day actions involving our "neighbors," they will continue to have an obvious role in answering questions about whether we are, or can be, a moral species.

This means that religion generally and specific communities of faith can be challenged with some simple, common-sense questions. What place will religions give to discoveries about nonhuman animals that emerge in the future? How might mainline religious institutions respond to their own subtraditions that become fully informed about other animals' realities and humans' current treatment and uses of other animals? Could individual believers or subtraditions prompt mainline traditions to respond to the ethics of contemporary practices such as factory farming and the decimation of wildlife? These questions drive at a simple question that challenges both religious and secular outlooks – how can humans, whether within or without religion, better understand nonhuman animals?

Because religious institutions have so much influence in cultures across the earth – worldwide, only about one-seventh of people count themselves as non-religious – religions have within their grasp an important leadership role regarding our relationship to the world around us. An increasing number of religious and non-religious humans have echoed some form of Thomas Berry's insight that "we cannot be truly ourselves in any adequate manner without all our companion beings throughout the earth. This larger community constitutes our greater self" (2005). Whether believers, churches, and religious institutions will respond to this challenge remains an unanswered question.

Works Cited

Berry, Thomas (2005) "Loneliness and Presence," Prologue to Paul Waldau and Kimberley Patton (eds), *A Communion of Subjects: Animals in Religion, Science and Ethics*, New York: Columbia University Press.

Deen (Samarrai), Mawil Y. Izzi (1990) "Islamic Environmental Ethics, Law, and Society," in J. Ronald Engel and Joan Gibb Engel (eds), *Ethics of Environment and Development: Global Challenge, International Response*, London: Bellhaven Press, pp. 189–98.

Gaffney, James (1986) "The Relevance of Animal Experimentation in Roman Catholic Ethical Methodology," in Tom Regan (ed.), *Animal Sacrifices: Religious Perspectives on the Use of Animals in Science*, Philadelphia: Temple University Press, pp. 149–70.

Kalechofsky, Roberta (1991) *Autobiography of a Revolutionary: Essays on Animal and Human Rights*, Marblehead, MA: Micah Publications.

Midgley, Mary (1984) *Animals and Why They Matter*, Athens, GA: University of Georgia Press.

Neihardt, John G. (1972 [1932]) *Black Elk Speaks: Being the Life Story of a Holy Man of the Oglala Sioux*, New York: Pocket Books.

Ryder, Richard D. (1970) *Speciesism*, Oxford (privately printed leaflet).

Sorabji, Richard (1993) *Animal Minds and Human Morals: The Origins of the Western Debate*, Ithaca, N.Y.: Cornell University Press.

Waldau, Paul (2001) *The Specter of Speciesism: Buddhist and Christian Views of Animals*, New York: Oxford University Press.

Additional Reading

Ascione, Frank R., and Arkow, Phil (eds) (1999) *Child Abuse, Domestic Violence, and Animal Abuse: Linking the Circles of Compassion for Prevention and Intervention*, West Lafayette, IN: Purdue University Press.

Goodall, Jane, and Bekoff, Marc (2002) *The Ten Trusts: What We Must Do to Care for the Animals We Love*, San Francisco: HarperSanFrancisco.

Goodall, Jane, with Berman, Phillip (1999) *Reason for Hope: A Spiritual Journey*, New York: Warner.

Harrod, Howard L. (1987) *Renewing the World: Plains Indian Religion and Morality*, Tucson: University of Arizona Press.

Lawrence, Elizabeth Atwood (1985) *Hoofbeats and Society: Studies of Human–Horse Interactions*, Bloomington: Indiana University Press.

Lonsdale, Steven (1982) *Animals and the Origins of Dance*, New York: Thames & Hudson.

Linzey, Andrew (1987) *Christianity and the Rights of Animals*, New York: Crossroad.
—— (1994) *Animal Theology*, Chicago: University of Illinois Press.
Regan, Tom (ed.) (1986) *Animal Sacrifices: Religious Perspectives on the Use of Animals in Science*, Philadelphia: Temple University Press.
Shepard, Paul (1996) *The Others: How Animals Made Us Human*, Washington, D.C. and Covelo, CA: Island Press/Shearwater Books.
Waldau, Paul (2000a) "Buddhism and Animals Rights," in Damien Keown (ed.), *Contemporary Buddhist Ethics*, Richmond, Surrey: Curzon Press, pp. 81–112.
—— (ed.) (2000b) *Society and Animals* 8(3) (special edition on "Religion and Animals").

Part II

The Problems

6

Speciesism in the Laboratory

Richard D. Ryder

Several factors in the 1970s contributed to the revival of the anti-vivisection and animal rights movements. Six of these have been identified, correctly I think, by Harlan B. Miller in *Ethics and Animals* (1983: 7). I would describe them thus:

- *The momentum of liberation.* Once colonialism, racism, and sexism had been intellectually challenged, then the next logical stage in the expansion of the boundaries of the moral in-group was an attack upon speciesism.
- *Increasing scientific evidence that nonhumans share intellectual and perceptual faculties in common with humankind.* Miller emphasizes recent evidence of high intelligence in apes. But, in addition, surely, the evidence that all vertebrate classes share with man the biochemical substances associated with the transmission of pain is of equal, or even greater, significance.
- *The ethical debate over abortion.* Miller claims that this had moved the "concept of a person" to the center of the stage.
- *The decline in dualistic views separating mind from body.* The greater acceptance that the substance of central nervous systems (as they exist in many animals) is the basis for mental life and consciousness. Increasing secularization reduced the influence of religiously based forms of speciesism.
- *The development of behavioral sciences (such as sociobiology and ethology) which attempt to draw conclusions about human behavior from observations of other*

animals. This has spread the view that *Homo sapiens* is just one species among other species.

• *The rise of the environmental and ecology movements*. This indicated an increasing "awareness of nature" and of "humanity's interdependence with other species."

Miller adds a seventh factor in parenthesis: the popularity of science fiction and recent advances in astronomy. These have promoted the view that the universe may contain other intelligences. The televised view of Earth from space, so I believe, has also improved our moral perspective.

All these factors affected the thinking of those of us who were involved in the revival of the animal protection movement. Above all, we were conscious of living in a post-Darwinian age when the moral implications of Darwinism were overdue for serious consideration. Maybe two world wars had had the effect of reducing human arrogance and deference to authority. Humans no longer saw themselves as being so different from the nonhuman animals. Some members of the younger generation rejected the double standards of their parents and the conspiracy of silence on a whole range of moral issues, among them our abuse of animals.

Two factors made the new animal experimentation reform campaign especially credible and supportable. The first was the emphasis we placed upon *the search for alternative humane techniques*. This search was led by animal welfare groups in America, Germany, and Britain. They not only propagated the idea that humane techniques should be sought but, in some cases, supplied the funds necessary for research into these new fields. Widespread initial skepticism among scientists was gradually dispelled as tissue and organ cultures and other techniques were developed and their relative validities established.

The second factor was the realization that *many experiments on animals are not performed for strictly medical purposes*. To many people it seems reasonable to argue that deliberately inflicted pain may be justified if the results significantly benefit humans medically. Commonly, however, such an analysis is used to justify inflicting pain on animals when the only benefits from particular experiments are found to be a new cosmetic, soap powder, or other inessential product, or greater knowledge of the effects of weapons. Academic psychological and other behavioral research can also fall into this less "necessary" category.

The Ethical Argument

From 1970 the so-called "Oxford Group" revived interest in the ethics of the human treatment of nonhuman animals with street protests, my writing of leaflets, and the publication of Stanley and Roslind Godlovitch and John Harris's *Animals, Men and Morals* (1971). Peter Singer's influential *Animal Liberation* of 1975 took our message from Oxford to the United States, and in the same year my *Victims of Science* precipitated debates in the UK Parliament and set in train events that would lead to new legislation controlling animal experimentation in 1986, in both the UK and the EU. I characterized the conventional prejudice against nonhumans as "speciesism" – drawing the parallel with similar forms of irrational discrimination such as racism, sexism, and ageism. Since Darwin, so I argued, there has been no justification for the moral gulf we impose between ourselves and our evolutionary relations. Abundant scientific evidence, based on neurological, behavioral, biological, and biochemical data, supports the view that many nonhumans can suffer pain and distress in the same sort of way that humans do. Considerations of intelligence, sophistication, autonomy, or species difference are morally irrelevant. What matters morally, we asserted, is the other's distress and pain, regardless of species (Godlovitch et al. 1971; Ryder 1975, 2001; Singer 1975); If nonhuman animals are sufficiently similar to humans for them to be used as scientific models in research, then they are sufficiently similar to be accorded a similar moral status.

The growing concern over the ethics of vivisection revived the reform movements on both sides of the Atlantic. Campaigners began to study the methods of regulation employed and to press for improvements.

The Elements of Reform

The licensing of experimenters and the inspection of laboratories are often the first steps in regulating vivisection. The reduction of secrecy and the admission of public opinion into the control process then follow. In Sweden, for example, experiments are allowed or disallowed by regional animal ethics committees on which lay, animal welfare, animal care (veterinary), and scientific interests are represented. The requirement to use alternative (non-animal) techniques (or lower organisms) wherever possible is sometimes the next stage. The control of pain or its prohibition are also key reforms, and in Britain, since 1986, procedures have been classified according to three levels of severity by the government licensing authority (see below).

Whether or not an experiment is essential depends upon one's point of view. To the experimenter, convinced of the importance of his or her own research, or to those in business determined to make a profit, almost any procedure may seem justified. But in certain fields, such as cosmetics testing, behavioral research, agricultural research, and weapons testing, the justification for inflicting pain wears thin in the opinion of most people. Clearly, decisions ought to be taken transparently, perhaps by a panel equally representative of the interests of the animals and the experimenters and arbitrated by a jury of intelligent lay persons.

In 1983 the Royal Society for the Prevention of Cruelty to Animals (RSPCA) sent the British government a report arguing that animal suffering is the single most significant issue in the political debate on vivisection and the main focus of public concern. The Society cited experiments in which irradiated mice took six months to die, monkeys dosed with weedkiller took a week, and other animals, desperately ill, took several weeks to die after being poisoned in military research.[1] The RSPCA had already established that certain body chemicals associated with the experience of pain in humans were also present in all other vertebrate classes. Their 1983 report, therefore, concluded that this new evidence, added to the older neurological and behavioral findings, strongly indicated that all vertebrates share a common capacity to experience pain. The RSPCA made clear its total opposition to any suffering in experimentation. The report went on to recommend that all those experimenting on animals should be required to show competence in modern techniques of anesthesia, analgesia, tranquillization, euthanasia, and animal care, and to use these skills as a matter of course. The physiological effects of analgesia might interfere with some experiments, but so also might the physiological effects of pain itself. An independent on-the-spot expert "animals' friend" within the laboratory should constantly monitor levels of suffering. The absence of certain behavioral or other signs should never be taken as proof of the absence of pain or distress, and as a general rule experimenters should record (and publish) descriptions of all steps taken to assess and maintain an animal's state of wellbeing. Many of these suggestions were enacted in the Animals (Scientific Procedures) Act of 1986.

The RSPCA report concluded by emphasizing the need for public accountability and recommended that experiments should be controlled by central and local ethical committees. These should have a composition balanced by equal representation between those representing the interests of the experimenters and those representing animal welfare, and should assess and balance pain against the probability of benefits.

Some Severe Experiments

Despite improvements in regulation, many experiments on animals continue to cause significant suffering.

- Recent procedures in the U.S., for example, include cats, rats, and rhesus monkeys being shaken and spun in the dark in order to measure the effects of experimental brain damage and eye movements. For example, juvenile rhesus monkeys were seated in a primate chair with their heads restrained in a position of 15 degrees nose-down relative to the stereotaxic horizontal. Some had rings anchored to their skulls by steel screws. The animals were placed inside the inner frame of a multi-axis turntable with three motor-driven gimbaled axes and rotated at various velocities (Hess and Angelaki 1997).
- In 2001 an American company patented a new technique for creating chronic pain. Current models for chronic pain in animals are created by sutures, lasers, freezing, nerve transactions, and irritants. These cause acute pain and, usually, significant nerve damage. The new technique causes pain in animals which lasts for "several months."[2]
- In Maryland, in 1996, in a study of septic shock, permanently tracheotomized beagle dogs were used. *E. coli*-infected clots were surgically placed in the dogs' peritoneum. Over the course of the next twenty-one days, ten of the sixteen dogs died (Eichacker et al. 1996).
- In Taiwan in 1997 spinal injuries were caused by dropping weights onto the spines of rats. It was found that greater injuries were caused by dropping the weights from greater heights (Hong et al. 1997).
- In Minneapolis in 1999 scientists studying bone cancer pain demonstrated a correlation between bone destruction, pain, and neurochemical changes in the spinal cord by injecting tumor cells into the femurs of mice. This replicated the symptoms of patients with bone cancer pain. It is known that such pain can be "intense" (Schwei et al. 1999).
- Since the 1990s many animals in America have been used to study the effects of high alcohol consumption and withdrawal. In studies of chimpanzees, monkeys, dogs, cats, and rodents, severe effects have been observed. These can include vomiting, tremor, anxiety, and seizures.

Convulsions have been induced in alcohol-withdrawal animals by lifting animals by the tail, giving electric shocks, or injecting chemicals directly into the brain (Becker 2000).

Legislation

There is much up-to-date legislation in the world relating to the use of animals in scientific procedures, for example Directive 86/609EC relating to the twenty-five member states of the EU, the U.S. Animal Welfare Act (as amended), and the New Zealand Animal Welfare Act 1999. Some features are mirrored across acts of legislation, but there are also variations and important differences. Much legislation states the requirement to use humane alternatives if available, defines minimum standards of housing and husbandry (which again vary across legislative area), stipulates the require-ment to undertake a pain/benefit assessment, or incorporates regimes for the scaling of pain severity and the invasiveness of procedures. In countries such as Canada, Sweden, Australia, New Zealand, and the USA, local Ethics or Animal Care and Use Committees have a considerable role in regulation, with less central government control; the local committees are responsible for implementing the mandates of the national legislation, for authorizing projects, and making sure researchers adhere to the law. These local com-mittees might be based at the individual establishment (e.g. Canada) or be regionally based, having responsibility for overseeing work in a particular area of the country (e.g. Sweden and Switzerland).

U.S. Law

The regulatory structure for laboratory animals in the USA involves several players. The U.S. Department of Agriculture (USDA) enforces the Animal Welfare Act. This Act was originally passed in 1966 and was then amended in 1970, 1976, and 1985. The original Act (then named the Laboratory Animal Welfare Act) dealt solely with the acquisition of dogs and cats for the laboratory. The 1970 amendments broadened the Act and covered the care of animals housed in laboratories but specifically excluded any over-sight of how they were used (except for a phrase requiring anesthesia and analgesia if it did not interfere with the research). The 1976 amendments did not deal with laboratory animals (the Act also covers animals on exhibit and the interstate transport of pets for sale). The 1985 amendments were passed in the wake of the two big scandals in American animal research in the early 1980s – the 1981 Silver Spring Monkeys case and the 1984 Head Trauma case at the University of Pennsylvania involving baboon research. These amendments required the establishment of Institutional Animal Care and Use Committees to review and approve protocols, and also focused attention on reducing animal pain and distress, promoting alternatives, and encouraging the psychological wellbeing of laboratory primates and dogs. There have been a couple of other minor legislative forays since 1985 (an Act tightening up on the use of random source dogs for research and an Act establishing a sanctuary/retirement program for laboratory chimpanzees).

The major weaknesses in the USDA oversight system include:

- the omission of mice, rats, and birds (because of the alleged expense involved in regulating these creatures, who make up 95 percent of all research animals used in the U.S.) and a focus only on six main categories – primates, dogs, cats, rabbits, hamsters, and guinea pigs;
- a very poor reporting system that has been plagued by late and inaccurate reporting and by simple numerical errors in the USDA-compiled annual report to Congress;
- a lack of focus on pain and distress (pain is essentially defined as "if it hurts a human being then, in the absence of contrary evidence, it should be assumed to hurt an animal"; there is no definition of distress);
- chronic under-funding of the regulatory structure and a lack of adequate training for the inspectors.

Other entities are also involved in U.S. laboratory animal oversight. The Public Health Service (PHS) (basically the National Institutes of Health [NIH] but the National Science Foundation and other entities like the Veteran's Administration and the USDA laboratories take their lead from the PHS) requires all recipients of federal research funds to follow certain policies and procedures, including the Guide for the Care and Use of Laboratory Animals. This Guide does cover mice, rats, and birds. The PHS provides funding to about 650 of the 2,000 or so research institutions, including all the large universities and research centers. Most of the corporations do not receive NIH funding so they are not bound by the PHS system, but the big ones are usually accredited by the Association for the Assessment and Accreditation of Laboratory Animal Care, which also uses the Guide.

Richard D. Ryder

British Law

The law controlling animal research in the UK is called the Animal (Scientific Procedures) Act 1986 (ASPA). It is often cited (perhaps wrongly) as the most advanced legislation in this field, so it will be considered here in detail. The law covers any scientific procedures carried out on an animal which *may have the effect of causing that animal pain, suffering, distress, or lasting harm.* It includes all vertebrate animals – mammals, birds, reptiles, amphibians, and fish – and one species of octopus.

The law works by a system of licenses. Three licences are required, covering:

- the program of research – this is called the *project license*;
- the person carrying out the work – this is called the *personal license*;
- the place where the research is carried out (including places where animals are bred for research) – this is called the *certificate of designation*.

Every designated establishment must have a person with overall responsibility for the day-to-day care of the animals, and a veterinary surgeon to advise on animal health and welfare. Each establishment must also have an ethics committee (now called an Ethical Review Process or ERP) to oversee all aspects of animal use.

The government department responsible for administering the Act is the Home Office, headed by the Home Secretary. The Home Office works through a team of inspectors. The Home Secretary also receives advice from the Animal Procedures Committee (APC). This committee is made up of independent experts – scientists, philosophers, lawyers, and animal welfarists.

Before a project license is granted, any adverse effects on the animals must be considered against the hoped-for benefits of the research. This so-called "cost/benefit assessment" is carried out first by the applicant for the license, then by the establishment's ERP, and finally by the Home Office inspectors. Alternatives to animals should be used where possible. Pain, distress, and discomfort to the animals should be minimized. Animals believed to be of the lowest level of consciousness must be used. Additional justification is required for the use of dogs, cats, primates, and horses and ponies.

Because the ASPA is perceived as the strictest system for controlling animal experiments in the world, its minimum standards are often wrongly interpreted as the best standards. This has encouraged complacency.

Animals require a varied and stimulating environment with plenty of space and opportunities for social interaction. The RSPCA considers that the minimum standards laid down in both UK and European legislation are inadequate to satisfy what is now known about animals' psychological, social, and behavioral needs. The RSPCA is also opposed to the import and export of laboratory animals because of the additional distress this causes, has many concerns about conditions for primates in overseas breeding centres, and does not believe that the search for alternatives, the cost/benefit procedure, the focus upon welfare and the relief of pain and distress, all emphasized by the Act, are being given sufficient emphasis in practice. Nor is the Act operated with any real transparency. Huge sums of taxpayers' money continue to be spent on animal research without the concerned taxpayer gaining real access. Unnecessary testing is rarely questioned by the government and no effort is made to explain to the public exactly what is being done to the animals in their name and allegedly for the public benefit. Like all legislation, this law needs to be intelligently and competently enforced.

In 1994 accredited training courses for license holders were made compulsory in Britain and, in the following year, a British ban was proposed on the use of great apes in laboratories and a near ban on the use of any wild-caught primates. In 1997 and 1998, at long last, there were bans on the use of animals to test cosmetics, cosmetic ingredients, tobacco, alcohol, and offensive weapons.

The Use of Great Apes

The UK (since 1997), New Zealand (since 1999), and Sweden (since 2003) now exclude the use of great apes for research and testing purposes. Although the Netherlands still has six chimpanzees on a hepatitis project, they will be the last, as the country has recently announced its intention not to allow further use. In Japan, academics have halted invasive chimpanzee research and are pressing for a total ban.[3] The U.S. has no such ban and currently there are 1,200 chimpanzees housed in laboratories in the U.S. (according to a recent survey cited in the July 2003 edition of *IAT Bulletin*). By contrast, the Republic of Ireland has a policy not to license projects involving the use of *any* primate species.

Alternatives to Experimentation
with Live Animals

The concept of the 3 R's of replacement, reduction, and refinement became a useful trinity in the scientific and reform communities of the 1990s. The 3 R's refer to:

- those techniques which *replace* experimental animals; the use of cell cultures generally or of sophisticated models and novel materials in some trauma research (e.g. car crash studies) are some examples of how imaginative scientists have created new techniques;
- those techniques which *reduce* the numbers of animals used;
- the reduction or abolition of pain or other suffering through the *refinement* of husbandry and procedures. This is now extended to include the positive concept of improving laboratory animal welfare.

All three approaches have some value, although replacement and refinement are generally accepted as being more morally important than mere reduction in the numbers of animals used.

Computer models of bodily function, physical models or films for teaching purposes, tissue cultures (i.e. growing living cells in a test tube), organ cultures, and magnetic resonance imaging (MRI) are all examples of techniques which have had the effect of successfully replacing some animals in research. Many of these techniques are more accurate and less expensive than using animals. Others need further research and development. Some, like the simple culturing of human cells, are inexpensive, while others require the purchase of new equipment, which can be costly.

One of the great drawbacks of tissue culture, as a method for testing chemical substances, drugs, or vaccines, has been the need to test new substances on all the systems of the body working together. A substance which is not poisonous to cells alone may become so after it is transformed by the liver, for example, into a new substance. On the other hand, what is poisonous to one species of animal may not affect another species. Rats and mice can react quite differently to the same substance. So can the human animal. As long ago as 1980 Professor George Teeling-Smith pointed out some of the problems of the statutory toxicity (poison) testing on animals, as it was at that time, in a paper entitled "A Question of Balance" (published by the Association of the British Pharmaceutical Industry):

The statutory bodies such as the Committee on Safety of Medicines which require these tests do so largely as an act of faith rather than on hard scientific grounds.

With thalidomide, for example, it is only possible to produce the specific deformities in a very small number of species of animal. In this particular case, therefore, it is unlikely that specific tests in pregnant animals would have given the necessary warning: the right species would probably never have been used. Even more strikingly, the practolol adverse reactions have not been reproducible in any species of animal except man. Conversely, penicillin in very small doses is fatal to guinea pigs. If it had been tested in those animals before being given to man, its systemic use in humans might well have been considered too hazardous and unethical.

Clearly, alternatives that are more scientifically valid than animals need to be found. The undoubted advantage of the tissue-culture approach is that it can use *human* rather than animal cells. Moreover, it can use different types of living human cell and even diseased cells, such as human cancer cells removed during normal surgery. (There are, of course, ethical problems with using human cells and tissues.)

Some of the heaviest users of animals are the firms which carry out routine toxicity testing of new products. Although the notorious LD50 Test is no longer supposed to be employed in Britain, cruel and clumsy acute toxicity tests are still in use. They may involve dosing animals with high doses of cosmetics or drugs, weedkillers, or consumer products, in order to see how many animals die within a certain time (for example, fourteen days). Many scientists attach little importance to the results of such crude procedures, yet some bureaucracies still obstinately and cruelly refuse to channel research funds into developing better alternative and humane techniques. The Draize Test (applying substances to the eyes of animals) is a similarly primitive procedure. This test, or similar eye-irritancy procedures, continue in use in Britain, the EU and the U.S. In the UK alone, in 2002, 1,271 procedures involved administering substances to the eyes of rabbits.[4] Another case is the testing of products for their carcinogenic potential. Thousands of animals perish miserably each year in such research, despite the fact that *human* cancer tumors cannot satisfactorily be produced in other species.

The Size of the Problem

The annual use of animals in laboratories worldwide has been put at between 40 and 100 million. Unfortunately, no accurate and comprehensive

Richard D. Ryder

figures are available on how many animals are used in the USA – or for what purposes they are used. The USDA does compile statistics on the use of dogs, cats, primates, rabbits, hamsters, and guinea pigs (as well as some wild animals and, recently, farm animals), but the most common laboratory animals – rats, mice, and birds, which make up around 90–5 percent of all animals used, are not counted. However, the U.S. Office of Technology Assessment estimated laboratory animal use in the U.S., *for all species of vertebrate*, to be 17 to 22 million animals annually during the mid-1980s. A more recent estimate is 20–5 million. In 2000 it was estimated that Canada uses around 1.95 million laboratory animals annually. A 1998 estimate for Japan was between 9 and 10 million and one for New Zealand produced a figure of 0.32 million. In 2003, the European Union released figures as shown in Table 6.1. Usage in Britain peaked at about 6 million in the years around 1970 (when the modern campaigns began). The British use of genetically modified (GM) animals has escalated at an alarming rate in recent years, however, rising from 631,000 in 2001 to 710,000 in 2002.

The British figures contain exceptional detail and may reveal features that are internationally typical. In 2001, in Britain, only 26.3 percent of licensed

Table 6.1 Number of laboratory animals in the European Union (m)

Belgium	0.79
Denmark	0.32
Germany	1.59
Greece	0.01
Spain	0.48
France	2.31
Ireland	0.07
Italy	0.99
Luxembourg	0.003
Netherlands	0.62
Austria	0.13
Portugal	0.04
Finland	0.23
Sweden	0.32
UK	1.91

procedures were classified as being for human medical or dental purposes, 29.7 percent were for the breeding of GM animals, and 17.4 percent were for toxicological purposes. Most of the latter (86 percent) were carried out to comply with national or international (e.g. OECD) safety-testing regulations. Just over half of the toxicological procedures carried out in 2001 were for the safety testing of drugs and vaccines. About 45,000 animals (1.75 percent), however, were used to test pesticides, food additives, and household products. Some twenty-three categories of animals are listed in the British figures for 2001: 83.6 percent of the total were rats and mice, but dogs, cats, primates, birds, fish, and horses were also used.

Levels of Suffering

Research projects in Britain are now officially classified as to the level of suffering that they may cause. There are three categories: mild, moderate, and substantial, depending on the intensity of suffering likely to occur, its duration, the number of animals likely to suffer, and the action taken to reduce suffering (see Table 6.2). (Experiments may also be "unclassified," which means the experiment is carried out under anaesthesia and the animal is killed without recovering consciousness.) These categories are very broad and the statistics only list how many *projects* fall into each category, not how many *animals*. This does not tell us about the criteria used to make these important yet difficult classifications.

Table 6.2 UK government classification of severity in licensed animal research

Level of severity (suffering)	Number of project licenses in force on 31 December 2001 (UK)	%
Mild	1,296	39
Moderate	1,811	55
Substantial	63	2
Unclassified	139	4
Total	3,309	100

Richard D. Ryder

Political Campaigning

Various commentators have seen the animal liberation movement as some sort of left-wing conspiracy. Yet, over the years, no evidence has appeared of any ulterior political motivation and, indeed, Marxists and socialists have usually been counted on the other side of the argument. Marxists are often great speciesists. Indeed, active discouragement of organized animal welfare was very much a feature of life in Eastern Europe during the Communist era. However, the European reform movement, since the 1990s, has included the parties of the center and the left – the Democratic Socialist, Social Democrat, and Liberal parties. This marks a change from the animal welfare movement of previous decades, which had become rather middle-class and conservative, a phenomenon deriving from the highly respectable position attained for the promotion of animal welfare in late nineteenth-century society on both sides of the Atlantic. Prior to the 1970s in Britain, center and left-wing politicians tended to be skeptical of animal welfare, and some viewed it as middle-class sentimentality – a preference for pets over people. This outlook was gradually changed by the new campaigns of the 1970s, the spate of serious publications on the subject, and the deliberate and successful attempts of the 1980s and 1990s to "put animals into politics." Campaigns led by Lord Houghton, Clive Hollands, and myself in Britain from 1970 led to an arousal of public awareness and, eventually, to the passage of the new laboratory animal legislation in London and the EU in 1986.

In the U.S. much progress was made by the late Christine Stevens and other animal groups in Washington during the 1950s and 1960s. After the publication of Peter Singer's *Animal Liberation* in New York in 1975, a new activist animal rights wing of the American movement developed and skilled campaigners such as Henry Spira, inspired by Singer's lectures, achieved important results. Alex Pacheco, Barbara Orlans, Tom Regan, Ingrid Newkirk, and many others followed up. The tactics followed a similar pattern to those in Europe: the presentation of evidence of atrocities to the media, public protest, and the focusing of public feeling onto politicians or other influential figures such as the heads of major testing companies. Some others took direct action including break-ins. The U.S. media were intrigued by the issue during the 1980s, but, as animal rights became part of popular culture, serious media interest waned during the following decade. The American scientific and academic establishments for the most part remained implacably hostile. Nevertheless, attempts were made to promote the "three R's" within the American laboratory community and Dr Andrew Rowan of the Humane Society of the U.S. initiated an important campaign to assess and eliminate the pain and distress inflicted on laboratory animals. In 1999 a coalition of representatives from the research, animal protection, zoo, and sanctuary communities, supported by the well-known primatologist Jane Goodall, successfully pressed for the introduction of the Chimpanzee Health Improvement Maintenance and Protection Act (CHIMP) by Rep. James Greenwood. This was signed into law by President Clinton on 20 December 2000, establishing a national sanctuary system for retired laboratory chimpanzees. Furthermore, supported by a major grant in 2003, the Florida-based Center for Captive Chimpanzee Care announced it would permanently care for some 300 chimpanzees and monkeys once used by the Coulston Foundation. Less successful was the campaign by a coalition of seven animal protection bodies to provide protection to laboratory birds, rats, and mice under the Animal Welfare Act. This failed in 2002 when Senator Jesse Helms, prompted by medical research organizations, amended the Farm Security Act so as to permanently deny protection to these species under the Animal Welfare Act.

The Political Animal Lobby (PAL) of the 1990s led the way in Europe by using not only personal contacts with ministers and media campaigns, backed by science and law, but also the legitimate funding of political institutions (Ryder 1989, 1998). In Europe, too, more than in the U.S., some good "insider" relationships have been established between scientists, animal welfarists, and politicians.

Governments tend to move only when pressed; when the pressure is released they usually cease to move. In the case of modern pressure-group politics the principal tools of the trade are media attention, the arousal and targeting of public opinion, and direct approaches to government and politicians supported by scientific, legal, and psephological evidence. European groups have excelled at these tactics. An early and classic example of this was the stopping of the slaughter of grey and common seals in Scotland in 1978. First, Greenpeace boats confronted the sealers and thus caught the attention of the media. The International Fund for Animal Welfare (IFAW) made the next major move by placing whole-page advertisements in the British press telling members of the public to "Write to the Prime Minister." (This caused James Callaghan to receive some 17,000 letters on this topic in one week – the most ever received on one subject by any Prime Minister in such a short period.) Finally, I headed an RSPCA deputation to the Secretary of State bearing some scientific findings which cast an element of doubt upon the scientific research of the government; this duly helped to provide the government with the excuse it by then needed to call off the seal slaughter. In this campaign the three elements (direct action attracting the media, the channeling of already aroused public feeling, and, finally, high-level political contact providing a face-saver for the government) all worked perfectly together.

Many politicians are sincerely moved by arguments, especially if these are backed by science and the law. But, ultimately, the effective incentives for politicians are votes and, sadly, money. Far more needs to be done in the future to tame the great international forces that now affect the welfare of animals around the world. The OECD, the World Trade Organization, the International Standards Organization, and even the United Nations now need to feel the skilled pressure of animal protectionists. There is also a need for better-educated and more humane government and science. These are the challenges for the twenty-first century.

Notes

I am particularly indebted to Dr Maggy Jennings, Dr Penny Hawkins, and Barney Reed of the RSPCA and to Dr Carmen Lee of Philadelphia and Dr Andrew Rowan of the Humane Society of the US for their assistance in bringing this chapter up to date in 2005.

1. *British Journal of Radiology* 49 (1976) and *European Journal of Cancer* 15 (1979); *British Journal of Experimental Pathology* 61 (1980), 62 (1981); *Toxicology* 15(1) (1979); *British Journal of Pharmacology* 70 (1980).
2. "Biogenic Rodent Model of Chronic Pain" (*www.neurodigm.com*).
3. *Nature* 417 (June 13, 2002), p. 686.
4. Home Office figures, 2003.

References

Becker, Howard C. (2000) "Animal Models of Alcohol Withdrawal," *Alcohol Research & Health* 24(2), 105–13.
Eichacker, P. Q., et al. (1996) "Serial Measures of Total Body Oxygen Consumption in an Awake Canine Model of Septic Shock," *American Journal of Respiratory Critical Care Medicine* 154(1), 68–75.
Godlovitch, Stanley, Godlovitch, Roslind, and Harris, John (1971) *Animals, Men and Morals*, London: Gollancz.

Hess, B. J., and Angelaki, D. E. (1997) "Kinematic Principles of Primate Vestibulo Ocular Reflex," *Journal of Neurophysiology* 78(4), 2203–16.

Hong, C. C., et al. (1997) "Induced Spinal Cord Injury," *Journal of Chinese Society of Veterinary Science* 23(5), 383–94.

Miller, Harlan B. (1983) "Introduction" to Harlan B. Miller and W. H. Williams (eds), *Ethics and Animals*, Totowa, N.J.: Humana Press.

Ryder, Richard D. (1975) *Victims of Science: The Use of Animals in Research*, London: Davis-Poynter; rev. edn, Fontwell, Sussex: Centaur Press Ltd (Dutch translation 1980; Norwegian 1984; Hungarian 1995).

—— (1989) *Animal Revolution: Changing Attitudes Towards Speciesism*, Oxford: Basil Blackwell; rev. edn, Oxford: Berg, 2000.

—— (1998) *The Political Animal: The Conquest of Speciesism*, Jefferson, N.C.: McFarland.

—— (2001) *Painism: A Modern Morality*, London: Opengate Press.

Schwei, Matthew J., Honore, Prisca, Rogers, Scott D., Salak-Johnson, Janeen L., Finke, Matthew P., Ramnaraine, Margaret L., Clohisy, Denis R., and Mantyh, Patrick W. (1999) "Neurochemical and Cellular Reorganization of the Spinal Cord in a Murine Model of Bone Cancer Pain," *The Journal of Neuroscience*, December 13, 10886–97.

Singer, Peter (1975) *Animal Liberation*, New York: Jonathan Cape.

7

Brave New Farm?

Jim Mason and Mary Finelli

In our mind's eye the farm is a peaceful place where calves nuzzle their mothers in a shady meadow, pigs loaf in the mudhole, and chickens scratch about the barnyard. These comforting images are implanted in us by calendars, coloring books, theme parks, petting zoos, and the countrified labeling and advertising of animal products.

The reality of modern farmed animal production, however, is starkly different from these scenes. Now, virtually all poultry products and most milk and meat in the U.S. come from animals mass-produced in huge factory-like systems. In some of the more intensive confinement operations, animals are crowded in pens and in cages stacked up like so many shipping crates. In these animal factories there are no pastures, no streams, no seasons, not even day and night. Growth and productivity come not from frolics in sunny meadows but from test-tube genetics and drug-laced feed.

Animal factories allow producers to maintain a larger number of animals in a given space, but they have created serious problems for consumers, farmers, and the environment, and they raise disturbing questions about the degree of animal exploitation that our society permits.

The animal factory is a classic case of technology run horribly amuck: it requires high inputs of capital and energy to carry out a simple, natural process; it creates a costly chain of problems and risks; and it does not, in fact, produce the results claimed by its proponents. Moreover, the animal factory pulls our society one long, dark step backward from the desirable goal of a sane, ethical relationship with the natural world and our fellow inhabitants.

Factories Come . . . Farms Go

Right under our noses agribusiness has wrought a sweeping revolution in the ways in which animals are kept to produce meat, milk, and eggs. It began in the years before World War II, when farmers near large cities began to specialize in the production of chickens to meet the constant demand for eggs and meat. By supplementing the birds' diet with vitamin D, they made it possible for them to be raised indoors without sunlight. The first mass-producers were able to turn out large flocks all the year round. Large-scale indoor production caught on fast around the urban market centers, but the new methods created a host of problems. Nightmarish scenes began to occur in the crowded, poorly ventilated sheds. Birds pecked others to death and ate their remains. Contagious diseases were rampant, and losses multiplied throughout the budding industry.

The boom in the chicken business attracted the attention of the largest feed and pharmaceutical companies, which put their scientists to work on the problems of mass-production. Someone found that losses from pecking and cannibalism could be reduced by burning off the tips of chickens' beaks with a blowtorch. Soon an automatic "debeaking" machine was patented, and its use became routine. Richer feeds made for faster-gaining birds and a greater number of "crops" of chickens each year. Foremost of the developments, however, was the discovery that sulfa drugs and antibiotics could be added to feed to help hold down diseases in the dirty, crowded sheds.

Chickens themselves were not entirely ready for mass-production, and the poultry industry set about looking for a better commercial bird. In 1946, the Great Atlantic and Pacific Tea Company (now A&P) launched the "Chicken of Tomorrow" contest to find a strain of chicken that could produce a broad-breasted body at low feed cost. Within a few years poultry breeders had developed the prototype for today's "broiler" – a chicken raised for meat who grows to a market weight of about five pounds in seven weeks or less. The pre-war ancestor of this bird took twice as long to grow to a market weight of about three pounds.

The egg industry went to work on engineering their own specialized chicken – the "layer" hen, who would turn out eggs and more eggs. Today's model lays twice as many eggs per year as did the "all-purpose" backyard chickens of the 1940s. Egg producers also tried to follow the "broiler" industry's factory ways, but they were faced with a major problem: confined hens produce loads of manure each week. "Broiler" producers had the manure problem with their large flocks too, but the birds were in and out within twelve weeks, and accumulations could be cleaned out after every few flocks. (Today, it can be years between complete litter changes.) Egg producers, however, kept their birds indoors for a year or more, so they needed a means of manure removal that would not disturb the hens or interfere with egg production. Unfortunately for the hens, they found it: producers discovered they could confine their chickens in wire-mesh cages suspended over a trench to collect droppings. At first they placed hens one to each cage, but when they found that birds were cheaper than wire and buildings, crowded cages became the rule. Although crowding caused the deaths of more hens, this cost was considered "acceptable" given the increased total egg output.

Having reduced chickens to the equivalent of living machinery, entrepreneurs and government scientists began looking about for ways to extend factory technology to other farmed animal species. In the 1960s they began developing systems for pigs, cattle, and sheep that incorporated the principles of confinement, mass-production, and automated feeding, watering, ventilation, and waste removal. The wire cage, which made everything possible for the egg industry, would not work for these heavier, hoofed animals. But slatted floors – rails of metal or concrete spaced slightly apart and built over gutters or holding pits – did much the same job. Now large numbers of animals could be confined indoors and held to rigid production schedules, for the laborious tasks of providing bedding and mucking out manure had been eliminated.

The basics of factory husbandry had been established. Now the job of refining mass-production systems and methods fell to husbandry experts, opening up a great new field for them. It opened up, as well, great new markets for the agribusiness companies that could profit from the expanded sales of feed, equipment, drugs, and the other products required by the new capital-intensive technology. Humanity and concern retreated further as animal scientists – funded by these companies and by government – worked out the "bugs" in the new systems.

The Factory Formula

Factory methods and equipment vary from species to species, but the principles are the same: keep costs down and manipulate animals' productivity upward. These principles ensure that animals are crowded in barren environments, restricted, stressed, and maintained on drug-laced, unnatural diets.

The modern chicken comes from the sterile laboratories of a handful of "primary breeders" worldwide. In the U.S., these companies sell animals for breeding to some 300 "multipliers" or hatcheries (down from 11,405 in 1934), which in turn produce the chicks who are used for egg and meat production. At the multipliers, birds have the run of the floor in the breeding houses, for freedom and exercise promote health and a higher percentage of fertile eggs.

If the hatchery is turning out birds for egg factories, the first order of business is to destroy half the "crop" of chicks. Males don't lay eggs, and the flesh of these specialized layer breeds is of poor quality – "not fit to feed," as one hatchery worker put it. These chicks, by the millions annually, have for decades been thrown into plastic bags to be crushed or suffocated. Large-scale hatcheries have moved toward the use of gas asphyxiation or "macerators," which grind up the live chicks at high speeds. About three-fourths of the female chicks ("pullets") are reared in cages, the other fourth raised loose in floor facilities. Shortly before they begin to lay eggs, at between eighteen and twenty weeks of age, they are moved to the egg factory.

Today, 98 percent of commercial layer hens in the U.S. are caged. At an industry average of eight birds per cage, each hen gets about 50 square inches of floor space. In 2002, under pressure from public opinion, the industry trade group United Egg Producers announced "Animal Care Certified" guidelines that will, over a six-year period, gradually increase the space allowance to a minimum of 67 inches per hen, or seven birds per cage. Studies have shown, however, that hens require 71–5 square inches of space just to stand and lie down, and about twice that much space to stretch their wings. In major egg-producing states, operations with flocks of 100,000 hens are common, some housing as many as 200,000 hens in a single building. The owner of a planned 2.4 million-hen facility explained: "We used to have one person for 10,000 chickens. Now we have one for every 150,000."

After a year in the cages, hens' egg productivity wanes and it becomes unprofitable to feed and house them. The manager may decide to use "force molting," a procedure which causes the birds to grow new feathers and accelerates and synchronizes another cycle of egg production. This is usually accomplished by reducing light and depriving the hens of food for ten to fourteen days. In a large study, mortality doubled during the first week of the molt and then doubled again during the second week. Aggression also increases among the starving birds. After a force molt or two the hens are deemed "spent" and are removed from the cages to make room for the next flock. There is a poor market for the birds in these days of mass-produced "broiler chickens," so they, too, are thrown into macerators, buried alive, or killed by having their neck broken. Now that these gruesome methods have created controversy, a few firms are beginning to experiment with other ways of killing hens, such as electrocution and gassing. Whatever the method of killing, millions go to renderers to be turned into companion-animal food and feed supplements, to incinerators, or to landfills.

With "broiler chickens," both sexes are kept and raised for meat. The chicks are dumped into a huge "shed" with some type of litter covering the floor. Not that these birds have it all that much better than their cousins in the layer cages: generations of inbreeding for rapid growth have produced crippled birds prone to heart attacks and a slew of other health problems. They spend their short lives packed together by tens of thousands on manure-soaked floors, breathing dust and ammonia. The situation is similar for turkeys, and the numbers are huge: roughly nine billion birds go through factory systems to slaughter each year in the USA alone (up from about 1.6 billion in 1960).

Specialized buildings similar to those used in the poultry industries are used to breed, wean, and fatten ("finish") pigs. About 83 percent of female pigs used for breeding ("sows") give birth in total confinement facilities, and some 82 percent of piglets are put in total confinement nurseries. While some operations keep male and female pigs to produce litters of piglets, most pigs marketed today are probably produced by artificial insemination. Roughly 70 percent of sows are artificially inseminated for at least their first two matings, according to United States Department of Agriculture (USDA) figures.

The factory sow's misery deepens in the "gestation crate," a stall so narrow that she cannot turn around or groom herself. It is the most common type of housing for female pigs used for breeding. She remains in it for her entire four-month gestation period. Her normal urges to forage, socialize, and build a nest are completely frustrated. As with cows, and birds used to breed fast-growing offspring, to prevent the sow from gaining weight and becoming unable to reproduce, her feed will be severely restricted, resulting in extreme hunger and distress. She may be fed only once every two days or so.

About a week before her piglets are due, she is moved to a narrow "farrowing crate." This device permits her to lie and stand, but she cannot walk or turn around; its purpose is to keep her in position only to eat, drink, and keep her teats exposed to the baby pigs. Soon after birth, the piglets' teeth are clipped; their tails are cut off, their ears are notched for identification, and males are castrated – all without any anesthetic. In a few weeks, the sow goes back to the breeding area, and the piglets are moved to pens in the "finishing" buildings, where they spend about sixteen weeks until they reach a slaughter weight of about 250 pounds.

Most of the milk produced in the U.S. comes from cows in intensive confinement, most commonly kept tethered to a stall. Increasingly popular in the West and Southwest are drylots: dirt or concrete lots devoid of vegetation and often without shade. They are only thoroughly cleaned once or twice a year, allowing manure to build up from the thousands of cows they hold. Partial tail amputation ("docking"), purportedly for cleanliness but actually for worker convenience, has become a popular practice.

From 1950 to 2000, owing to genetics and other factors, the number of cows used for milk production in the U.S. decreased by 67 percent while the amount of milk produced tripled. By 2002, over 20 percent of the 9 million cows were being injected with synthetic bovine growth hormone to increase milk production. (The drug is banned in other countries due to animal health concerns.) The dramatic increase in milk production has been accompanied by deterioration in most measures of cow health. High-producing cows are particularly prone to metabolic disorders, lameness, mastitis (inflammation of the udder, a disease that costs the dairy industry $1.7 billion annually), and infertility. Crowding also leads to a higher incidence of "production diseases." Although cows do not reach full maturity until four years of age, they are typically sent to slaughter by about five years. Even at that early age many are already debilitated, the problem of non-ambulatory ("downer") animals being most common with the dairy industry.

Veal production has been considered by many to be the cruelest of all the confinement systems. In the U.S., every year about 750,000 calves – mostly males, who are of little use to the dairy industry – are taken from their mothers within a day of birth and turned into sickly, neurotic animals to provide the luxury-grade "milk-fed" veal preferred by gourmet cooks and fancy restaurants. The young calves, stressed by separation from their mothers, are placed in narrow wooden stalls, lined up row on row in the confinement building. For between eighteen and twenty weeks, each calf is confined to a space scarcely larger than his own body, and is tied at the neck to restrict movement further. He is fed only "milk replacer," a liquid mixture of dried milk products, starch, fats, sugar, antibiotics, and other additives. The milk replacer is deficient in iron to induce subclinical anemia

– a necessary condition if the producer's calves are to have flesh white enough to fetch the market price for "prime" veal. No hay or other roughage is permitted, for that too might darken the flesh. Even the wooden stalls and neck chains are part of the plan, as these restrictions keep the calf from licking his own urine and feces to satisfy his craving for iron.

In "beef cattle" feedlots, stress from crowding, exposure, and an unnatural diet adversely affect the animals' health. Liver abscesses are common in these animals because their digestive tracts are geared more to roughage than to the steady diet of high-energy grain and growth promotants that they receive. Cattle may be dehorned and branded, and males are castrated, all without anesthesia.

Ducks are raised both for meat and to produce foie gras ("fatty liver"), which involves a most brutal practice. Total confinement housing is the most common method of raising ducks, with thousands of birds kept in a single, dark building. Being aquatic animals, they need to submerse their head in water in order to keep their eyes healthy. But the only water they are provided with is for drinking, from nipple-like devices. The tip of their sensitive bill is burned off with a hot knife, often resulting in chronic pain and debilitation. At about four months of age, ducks used for foie gras are put in small pens or are kept virtually immobilized in individual cages. For two to three weeks, up to two pounds of a corn/fat mixture are forced down their throat through a 12- to 16-inch pipe attached to a motorized pump. The massive quantities of food cause the bird's liver to swell to up to ten times its normal size, a clinical disease state called "hepatic steatosis." Many of the birds also suffer blindness, lameness, throat injuries, and ruptured livers.

Aquatic animals account for 16 percent of the animal protein consumed worldwide. Official figures on the number of aquatic animals killed for food in the U.S. are not kept but estimates exceed 15 billion annually. This is far more than all the other farmed animal species combined. Aquaculture, the factory farming of aquatic species, supplies 30 percent of all seafood consumed globally, up from 10 percent two decades ago. It's a $56 billion global enterprise that is rapidly being consolidated by a few big companies. About a third of the seafood consumed in the U.S., including nearly all of the catfish and trout and about two-thirds of the salmon and shrimp, is from captive-raised animals. With wild fish populations having been drastically reduced, in order to just maintain world fish consumption levels it is predicted that aquaculture will have to grow seven-fold in the next twenty-five years.

Aquaculture is being promoted as the "Blue Revolution," an aquatic version of the Green Revolution which vastly multiplied agricultural output in non-industrialized countries. Critics warn of environmental havoc, as was seen with the Green Revolution. Algicides, pesticides, antibiotics, and other drugs are heavily used in aquaculture, and federal inspection of fish farms is lacking. Coastal waters are degraded by the discharge of aqua-farm chemicals and wastes, with shrimp farming said to be particularly destructive. Environmentally superior techniques are expensive and difficult to employ on a large-scale basis. Feed conversion is also inefficient. For example, between two and five pounds of other fish are needed as feed to produce one pound of farmed salmon.

Increasingly, fish are being raised in cages floating in the ocean. Sea lice proliferate in these crowded confines, boring holes in the skin of fish and feasting on their flesh. Schools of fish inevitably escape through torn nets, flooding, or accidental release during transport. Once free, they spread disease and compete with wild native fish. Genetically engineered fish, made to grow at much faster rates, pose an even greater potential threat.

Many farmed fish species spend most of their lives in steel buildings, crowded into shallow, cement troughs. According to the 2002 Compassion in World Farming report "In Too Deep," twenty-seven one-foot-long trout share the equivalent of a bathtub of water. At high densities, fish exhibit abnormal behaviors, such as increased aggression; suffer widespread injuries, deformities, and disease; and have high parasitic infestations. Scientific research has shown that fish are capable of experiencing pain and distress. Veterinary medicine for fish is very limited, and pre-slaughter mortality rates are high.

Fish are commonly starved for seven days or more prior to slaughter. To increase shelf life, many are left to suffocate on bins of ice. Others are rendered immobile rather than insensible at slaughter, resulting in their being processed while still alive and fully capable of immense suffering. Stunning methods include clubbing and gassing. Slaughter methods include bleeding and electrocution. Less inhumane methods are being researched.

Factory Problems, Factory Solutions

The industrialization of animal production has provided farmers with tighter controls over their herds and flocks and it has eliminated much of the labor of feeding, waste removal, and other chores, but it has also created a whole new set of problems for producers. These problems have in turn created whole new industries of research and experts who churn out increasingly elaborate management schemes and expensive inputs needed to keep the factory system producing. Continual manipulations of animals' heredity, anatomy, physiology, and environment are required to hold down health problems and maintain mass commodity production at a profitable level. Chief among these factory-caused health problems is stress.

In confinement, animals are subjected to a variety of stressors. In addition to acute stresses such as early weaning, debeaking, dehorning, tail docking, and castration, other causes of stress in the factory farm are constant. The animals have no relief from crowding and monotony. In a less restrictive environment they would relieve boredom by moving; confined animals cannot. Nor have they relief from social disturbances caused by factory conditions. When animals are crowded and agitated, they are more likely to fight. In the restricted space of confinement pens, less aggressive animals cannot get away to make the instinctive show of submission. With caged birds, for example, each cage contains a small "flock," with one member at the bottom of the social ladder. This unfortunate bird cannot escape her tormentors. When growing pigs are moved to larger pens and mixed with unfamiliar pigs, fighting can occur, leaving pigs injured or dead.

In pigs, stress-induced aggression or "cannibalism" takes the form of tail biting, best described by a swine expert for Hog Farm Management back in 1976, when such practices had not yet raised controversy and farming publications were more plainspoken than they are today: "Acute tail biting is often called cannibalism and frequently results in crippling, mutilation and death. . . . Many times the tail is bitten first and then the attacking pig or pigs continue to eat further into the back. If the situation is not attended to, the pig will die and be eaten."

In dealing with these stress-related problems, animal-factory managers manipulate both animal and environment rather than eliminate the primary underlying cause – crowded, inappropriate conditions. Prevented from forming stable social structures, birds may engage in abnormal and potentially injurious pecking behavior. (Genetics and other faulty management factors can also precipitate this.) To control it, birds are debeaked, an operation that removes the front third to one-half of the bird's beak. Chickens used by the egg industry and those used for breeding purposes are debeaked anywhere from one day to eighteen weeks of age. The procedure is sometimes later repeated. Turkeys and ducks are also debeaked, but today's "broilers" are not because they are too young and listless to become aggressive. According to United Egg Producers, welfare impairments "may include the bird's ability to feed itself following beak trimming, short-term pain, perhaps chronic pain, and acute stress." Poultry ethologist Dr Ian Duncan explains that the tip of the beak is richly innervated and contains pain receptors. Therefore, cutting and heating the beak will lead to acute pain. Additionally, the behavior of debeaked birds is radically altered for many weeks, which, along with neurophysiological evidence, indicates the birds experience chronic pain. Dr Duncan states: "Chopping off parts of young animals in order to prevent future welfare problems is a very crude solution." (Incidentally, the poultry industry coined the term "debeaking" and used it for generations until the controversies over factory methods surfaced; since then it has preferred the term "beak trimming.")

At the same time they are debeaked, turkeys and some chickens have part of their toes amputated, often by the same hot-knife machine. This is done to prevent them from using their claws to cause injuries. The combs and wattles of males used for breeding are also cut off to prevent them from being injured, since injuries reduce production. All of these procedures are performed without anesthesia.

Problematic genetics and production demands take their toll on stressed animals in other ways. Pigs bred for leanness and rapid growth are prone to a condition that we would probably call "shock" if it occurred in humans; the pig industry calls it "porcine stress syndrome," or simply "PSS." Pigs may literally drop dead from stress when they are weaned, moved to a new pen, mixed with strange pigs, or shipped to market. Cattle bred similarly for meat production are also highly excitable, making them hard to manage and prone to injury. A condition affecting about a third of flocks in the U.S. egg industry is termed "caged layer fatigue." The exhausted birds have brittle or broken bones and a pale, washed-out appearance in their eyes, combs, beaks, and feet. The relentless calcium demand for eggshell production causes the mineral to be withdrawn from hens' bones and muscles. Afflicted birds are left unable to stand and may die if unable to reach food or water. It occurs only in caged birds, due to their lack of exercise, and is exacerbated by crowding. In "broiler" operations, "Acute Death Syndrome," also known as "Flip-Over Syndrome," occurs in fast-growing birds. They have been observed suddenly jumping into the air, giving a loud squawk, and falling over dead. Metabolic diseases associated with fast growth have become more of a problem than infectious diseases for the poultry meat industry. One chicken farmer wrote, "Aside from the stupendous rate of growth . . . the sign of a good meat flock is the number of birds dying from heart attacks."

To speed up reproductive cycles, babies are prematurely separated from their mothers. In nature, a calf might nurse and run with his or her mother for about a year; on a dairy farm they're lucky to spend more than a day together. Sows and their piglets are left together an average of about nineteen days (down from fifty-six days). In addition to the manipulation of sex and reproduction, managers control lighting to increase production. Egg producers try to create the illusion of perpetual spring by keeping the lights on a little longer each day.

Biotech Barnyard

Not satisfied with the innovations described above, some scientists are now looking at the prospect of cloning and genetic engineering to further optimize production. These reproduction technologies raise grave concerns.

Cloning can be carried out with embryo cells or with somatic (i.e. body) cells. In the technically simplest form, egg and sperm from prized animals are "harvested" and combined in a laboratory to form an embryo. Once the cell has multiplied to a certain stage it is divided and each section is implanted as a separate embryo into a lesser valued surrogate mother for gestation. This enables more highly valued animals to be produced than could be through normal reproduction. This type of cloning, called "embryo splitting" or "embryo twinning," has been commercially employed for a decade or two but on an extremely limited basis due to its expense and the unpredictability of results. In the more highly publicized form of cloning, somatic cell nuclear transfer (SCNT), a nearly exact genetic copy of a parent animal is produced by putting the nucleus of a differentiated cell from the parent into a denucleated egg cell from a surrogate mother, who then gestates the embryo. In theory, farmed animals with particularly desirable characteristics can be mass-produced this way. In practice, however, hundreds of attempts are needed to produce a single healthy animal. In the U.S., the Food and Drug Administration has asked that animals produced this way, and products from them, not be allowed in the human or animal food supply on account of food safety and animal welfare concerns.

Genetic engineering has been used to insert genes from another life form – usually another species and not necessarily an animal – into animals in order to produce specific benefits for humans. It is hoped that these "transgenic" animals will have an increased quantity and quality of food and fiber production, or will produce pharmaceutical proteins in their milk, eggs, or urine: animal "pharming." Additional research is underway to produce transgenic pigs with organs that will be able to be transplanted into humans without being rejected.

Repeatedly subjecting individual animals to invasive procedures in order to obtain eggs for cloning is likely to cause them pain and distress. "Large Offspring Syndrome" occurs with cloned cattle and sheep, putting the animals used as surrogate mothers at increased risk for difficult pregnancies and caesarean sections. Attempts to clone animals through SCNT often produce deformed animals who suffer and die at an early age. Genetically engineered animals may also suffer from bizarre maladies. Additionally, opponents argue that these technologies will only benefit large corporations while further exacerbating the loss of small farms, and that poor countries won't be able to afford them.

Human Health Concerns

"In current agricultural practice, raising animals for food depends heavily on the use of pharmacologically active compounds: drugs," states a 1999 National Academy of Science report. ("Broiler chicken" feed, for example, almost always contains an antibiotic, a coccidiostat for internal parasites and improved feed efficiency, and arsenic to color the birds' skin yellow and increase growth.) This is no wonder because factory animals are genetically more susceptible to infectious diseases, and the stresses of factory life further debilitate their immune defenses. Animal factories breed germs – leaner, meaner germs and more kinds of them – that easily spread throughout the crowded, dirty buildings. Stressed from discomfort and frustration, and breathing dusty, noxious air, factory animals are highly vulnerable to infection. If not suppressed with drugs and chemistry, flocks and herds would be even more disposed to disease epidemics.

Antibiotics have been the main tool for growth promotion and disease control since the 1950s. Nearly all U.S. factory animals – poultry, pigs, cattle in feedlots, and calves raised for veal – routinely get antibiotic-laced feed. In 2001, the Union of Concerned Scientists (UCS) "conservatively" estimated that 24.6 million pounds of antibiotics was administered to U.S. cattle, pigs, and poultry for non-therapeutic purposes. According to UCS, this was equivalent to 70 percent of the country's total anti-microbial use, and eight times the amount used in human medicine.

Individual bacteria that are able to withstand the effects of antibiotics can multiply, creating resistant bacteria. As bacteria evolve very rapidly, many species have developed resistance to our "wonder drugs." For example, the types of bacteria that cause diarrhea, septicemia, salmonella, gonorrhea, pneumonia, tuberculosis, typhoid, and childhood meningitis have long developed drug-resistant strains. Harmless bacteria that develop resistance can transfer resistant genes to infectious bacteria. So, if you are infected by one of these strains, a course of antibiotics will not help as it might have a decade or so ago. Because of this, the World Health Organization (WHO) and the American Medical Association recommend that antibiotics not be used to promote animal growth. The European Union is set to ban the practice in 2006. It has already been banned in Denmark and Sweden.

The factory system has also created an alarming new kind of pollution. Reportedly, up to 75 percent of an antibiotic may pass undigested through an animal's body. The trillions of pounds of manure produced in the U.S. every year (1.4 billion tons in 1997) contain antibiotics and astronomical amounts of bacteria, including antibiotic-resistant bacteria. Much of the manure is used as fertilizer, from which resistant bacteria can leach into the soil and groundwater, altering microbial ecosystems in the environment.

Top "broiler" companies recently announced that they are phasing out the use of certain antibiotics that are similar to ones used in human medicine, and leading fast-food chains say they are no longer purchasing chickens treated with certain antibiotics. The National Chicken Council claims overall antibiotic usage in animals of all kinds has been in decline since 1999. However, industry data don't provide specifics about antibiotic use and the government doesn't collect such data. If there has in fact been a decline, at least part of the reason for the industry change may be because antibiotics have lost much of their growth-promoting effectiveness.

Over the past three decades, many studies have pointed to the dangers posed by rampant chemical and pharmaceutical use and abuse in animal factories. There are many instances of widespread sales and abuse of illegal drugs, and there are many instances of abuses of legal drugs. For example, in late March 2004, U.S. federal regulators discovered that growth hormones were being used in up to 90 percent of calves raised for veal production, an illegal practice the industry admitted to having engaged in for decades. USDA testing for drugs in animal tissues has been much criticized. A string of reports, including ones by the Government Accountability Office, have concluded that the government's inspection and testing programs are inadequate to protect the public from either drug residues or bacterial contamination.

Aside from drug-resistant diseases, people (and other animals) can come down with "ordinary" food poisoning caused by the animal factory's prolific production of germs. Some of these cases are not so ordinary, with factory farms and the debilitated animals in them providing the ideal environment in which pathogenic bacteria and viruses can become more virulent. The Centers for Disease Control and Prevention (CDC) estimates that food-borne diseases cause approximately 76 million illnesses, 325,000 hospitalizations, and 5,000 deaths in the U.S. each year. Other public health authorities put the food-poisoning estimates at 250 million illnesses and 9,000 deaths each year. In an analysis of food-borne illnesses occurring between 1990 and 2003, the Center for Science in the Public Interest found seafood, poultry, beef, and eggs to be among the top five vehicles for which a single food was identified as responsible. Collectively, they were responsible for 88 percent of the outbreaks and 79 percent of the cases. Two of the most common pathogens, salmonella and *E. coli*, are most frequently linked to animal waste that can contaminate produce via the billions of pounds of manure spread on cropland as fertilizer. In addition to acute illness, animal products pose long-term risks to human health due to their cholesterol and fat content, and their lack of fiber and complex carbohydrates. This combination is implicated in heart disease, cancers, obesity, kidney disease, diabetes, hypertension, and other chronic illnesses.

The recklessness of the factory system manifested for industry, governments, and consumers when "mad cow disease" (bovine spongiform encephalopathy [BSE]) was identified in 1986. The disease, caused by feeding cattle the rendered remains of sheep, also infected human beef consumers. Since then, there have been some 190,000 reported cases of BSE in twenty-five countries, with several million cattle killed in an attempt to eradicate the disease. There have been 153 cases of the human form of the disease, new variant Creutzfeldt–Jakob Disease, which is always fatal. It has now been found that the disease can spread through the blood supply. Some scientists warn that the human cases may just be the beginning of a "timebomb."

Avian influenza (AI) is another disease that has crossed the species barrier. Wild aquatic birds are the natural hosts of AI. The viruses ordinarily do not cause disease in them, but in a new host, such as chickens, they dangerously mutate. According to Dr Robert Webster, director of the World Health Organization Collaborating Center for Studies on the Ecology of Influenza in Animals and Birds, humans have created optimal conditions to generate flu epidemics. A single factory farm provides hundreds of billions of replication cycles with an exponentially greater risk of a pathogenic strain arising. In early 2004, virulent AI raced through Asia, infecting thirty-four people, twenty-three of them fatally. An estimated 200,000,000 birds were killed in an attempt to control the disease. If avian virus merges with a human virus, it could more easily transmit between people and rapidly spread. Some scientists fear avian influenza may become the human plague of the twenty-first century.

Farmers (and the Rest of Us) Are Victims Too

Ironically, the trend toward complex, expensive husbandry systems hurts farmers and rural communities. Those huge buildings full of specialized floors and feeding equipment don't come cheap. Financial burdens are so great that factory farmers must continuously keep their buildings at capacity, working longer and harder than ever just to meet their loan payments. The tendency to operate at capacity in order to cover capital costs creates chronic overproduction in the poultry, pork, and dairy industries and drives down market prices. In this situation, many smaller and non-factory farmers cannot make a living so they quit raising animals altogether. Moreover, the high capital investment required tends to attract agribusiness companies, urban investors, and other non-farm interests with deep pockets. Thus, more and more production has fallen into the hands of the largest, most intensive operations. Government subsidies have also helped accelerate this trend.

The poultry industry, the originator of factory systems, offers a clear example of how the trend toward capital intensification affects farmers. Chickens and eggs, along with pigs, used to be the mainstay of the small, independent family farm before the poultry scientists and agribusiness companies got involved. In 1950, independent operators raised 95 percent of the chickens produced for meat. Today, nearly all chickens raised for meat are produced and processed under contracts between "growers" and processors. Prior to 1950, nearly all egg production was conducted by independent operators. Today, nearly 40 percent of eggs are produced under contract, with the remainder produced through vertical integration (whereby various stages of production and processing are controlled by a single company). The farm family has been reduced to the status of "poultry peons" who turn out company birds on company feed according to company schedules and specifications. Similarly, in 1970 nearly all pigs were sold on the open market. By 2001, only about 25 percent were, the rest having been produced under contract.

There are many, many costs in the new factory methods and systems for raising animals, although agribusiness experts would have us hear only their talk of benefits. They are fond of using cost/benefit analyses to justify crowding animals, the use of antibiotics in feed, and converting farming communities to factory towns. They assert that the benefits to consumers from these practices outweigh the risks involved. But if this sort of test is to have any validity in agricultural affairs it must take into account all the costs of factory methods, which harm:

- farmed animals, who are restricted, mutilated, manipulated, and ultimately killed;
- the health of consumers, who are put at much greater risk for both acute and chronic disease;
- the land, much of which is used to grow animal feed or is degraded by overgrazing;
- wildlife, whose habitat is destroyed and who are killed by agricultural predator control programs;
- the environment, polluted by pesticides and toxic animal wastes;
- our limited supply of fossil fuels, their procurement causing environmental destruction and escalating international strife;
- the atmosphere, polluted by fossil fuel use and methane gas, generated by the immense numbers of ruminant farmed animals, adding to global warming;
- prospects for alleviating world hunger, by the depletion of fresh water and other natural resources;
- farm families and rural communities, whose livelihood is stolen by high-tech factory systems;
- citizens, who pay for subsidies that prop up costly systems, and farmers – and ultimately all residents – in other countries who are unable to compete with the "cheap" imports;
- human dignity and self-respect, as a result of carrying on all of the above and on such a massive scale.

Quite possibly the greatest threat factory farming poses now is its expansion in "developing" countries. Worldwatch Institute's *State of the World 2004* explains:

Global meat production has increased more than fivefold since 1950, and factory farming is the fastest growing method of animal production world-wide. Industrial systems are responsible for 74 percent of the world's total poultry [meat], 50 percent of pork production, 43 percent of the beef, and 68 percent of the eggs. Industrial countries dominate production, but developing nations are rapidly expanding and intensifying their production systems. According to the U.N. Food and Agriculture Organization (FAO), Asia has the fastest-developing livestock sector, followed by Latin America and the Caribbean.

Laws and Standards

Farmed animals in the U.S. have little to no legal protection. Hundreds of millions of them die every year prior to the time they would be slaughtered, yet there is no federal law that regulates the treatment of farmed animals on farms. (Farmed animals are essentially exempted from the protections of the Animal Welfare Act.) The Twenty-Eight Hour Law prohibits the transport of animals across state lines for more than twenty-eight hours without being unloaded for at least five hours of rest with access to food and water. However, the law does not apply to trucks, by far the most common means of transporting farmed animals. Furthermore, the law is rarely enforced and the maximum penalty is only $500. The Humane Methods of Slaughter Act requires that slaughter "be carried out only by humane methods" to prevent "needless suffering." Yet birds and fish, who constitute about 98 percent of slaughtered animals, are not covered by the Act. In a 1996 slaughterplant audit commissioned by the USDA, 64 percent of the cattle plants and 36 percent of the pig and sheep plants were rated "not acceptable" or a "serious problem" in regard to stunning procedures. Enforcement of the law was found to be so lacking that, in 2002, Congress passed a resolution entitled Enforcement of the Humane Slaughter Act of 1958. In February 2004, the government's General Accounting Office reported that the Act was still not being adequately enforced.

In the absence of federal law, state law does little better. The majority of U.S. states exempt customary farming practices from their anti-cruelty statutes, and it is industry that determines what is customary. In other words, industry determines what is an acceptable way to treat farmed animals. Convictions are extremely difficult and infrequent, and fines are relatively minimal. Forty-one states currently have animal anti-cruelty statutes with felony penalties, but only in seven states do they effectively apply to farmed animals. In Florida in 2002, a law banning gestation crates for pregnant pigs was passed by a 55 percent majority vote. It is said to be the first U.S. measure banning a particular farming practice on the grounds of cruelty. However, ballot initiatives are difficult and expensive, and twenty-six states do not allow them.

Industry – including farmed-animal trade groups, supermarkets, and fast-food restaurant chains – has recently responded to public pressure by formulating minimal, voluntary standards, some with third-party inspections. But there are grounds for skepticism about the efficacy of industry codes and standards. In the U.S., the United Egg Producers authorized the use of an "Animal Care Certified" logo to mark cartons of eggs from operations enrolled in their welfare standards program. In 2004, the Better Business Bureau deemed this logo misleading because the program did not ensure that animals were cared for. In the same year, an undercover investigation by People for the Ethical Treatment of Animals (PETA) at a slaughterplant operated by Pilgrim's Pride, the second largest chicken company in the U.S., revealed sadistic abuse of birds, involving laborers, supervisors, foremen, and managers. In responding, the President and CEO assured the public that "Pilgrim's Pride strictly adheres to the animal welfare program recommended by the National Chicken Council (NCC)."

The national organic standards, implemented by the USDA in 2001 after a decade of formulation, require outdoor access for farmed animals, with notable exceptions. However, the standards are vague about the type of space, and do not specify the amount of space or the length of time animals must have access to it.

Animal advocacy organizations have also formulated farmed-animal welfare standards. They include the Animal Welfare Institute, American Humane ("Free Farmed"), and Humane Farm Animal Care ("Certified Humane"), the latter two of which are predicated on the Freedom Food program of the UK's Royal Society for the Protection of Animals (RSPCA). Additionally, Whole Foods Market, the world's largest retailer of natural and organic foods, is in the process of devising standards (see Karen Dawn's interview with John Mackey and Lauren Ornelas later in this volume). Promoted as "humane," such standards lead to conditions that are at best less inhumane than conventional production practices. For example, Certi-fied Humane – which is endorsed by the American Society for the Pro-tection of Animals (ASPCA), Animal People, the Humane Society of the U.S., and ten other humane societies and SPCAs – does not require out-door access for animals. It also, among other objectionable points, permits castration, tail docking, dehorning, and debeaking, all without anesthesia, albeit with limitations.

Farmed-animal abuse didn't begin with factory farming nor is it unique to it. Welfare standards for alternative production are usually vague if not altogether lacking, and auditing programs are being questioned. While alternative, "humane" animal agriculture is growing in popularity and may be preferable to factory farming, virtually all animal agriculture involves a substantial degree of animal suffering and death. As long as eating meat is considered acceptable, farmed animals will not rise above the status of consumables. Eating eggs and dairy products may actually be worse than eating meat, since the hens and cows used to produce them are among the animals who suffer the longest and the worst, after which they, too, are killed. We need to question the very concept of marketing sentient beings. Welfare reforms can lessen their suffering but will not make it right.

8

Outlawed in Europe

Clare Druce and Philip Lymbery

Animal welfare has been undergoing a revolution in Europe. Across the continent, people have awakened to the fact that animals are sentient beings, capable of feeling pain and suffering. The second half of the twentieth century saw the rapid rise of factory farming systems in the USA and Europe. Hundreds of millions of farm animals were put in cages or crates and crammed into windowless sheds. Three classic factory farm methods epitomized this approach: veal crates for calves, stall and tether-cages for pregnant pigs, and battery cages for laying hens.

All three of these classic systems of the 1960s were targeted by the European animal movement from the 1970s to the 1990s. As a result of this protracted, many-faceted campaign, the European Union (EU) agreed to outlaw veal crates for calves, battery cages for hens, and the prolonged use of sow stalls and tethers for pigs – three monumental victories for animal welfare. During this period, the EU also agreed on a legally binding protocol that recognizes animals as sentient beings rather than just "agricultural products." Now the ten new member nations that joined the EU in 2004 will also be bound by these decisions, thus bringing hundreds of millions more animals within their scope.

The fact that animal welfare is now seen in Europe as an important public and political issue gives real cause for optimism. The campaign in Europe has reached "critical mass," something that has so far eluded the farm animal welfare reform movement in the USA. Yet the ripples from

This essay draws on material first published in Clare Druce and Philip Lymbery, *Outlawed in Europe: How America is Falling Behind Europe in Farm Animal Welfare* (2002), a report commissioned by Animal Rights International, and published by Archimedian Press, PO Box 532, Woodbury, CT, USA.

Europe's humane revolution are being felt far and wide. The factory farm industry internationally is voicing fears of a domino effect around the world.

What follows is a summary of the key farm animal welfare reforms in the European Union, together with background information on the issues as they affect animals in Europe, and examples of the legislation enacted.

Sow Stalls and Tethers

Sow stalls and tethers, known in the USA as "gestation crates," are two similar systems for keeping pregnant pigs in close confinement. In both systems, the sow is prevented from being able to exercise or even turn round for nearly four months at a time. Her entire sixteen-week pregnancy will be spent in a narrow metal-barred stall that is barely bigger than the sow herself. Sow stalls are typically about 0.6 meters, or 24 inches, wide and 2 meters, or 78 inches, long. Bedding material is not normally provided.

Alternatively, the sow may be tethered to the concrete floor by a heavy collar and chain around her neck or strapped around her middle. Metal bars will partially enclose her to prevent neighboring animals from fighting. They are kept caged or chained like this in rows, and forced to stand or lie on an uncomfortable floor of concrete and slats.

Evidence of Suffering in Sow Stalls and Tethers

In response to public concern about the welfare of sows in stalls and tethers in several member nations of the European Union, the European Commission, which makes recommendations on these matters to the EU Council of Agriculture Ministers, asked its expert Scientific Veterinary Committee (SVC) to investigate the issue. The official report from the SVC (1997) found that sow stalls have "major disadvantages" for welfare.

As the SVC noted, sows kept in stall and tether systems often suffer a range of health problems. Compared with those kept in humane alternative systems that allow freedom of movement, confined sows are more likely to suffer foot injuries, lameness, and long-term pain from infected cuts and abrasions. Lack of exercise leads to weakened bones and muscles. Their inability to move freely also causes greater levels of urinary infections. They may suffer heart problems, which can be evident by higher mortalities due to stress when being transported for slaughter.

Foraging and exploring are important behaviors for a sow. Studies of pigs kept in semi-natural conditions show that they are social and inquisitive animals, with a level of intelligence equivalent to the average dog. Experts estimate that pigs will naturally spend 75 percent of their time rooting in the soil, foraging and exploring. Sow stalls render these behaviors impossible.

Confined sows carry out meaningless, repetitive motions, known as stereotypies. Experts regard these abnormal behaviors as outward signs of stress and suffering. They are the only behavioral means available for the highly frustrated sow to attempt to "cope" with her confinement. Stereotypic behaviors include bar-biting, sham-chewing (chewing the air), shaking the head from side to side, repeated nosing in the empty feed trough, and attempting to root at the concrete floor.

Newly confined sows do not show stereotypic behaviors immediately. The animal's initial reaction is to try to escape. After a while, the sow appears to quieten down and can become abnormally inactive and unresponsive. The SVC says that this indicates clinical depression in the sow.

Many sows are also kept hungry throughout much of their lives. Sows are normally fed restricted rations of concentrated feed. These provide for the nutritional requirements of the sow, but lack the bulk or roughage needed to satisfy her hunger. Confinement prevents the sow from searching for additional food and adds to the suffering involved in the system. The SVC reported: "The food provided for dry sows is usually much less than that which sows would choose to consume, so the animals are hungry throughout much of their lives."

The SVC's report found that "the major disadvantages for sow welfare of housing them in stalls are indicated by high levels of stereotypies, of unresolved aggression and of inactivity associated with unresponsiveness, weaker bones and muscles and the clinical conditions mentioned above." The report stated, "In general, sows prefer not to be confined in a small space" and they "find the confinement aversive." Overall, the SVC concluded, "Since overall welfare appears to be better when sows are not confined throughout gestation [pregnancy], sows should preferably be kept in groups."

Not surprisingly, the European Commission acknowledged that sow stalls "are causing serious welfare problems to the animals" (EU Commission 2001). Its accompanying communication to new legislative proposals also pointed to SVC conclusions that serious problems exist "even in the best stall-housing system," and stated that "No individual pen should be used which does not allow the sow to turn around easily."

The Legal Situation

European Union law will prohibit the use of sow tethers by 2006. A recent review of EU pig welfare law included an agreed ban on individual sow stalls for pregnant pigs from 1 January 2013, as well as a requirement for permanent access to manipulable materials like straw. The revised directive does, however, allow sows to be kept in stalls for the first four weeks after mating. Although imperfect, this reform represents a major step forward as sows would normally spend sixteen weeks in stalls, unable even to turn around.

A number of EU countries have taken unilateral action over sow stalls. This system is already banned in the UK and Sweden. All the UK's 600,000 breeding sows are now kept in more humane alternative systems. Most are kept in group-housing indoors, whilst about a quarter are kept outdoors. Laws have also been passed to prohibit stalls in the Netherlands, Denmark, and Finland.

Veal Crates for Calves

There can be few more poignant images of factory farming than that of a young calf incarcerated in a wooden veal crate, another system where the animal cannot exercise or even turn round. The suffering of tiny calves in their "premature coffins" rocked the UK in a major campaign in the 1980s. Peter Roberts, the founder of leading anti-factory farming group Compassion In World Farming, took a test case against the veal crate-farming monks of Storrington Priory. The case achieved massive publicity. It also sparked perhaps the biggest consumer boycott ever known in Britain. Veal literally became a dirty word. Consumers avoided the product *en masse*. Veal farms were forced to switch to more humane methods or go out of business. The campaign was finally won when the UK government declared that the veal crate would be banned from 1990.

But that was not the end of the extraordinary public reaction to the crate. Popular protest again erupted in 1994/5 against the export of live calves to veal crates on the European continent. The campaign spread to neighboring countries and achieved worldwide media coverage. It resulted in the European Union agreeing to ban the veal crate. This was a victory without precedent. Never before had the EU legislated to ban a farming system on welfare grounds. From 2007, calves will no longer legally be kept in narrow crates.

The System

Veal crates are narrow, solid-sided wooden boxes for rearing surplus dairy calves for slaughter. The crates are so narrow that within a short time the calves are unable to turn round. Exercise is rendered impossible. The calves may be fully enclosed by the crate itself, or they may be chained in, or yoked by having their head held frontward by parallel metal-bars that suppress freedom of movement even further.

Floors usually consist of uncomfortable wooden slats that are devoid of bedding. Rows of crates are housed in darkened sheds. The calves are fed an all-liquid diet that is deficient in iron. This deliberate deficiency helps to keep the flesh pale, and makes for "white" veal prized by some gourmets. The lack of roughage in the diet prevents the animals' rumen from developing properly. The calves often make desperate attempts to gain roughage by licking at the crate sides or at their own hair. The latter can lead to hairballs forming in the stomach, causing digestive problems. After four to six months of isolation, the calf is released from the crate for slaughter. Deprived of exercise for much of their lives, some can barely walk to their end.

Evidence of Suffering in Veal Crates

In 1995, the European Commission's Scientific Veterinary Committee published a major Report on the Welfare of Calves. Having reviewed the wide range of evidence, the SVC made a number of important conclusions:

- Conclusion 4: "The best conditions for rearing young calves involve leaving the calf with the mother in a circumstance where the calf can suckle and can subsequently graze and interact with other calves."
- Conclusion 10: "The welfare of calves is very poor when they are kept in small individual pens with insufficient room for comfortable lying, no direct social contact and no bedding or other material to manipulate."
- Conclusion 12: Good husbandry "is needed to minimize disease in group housing conditions but results that are as good as those from individual housing can be obtained."

- Conclusion 15: "In order to provide an environment which is adequate for exercise, exploration and free social interaction, calves should be kept in groups."
- Conclusion 20: Calves given an all-liquid, iron-deficient diet "can have serious health problems, can show serious abnormalities of behaviour, and can have substantial abnormalities in gut development."

The strength of these conclusions, together with overwhelming public condemnation of the veal crate, persuaded the EU to enact the ban on this system from 2007.

The Legal Situation

EU legislation lays down minimum standards for calf rearing (Council Directive 97/2/EC). This prohibits the housing of calves in individual pens or boxes after the age of eight weeks. Up to eight weeks, any individual pen must not have solid walls. Instead, the walls must be perforated to allow calves visual and tactile contact with other calves. The legislation also stipulates that any individual calf pen shall be at least equal in width to the height of the calf at the withers (shoulders), measured in the standing position. The length of the pen shall be at least equal to the body length of the calf measured from the tip of the nose to the caudal edge of the tuber ischii (pin bone), multiplied by 1.1. This effectively ensures that the calf has at least enough room to turn round. After eight weeks old, calves must be housed in groups.

These provisions came into force for new or rebuilt farm units from January 1998, and will apply to all holdings after December 31, 2006. Additional requirements to ensure an appropriate diet with minimum levels of iron and fibrous food were laid down by the European Commission (97/182/EC).

Laying Hens in Battery Cages

Endless rows of battery cages in long sheds have come to epitomize factory farming. In the battery system, hens kept to produce eggs are crammed into a cage so small that they cannot stretch their wings, let alone walk, or peck and scratch at the ground. Under these conditions, hens are prevented from performing most of their natural behaviors, such as dust-bathing, perching, or laying their eggs in a nest. Up to 90,000 caged hens can be crammed into one windowless shed. The cages in Europe are stacked between four and nine cages high. Japan is said to have the world's highest battery cage unit, with cages stacked eighteen tiers high.

The world laying hen population is currently estimated at 4,700 million. The USA has 270 million laying hens, and is the third largest egg producer, behind China (800 million) and the EU (which had 271 million hens before it added ten new member nations in 2004). An estimated 70–80 percent of the world's laying hens are kept in cages, mostly in so-called "developed" countries.

Evidence of Suffering

In 1996, the Scientific Veterinary Committee published a report acknowledging the behavioral needs of hens, and the welfare problems caused by caging. There is clear scientific evidence that hens suffer in battery cages. Such conditions, as noted, prevent the hens performing their natural behaviours, and cause their bodies to degenerate through lack of exercise. Confined to the cage, the hen is unable to forage by scratching and pecking at the ground. Under natural conditions, a large proportion of a hen's day would be spent looking for food. Denied this simple activity, the hen's claws can grow long and twisted. They can even grow around the wire mesh of the cage floor, to be torn off when the unit is "depopulated" for slaughter. The slope of the floor (designed to allow eggs to roll away once laid) puts painful pressure on the hen's toes, causing damage to her feet.

After reviewing the evidence, the Scientific Veterinary Committee report found that:

> Hens have a strong preference for laying their eggs in a nest and are highly motivated to perform nesting behaviour.

> Hens have a strong preference for a littered floor for pecking, scratching and dust-bathing.

> Hens have a preference to perch, especially at night.

All of these behaviors are denied to caged hens. The report concluded that:

Battery cage systems provide a barren environment for the birds. . . . It is clear that because of its small size and its barrenness, the battery cage as used at present has inherent severe disadvantages for the welfare of hens.

The Legal Situation – Minimum Legal Standards for Battery Hens

On June 15, 1999 the EU Council of Agriculture Ministers agreed to ban the use of conventional battery cages from 2012. The Laying Hens Directive (Council Directive 1999/74/EC) forbade the introduction of newly built battery cages from 2003, and from that date space requirements for existing conventional battery cages were increased from 450 to 550 square centimeters per bird. (For comparison, the typical stocking density in U.S. egg units allows only about 300 square centimeters, or 48 square inches, per bird.) Under the new Directive, so-called "enriched" cages, in which hens must have at least 750 square centimeters per hen, a nest, litter, and perches, will still be allowed.

The European Commission is due to submit a report to the Council on the various systems of egg production (the due date was to have been January 1, 2005). The Commission will then bring out further proposals taking into account the conclusions of the report and the outcome of World Trade Organization negotiations.

The abolition of the battery cage throughout the EU will rectify a situation where hens are kept in such a way that they cannot fulfil the most minimal requirements of animal welfare.

Conclusion

The sweeping farm animal reforms in Europe represent the most remarkable victory yet by the animal welfare movement. A movement of ordinary citizens, with financial resources dwarfed by those of the industry they were seeking to change, has succeeded in transforming a vast industry and dramatically changing the lives of hundreds of millions of animals, allowing them to perform natural behaviors previously ruled out by their harsh confinement. In terms of the extent to which these reforms will, if all goes according to plan, reduce animal suffering, they almost certainly surpass anything else that the animal welfare movement has ever achieved, anywhere in the world. Yet these victories are still not entirely secure. When Europe goes ahead with its plans to phase out the worst forms of factory farm animal confinement, there is a danger that animal products from countries that have not prohibited these ways of treating animals will be imported into Europe, undercutting European products in price. If the European Union seeks to prohibit such imports it will almost certainly find itself the target of a case brought against it under the rules of the World Trade Organization. Although Europe will not be giving any advantage to domestic producers over foreign ones – which is all that the WTO says its trade rules are supposed to prevent – it is possible that, under the current WTO rules, such a case could succeed. It will take a determined effort by the citizens of Europe and other nations to ensure that the WTO does not undermine these important gains for farm animals.

References

EU Commission (2001) Communication from the Commission to the Council and the European Parliament on the welfare of intensively kept pigs in particular taking into account the welfare of sows reared in varying degrees of confinement and in groups. Proposal for a Council Directive amending Directive 91/630/EEC laying down minimum standards for the protection of pigs. Brussels, January 16. COM (2001) 20 final.

Scientific Veterinary Committee, Animal Welfare Section (SVC) (1995) Report on the Welfare of Calves. European Commission, Brussels.

—— (1996) Report of the Scientific Veterinary Committee, Animal Welfare Section, on the Welfare of Laying Hens. Brussels, October 30.

—— (1997) The Welfare of Intensively Kept Pigs. Brussels: Scientific Veterinary Committee.

9

Against Zoos

Dale Jamieson

Zoos and Their History

We can start with a rough-and-ready definition of zoos: they are public parks which display animals, primarily for the purposes of recreation or education. Although large collections of animals were maintained in antiquity, they were not zoos in this sense. Typically these ancient collections were not exhibited in public parks, or they were maintained for purposes other than recreation or education.

The Romans, for example, kept animals in order to have living fodder for the games. Their enthusiasm for the games was so great that even the first tigers brought to Rome, gifts to Caesar Augustus from an Indian ruler, ended up in the arena. The emperor Trajan staged 123 consecutive days of games in order to celebrate his conquest of Dacia. Eleven thousand animals were slaughtered, including lions, tigers, elephants, rhinoceroses, hippopotami, giraffes, bulls, stags, crocodiles, and serpents. The games were popular in all parts of the empire. Nearly every city had an arena and a collection of animals to stock it. In fifth-century France there were twenty-six such arenas, and they continued to thrive until at least the eighth century.

In antiquity rulers also kept large collections of animals as a sign of their power, which they would demonstrate on occasion by destroying their entire collections. This happened as late as 1719 when Elector Augustus II of Dresden personally slaughtered his entire menagerie, which included tigers, lions, bulls, bears, and boars.

The first modern zoos were founded in Vienna, Madrid, and Paris in the eighteenth century and in London and Berlin in the nineteenth. The first American zoos were established in Philadelphia and Cincinnati in the 1870s.

Today in the United States alone there are hundreds of zoos, and they are visited by millions of people every year. They range from roadside menageries run by hucksters, to elaborate zoological parks staffed by trained scientists.

The Roman games no longer exist, though bullfights and rodeos follow in their tradition. Nowadays the power of our leaders is amply demonstrated by their command of nuclear weapons. Yet we still have zoos. Why?

Animals and Liberty

Before we consider the reasons that are usually given for the survival of zoos, we should see that there is a moral presumption against keeping wild animals in captivity. What this involves, after all, is taking animals out of their native habitats, transporting them great distances, and keeping them in alien environments in which their liberty is severely restricted. It is surely true that in being taken from the wild and confined in zoos, animals are deprived of a great many goods. For the most part they are prevented from gathering their own food, developing their own social orders, and generally behaving in ways that are natural to them. These activities all require significantly more liberty than most animals are permitted in zoos. If we are justified in keeping animals in zoos, it must be because there are some important benefits that can be obtained only by doing so.

Against this it might be said that most mammals and birds added to zoo collections in recent years are captive-bred. Since these animals have never known freedom, it might be claimed that they are denied nothing by captivity. But this argument is far from compelling. A chained puppy prevented from playing or a restrained bird not allowed to fly still have interests in engaging in these activities. Imagine this argument applied to humans. It would be absurd to suggest that those who are born into slavery have no interest in freedom since they have never experienced it. Indeed, we might think that the tragedy of captivity is all the greater for those creatures who have never known liberty.

The idea that there is a presumption against keeping wild animals in captivity is not the property of some particular moral theory; it follows from most reasonable moral theories. Either we have duties to animals or we do not. If we do have duties to animals, surely they include respecting those interests which are most important to them, so long as this does not conflict with other, more stringent duties that we may have. Since an interest in liberty is central for most animals, it follows that if everything else is equal, we should respect this interest.

Suppose, on the other hand, that we do not have duties to animals. There are two further possibilities: either we have duties to people that sometimes concern animals, or what we do to animals is utterly without moral import. The latter view is quite implausible, and I shall not consider it further. People who have held the former view, that we have duties to people that concern animals, have sometimes thought that such duties arise because we can "judge the heart of a man by his treatment of animals," as Kant (1963: 240) remarked in "Duties to Animals." It is for this reason that he condemns the man who shoots a faithful dog who has become too old to serve. If we accept Kant's premise, it is surely plausible to say that someone who, for no good reason, removes wild animals from their natural habitats and denies them liberty is someone whose heart deserves to be judged harshly. If this is so, then even if we believe that we do not have duties to animals but only duties concerning them, we may still hold that there is a presumption against keeping wild animals in captivity. If this presumption is to be overcome, it must be shown that there are important benefits that can be obtained only by keeping animals in zoos.

Arguments for Zoos

What might some of these important benefits be? Four are commonly cited: amusement, education, opportunities for scientific research, and help in preserving species.

Amusement was certainly an important reason for the establishment of the early zoos, and it remains an important function of contemporary zoos as well. Most people visit zoos in order to be entertained, and any zoo that wishes to remain financially sound must cater to this desire. Even highly regarded zoos have their share of dancing bears and trained birds of prey. But although providing amusement for people is viewed by the general public as a very important function of zoos, it is hard to see how providing such amusement could possibly justify keeping wild animals in captivity.

Most curators and administrators reject the idea that the primary purpose of zoos is to provide entertainment. Indeed, many agree that the pleasure we take in viewing wild animals is not in itself a good enough reason to keep them in captivity. Some curators see baby elephant walks, for example, as a necessary evil, or defend such amusements because of their role in educating people, especially children, about animals. It is sometimes said that people must be interested in what they are seeing if they are to be educated about it, and entertainments keep people interested, thus making education possible.

This brings us to a second reason for having zoos: their role in education. This reason has been cited as long as zoos have existed. For example, in its 1898 annual report, the New York Zoological Society resolved to take "measures to inform the public of the great decrease in animal life, to stimulate sentiment in favor of better protection, and to cooperate with other scientific bodies . . . [in] efforts calculated to secure the perpetual preservation of our higher vertebrates." Despite the pious platitudes that are often uttered about the educational efforts of zoos, there is little evidence that zoos are very successful in educating people about animals. Indeed, a literature review commissioned by the American Zoo and Aquarium Association (available on their website) concludes that "[l]ittle to no systematic research has been conducted on the impact of visits to zoos and aquariums on visitor conservation knowledge, awareness, affect, or behavior." The research that is available is not encouraging. Stephen Kellert has found that zoo-goers display the same prejudices about animals as the general public. He is quoted in *The New York Times* (December 21, 1993, p. B 9) as saying that "[a] majority expressed willingness to eliminate whole classes of animals altogether, including mosquitoes, cockroaches, fleas, moths, and spiders." His studies have even indicated that people know less about animals after visiting a zoo than they did before. One reason why some zoos have not done a better job in educating people is that many of them make no real effort at education. In the case of others the problem is an apathetic and unappreciative public.

Edward G. Ludwig's (1981) study of the zoo in Buffalo, New York, revealed a surprising amount of dissatisfaction on the part of young, scientifically inclined zoo employees. Much of this dissatisfaction stemmed from the almost complete indifference of the public to the zoo's educational efforts. Ludwig's study indicated that most animals are viewed only briefly as people move quickly past cages. The typical zoo-goer stops only to watch baby animals or those who are begging, feeding, or making sounds. Ludwig reported that the most common expressions used to described animals are "cute," "funny-looking," "lazy," "dirty," "weird," and "strange." More recently, Frans de Waal has noted that after spending two or three minutes watching chimpanzees, zoo-goers often say as they walk away, "Oh, I could watch them for hours!"

Of course, it is undeniable that some education occurs in some zoos. But this very fact raises other issues. What is it that we want people to learn from visiting zoos? Facts about the physiology and behavior of various animals? Attitudes towards the survival of endangered species? Compassion for the fate of all animals? To what degree does education require keeping wild animals in captivity? Couldn't most of the educational benefits of zoos be obtained through videos, lectures, and computer simulations? Indeed, couldn't most of the important educational objectives better be achieved by exhibiting empty cages with explanations of why they are empty?

A third reason for having zoos is that they support scientific research. This, too, is a benefit that was pointed out long ago. Sir Humphrey Davy, one of the founders of the Zoological Society of London, wrote in 1825: "It would become Britain to offer another, and a very different series of exhibitions to the population of her metropolis; namely, animals brought from every part of the globe to be applied either to some useful purpose, or as objects of scientific research – not of vulgar admiration!" (cited in Scherrin 1905: 16). Zoos support scientific research in at least three ways: they fund field research by scientists not affiliated with zoos; they employ other scientists as members of zoo staffs; and they make otherwise inaccessible animals available for study.

We should note first that very few zoos support any real scientific research. Fewer still have staff scientists with full-time research appointments. Among those that do, it is common for their scientists to study animals in the wild rather than those in zoo collections. Much of this research, as well as other field research that is supported by zoos, could just as well be funded in a different way – say, by a government agency. The question of whether there should be zoos does not turn on the funding for field research which zoos currently provide. The significance of the research that is actually conducted in zoos is a more important consideration.

Research that is conducted in zoos can be divided into two broad categories: studies in behavior and studies in anatomy and pathology.

Behavioral research conducted on zoo animals is controversial. Some have argued that nothing can be learned by studying animals that are kept in the unnatural conditions that obtain in most zoos. Others have argued that captive animals are more interesting research subjects than are wild animals: since captive animals are free from predation, they exhibit a wider range of physical and behavioral traits than do animals in the wild, thus permitting researchers to view the full range of their genetic possibilities. Both of these positions are surely extreme. Conditions in some zoos are natural enough to permit some interesting research possibilities. But the claim that captive animals are more interesting research subjects than those in the wild is not very plausible. Environments trigger behaviors. No doubt a predation-free environment triggers behaviors different from those of an animal's natural habitat, but there is no reason to believe that better, fuller, or more accurate data can be obtained in predation-free environments than in natural habitats.

Studies in anatomy and pathology have three main purposes: to improve zoo conditions so that captive animals will live longer, be happier, and breed more frequently; to contribute to human health by providing animal models for human ailments; and to increase our knowledge of wild animals for its own sake.

The first of these aims is surely laudable, if we concede that there should be zoos in the first place. But the fact that zoo research contributes to improving conditions in zoos is not a reason for having them. If there were no zoos, there would be no need to improve them.

The second aim, to contribute to human health by providing animal models for human ailments, appears to justify zoos to some extent, but in practice this consideration is not as important as one might think. There are very severe constraints on the experiments that may be conducted on zoo animals. In a 1982 article, Montali and Bush drew the following conclusion:

> Despite the great potential of a zoo as a resource for models, there are many limitations and, of necessity, some restrictions for use. There is little opportunity to conduct overly manipulative or invasive research procedures – probably less than would be allowed in clinical research trials involving human beings. Many of the species are difficult to work with or are difficult to breed, so that the numbers of animals available for study are limited. In fact, it is safe to say that over the past years, humans have served more as "animal models" for zoo species than is true of the reverse.

Whether for this reason or others, many of the experiments that have been conducted using zoo animals as models for humans seem redundant or trivial. For example, the article cited above reports that zoo animals provide good models for studying lead toxicity in humans, since it is common for zoo animals to develop lead poisoning from chewing paint and inhaling polluted city air. There are available for study plenty of humans who suffer from lead poisoning for the same reasons. That zoos make available some additional nonhuman subjects for this kind of research seems at best unimportant and at worst deplorable.

Finally, there is the goal of obtaining knowledge about animals for its own sake. Knowledge is certainly something which is good and, everything being equal, we should encourage people to seek it for its own sake. But everything is not equal in this case. There is a moral presumption against keeping animals in captivity. This presumption can be overcome only by demonstrating that there are important benefits that must be obtained in this way if they are to be obtained at all. It is clear that this is not the case with knowledge for its own sake. There are other channels for our intellectual curiosity, ones that do not exact such a high moral price. Although our quest for knowledge for its own sake is important, it is not important enough to overcome the moral presumption against keeping animals in captivity.

In assessing the significance of research as a reason for having zoos, it is important to remember that very few zoos do any research at all. Whatever benefits result from zoo research could just as well be obtained by having a few zoos instead of the hundreds which now exist. The most this argument could establish is that we are justified in having a few very good zoos. It does not provide a defense of the vast majority of zoos which now exist.

A fourth reason for having zoos is that they preserve species that would otherwise become extinct. As the destruction of habitat accelerates and as breeding programs become increasingly successful, this rationale for zoos gains in popularity. There is some reason for questioning the commitment of zoos to species preservation: it can be argued that they continue to remove more animals from the wild than they return. In the minds of some skeptics, captive breeding programs are more about the preservation of zoos than the preservation of endangered species. Still, without such programs, the Pere David Deer, the Mongolian Wild Horse, and the California Condor would all now be extinct.

Even the best of such programs face difficulties, however. A classic study by Katherine Ralls, Kristin Brugger, and Jonathan Ballou (1979) convincingly argues that lack of genetic diversity among captive animals is a serious problem for zoo breeding programs. In some species the infant mortality rate among inbred animals is six or seven times that among noninbred animals. In other species the infant mortality rate among inbred animals is 100 percent.

Moreover, captivity substitutes selection pressures imposed by humans for those of an animal's natural habitat. After a few years in captivity, animals can begin to diverge both behaviorally and genetically from their relatives in the wild. After a century or more it is not clear that they would be the same animals, in any meaningful sense, that we set out to preserve.

There is also a dark side to zoo breeding programmes: they create many unwanted animals. In some species (lions, tigers, and zebras, for example) a few males can service an entire herd. Extra males are unnecessary to the program and are a financial burden. Some of these animals are sold and end up in the hands of individuals and institutions which lack proper facilities. Others are shot and killed by Great White Hunters in private hunting camps. An article in *US News* (August 5, 2002) exposed the widespread dumping of "surplus" animals by some of America's leading zoos. The reporter even found two endangered gibbons in a filthy cage with no water, in a bankrupt roadside zoo just off Interstate 35 in Texas. The *San Francisco Chronicle* (February 23, 2003) reports that there are now more tigers in private hands than in the wild. There is a flourishing trade in exotic animals fed by more than 1,000 internet sites, and publications such as the *Animal Finders' Guide*, which is published eighteen times per year. A recent browse finds advertisements for coyote pups ($250), baboons ($4,000 for a pair), a declawed female black bear ($500), a 12-year-old female tiger ($500), and much more. In order to avoid the "surplus" problem, some zoos have considered proposals to "recycle" excess animals: a euphemism for killing them and feeding their bodies to other zoo animals.

The ostensible purpose of zoo breeding programs is to reintroduce animals into the wild. In this regard the California Condor is often portrayed as a major success story. From a low of 22 individuals in 1982, the population has rebounded to 219, through captive breeding. Since 1992 condors have been reintroduced, but most have not survived and only six eggs have been produced in the wild. Most eggs have failed to hatch, and only one chick has fledged. Wolf reintroductions have also had only limited success. Wolves, even when they have learned how to hunt, have often not learned to avoid people. Familiarity with humans and ignorance about their own cultures have devastated reintroduced populations of big cats, great apes, bears, rhinos, and hippos. According to the philosopher Bryan Norton, putting a captive-bred animal in the wild is "equivalent to dropping a contemporary human being in a remote area in the 18th or 19th century and saying, 'Let's see if you can make it'" (quoted in Derr 1999). In a 1995 review, Ben Beck, Associate Director of the National Zoological Park in Washington, found that of 145 documented reintroductions involving 115 species, only 16 succeeded in producing self-sustaining wild populations, and only half of these were endangered species.

Even if breeding programs were run in the best possible way, there are limits to what can be done to save endangered species in this way. At most, several hundred species could be preserved in the world's zoos, and then at very great expense. For many of these animals the zoo is likely to be the last stop on the way to extinction. Zoo professionals like to say that they are the Noahs of the modern world and that zoos are their arks, but Noah found a place to land his animals where they could thrive and multiply. If zoos are like arks, then rare animals are like passengers on a voyage of the damned, never to find a port that will let them dock or a land in which they can live in peace. The real solution, of course, is to preserve the wild nature that created these animals and has the power to sustain them. But if it is really true that we are inevitably moving towards a world in which mountain gorillas can survive only in zoos, then we must ask whether it is really better for them to live in artificial environments of our design than not to be born at all.

Even if all these questions and difficulties are overlooked, the importance of preserving endangered species does not provide much support for the existing system of zoos. Most zoos do very little breeding or breed only species which are not endangered. Many of the major breeding programs are run in special facilities which have been established for that purpose. They are often located in remote places, far from the attention of zoo-goers. (For example, the Wildlife Conservation Society [formerly the New York Zoological Society] operates its Wildlife Survival Center on St Catherine's Island off the coast of Georgia, and the National Zoo runs its Conservation and Research Center in the Shenandoah Valley of Virginia.) If our main concern is to do what we can to preserve endangered species at any cost and in any way, then we should support such large-scale breeding centers rather than conventional zoos, most of which have neither the staff nor the facilities to run successful breeding programs.

The four reasons for having zoos which I have surveyed carry some weight. But different reasons provide support for different kinds of zoo. Preservation and perhaps research are better carried out in large-scale animal preserves, but these provide few opportunities for amusement and education. Amusement and perhaps education are better provided in urban zoos, but they offer few opportunities for research and preservation. Moreover, whatever benefits are obtained from any kind of zoo, we must confront the moral presumption against keeping wild animals in captivity. Which way do the scales tip? There are two further considerations which, in my view, tip the scales against zoos.

First, captivity does not just deny animals liberty but is often detrimental to them in other respects as well. The history of chimpanzees in the zoos of Europe and America is a good example.

Chimpanzees first entered the zoo world in about 1640 when a Dutch prince, Frederick Henry of Nassau, obtained one for his castle menagerie. The chimpanzee didn't last very long. In 1835 the London Zoo obtained its first chimpanzee; he died immediately. Another was obtained in 1845; she lived six months. All through the nineteenth and early twentieth centuries zoos obtained chimpanzees who promptly died within nine months. It wasn't until the 1930s that it was discovered that chimpanzees are extremely vulnerable to human respiratory diseases, and that special steps must be taken to protect them. But for nearly a century zoos removed them from the wild and subjected them to almost certain death. Even today there are chimpanzees and other great apes living in deplorable conditions in zoos around the world.

Chimpanzees are not the only animals to suffer in zoos. It is well known that animals such as polar bears, lions, tigers, and cheetahs fare particularly badly in zoos. A recent (2003) report in *Nature* by Ros Clubb and Georgia Mason shows that repetitive stereotypic behavior and high infant mortality rates in zoos are directly related to an animal's natural home range size. For example, polar bears, whose home range in the wild is about a million times the size of its typical zoo enclosure, spend 25 percent of their days in stereotypic pacing and suffer from a 65% infant mortality rate. These results suggest that zoos simply cannot provide the necessary conditions for a decent life for many animals. Indeed, the Detroit Zoo has announced that, for ethical reasons, it will no longer keep elephants in captivity. The San Francisco Zoo has followed suit.

Many animals suffer in zoos quite unnecessarily. In 1974 Peter Batten, former director of the San Jose Zoological Gardens, undertook an exhaustive study of two hundred American zoos. In his book *Living Trophies* he documented large numbers of neurotic, overweight animals kept in cramped, cold cells and fed unpalatable synthetic food. Many had deformed feet and appendages caused by unsuitable floor surfaces. Almost every zoo studied had excessive mortality rates, resulting from preventable factors ranging from vandalism to inadequate husbandry practices. Batten's conclusion was: "The majority of American zoos are badly run, their direction incompetent, and animal husbandry inept and in some cases non-existent" (1976: ix).

Many of these same conditions are documented in Lynn Griner's (1983) review of necropsies conducted at the San Diego Zoo over a fourteen-year period. This zoo may well be the best in the country, and its staff are clearly well trained and well intentioned. Yet this study documents widespread malnutrition among zoo animals; high mortality rates from the use of anesthetics and tranquilizers; serious injuries and deaths sustained in transport; and frequent occurrences of cannibalism, infanticide, and fighting almost certainly caused by overcrowded conditions.

The Director of the National Zoo in Washington resigned in 2004 when an independent review panel commissioned by the National Academy of Sciences found severe deficiencies at the zoo in animal care, pest control, record keeping, and management that contributed to the deaths of twenty-three animals between 1998 and 2003, including, most spectacularly, the loss of two pandas to rat poison. Despite the best efforts of its well-paid public relations firm, it is difficult to trust an institution that cannot avoid killing its most charismatic and valuable animals in such a stupid and unnecessary way.

The second consideration which tips the scales against zoos is more difficult to articulate but is, to my mind, even more important. Zoos teach us a false sense of our place in the natural order. The means of confinement mark a difference between humans and other animals. They are there at our pleasure, to be used for our purposes. Morality and perhaps our very survival require that we learn to live as one species among many rather than as one species over many. To do this, we must forget what we learn at zoos. Because what zoos teach us is false and dangerous, both humans and other animals will be better off when they are abolished.

References

Batten, P. (1976) *Living Trophies*, New York: Thomas Y. Crowell Co.

Beck, B. (1995) "Reintroduction, Zoos, Conservation, and Animal Welfare," in B. Norton, M. Hutchins, E. F. Stevens, and T. L. Maple (eds), *Ethics on the Ark: Zoos, Animal Welfare, and Wildlife Conservation*, Washington, D.C.: Smithsonian Institution Press, pp. 155–63.

Clubb, R., and Mason, G. (2003) "Animal Welfare: Captivity Effects on Wide-Ranging Carnivores," *Nature*, October 2; 425(6957), 473–4.

Derr, M. (1999) "A Rescue Plan for Threatened Species," *New York Times*, January 19.

Griner, L. (1983) *Pathology of Zoo Animals*, San Diego: Zoological Society of San Diego.

Kant, I. (1963) *Lectures on Ethics*, trans. L. Infield, New York: Harper.

Ludwig, E. G. (1981) "People at Zoos: A Sociological Approach," *International Journal for the Study of Animal Problems* 2(6), 310–16.

Montali, R., and Bush, M. (1982) "A Search for Animal Models at Zoos," *ILAR News* 26(1), Fall.

Ralls, K., Brugger, K., and Ballou, J. (1979) "Inbreeding and Juvenile Mortality in Small Populations of Ungulates," *Science* 206, 1101–3.

Scherrin, H. (1905) *The Zoological Society of London*, New York: Cassell and Co., Ltd.

10

To Eat the
Laughing Animal

Dale Peterson

I first heard an ape laugh while following a large group of wild chimpanzees in the great Tai Forest of Côte d'Ivoire, West Africa, as they moved on their daily circuit, a complex progression from food to food to food, from obscure fruits to tender herbs to hard nuts.

These West African chimpanzees are well known for their stone- and hardwood-tool-using culture, and at two or three moments during the day I paused to watch a large number of the nomadic apes assemble in a glade of African walnut trees (*Coula edulis*), pick up the stone and wood hammers they had previously left lying about on the ground, place individual ripe walnuts on top of stone and wood anvils, and then methodically crack open the hard walnut shells to get at the meat inside. That whole procedure was astonishing, particularly since the hammers seemed indistinguishable from rough human artifacts and also since the apes themselves (looking about, picking up walnuts in their hands, walking upright to carry them over to the tools, and squatting intently while they hammered away) seemed to me then hardly distinguishable from people. But my biggest shock that day came from watching a couple of juvenile chimps wrestling, teasing each other, tumbling and chasing – and laughing, laughing their heads off. It was not an action that simply *reminded* me of human laughter or merely *seemed* like human laughter. It was without question genuine laughter, virtually identical to human laughter minus some of

An earlier version of this chapter appeared in *Gastronomica*, Spring 2003.

the vocalized overlay (producing a gasping, panting, frenetic sort of wood-sawing sound).

Since then, I have observed chimpanzee laughter at other times, in other places. I have also seen wild-born bonobos and gorillas laugh, again apparently as a frantic expression of delight and mirth. And I have been told by experts that orangutans, too, sometimes laugh.

Animal play is not surprising, and one can easily believe that neurologically complex animals experience complex pleasure, something akin to "mirth" or, perhaps, an irresistible sensation of emotional lightness. But laughter? The laughter of apes is entirely different from any mere facial upturn of pleasure: a dog's smile, for instance. And it is another thing altogether from the high-pitched hyena vocalizations, sometimes described as "laughter" but completely unassociated with play or pleasure. Laughter may be among the most fragile and fleeting of vocal utterances. What does it mean? That apes laugh is undeniable. That their laughter means anything significant is a matter of opinion. Still, the laughter of apes provokes us to consider the possibility of an underlying complexity of cognition and intellect, to wonder about the existence of an ape mind.

The great apes – the three species commonly known as chimpanzees, bonobos, and gorillas in Africa, and orangutans in Southeast Asia – are special animals because they are so close to human.

This idea is one long held in several though not all African traditions and now, increasingly, in the European tradition. One of the earliest European reports on the existence of the great apes in Africa, English sailor Andrew Battell's tale (told to a collector of explorers' narratives probably in 1607) of two types of humanoid "monsters" in Africa may have provided the seminal inspiration for Shakespeare's evocatively humanoid "howling monster" Caliban, in *The Tempest* (1611). A few live apes created some more generalized interest, as they began arriving in Europe by the middle of the seventeenth century; and in 1698, British physician Edward Tyson dissected the recently deceased body of the first live chimpanzee ever to appear in England and announced before the Royal Society the existence of *Homo Sylvestrius*, an animal with a profound anatomical similarity to humans. That sort of rather casual enthusiasm was, during the nineteenth century, replaced by less casual studies in comparative anatomy. Charles Darwin himself was inspired to speculate that the African great apes would most likely turn out to be our own closest living relatives, though he lacked the data to prove it.

Around the turn of the twentieth century, George Nuttall, an American expert on ticks lecturing in bacteriology at Cambridge University, pressed the comparative science beyond observable anatomy by examining the molecular structure of blood from different species, via antibody reactivity, and demonstrated the surprising fact that the blood of apes resembles human blood far more than it resembles monkey blood. By mid-century, behavioral studies in the field began adding to the picture – perhaps most dramatically through Jane Goodall's first observations in 1960 that the chimpanzees of Gombe Stream Reserve in East Africa were making and using simple tools to capture termites. Subsequent behavioral research shows that wild chimpanzees fashion and exploit an impressive variety of tools according to locally different cultural traditions and that they live in provocatively human-like social systems, complete with a Machiavellian style of male power-politics and lethal, male-driven territorial wars between adjacent chimp communities. Around the same time, laboratory projects in the United States and Japan were starting to demonstrate the astonishing reality that apes – all four species – are capable of learning and using sign language for communication purposes. Some of those early studies still continue at full strength, as I write, and they have successfully responded to the earliest cries of disbelief from astonished skeptics.

By the end of the twentieth century, techniques and technologies for genetic analysis had become sophisticated enough that it was possible not only to demonstrate to the satisfaction of every scientifically informed observer the undeniable reality of this closeness between humans and the great apes, but also to quantify it. The numbers go like this. Humans and orangutans share 96.4 percent of their genetic code. Humans and gorillas are genetically 97.7 percent identical. And, finally, humans share with both chimpanzees and bonobos an amazing 98.7 percent of their DNA. Genetically, you and I are 98.7 percent identical to both those ape species.

A somewhat careless reader required to examine two books in which 98.7 percent of the words, sentences, and paragraphs are identical and placed in the identical order might complain at the serious injustice of having been forced to read the same book twice. A moderately careful reader, perhaps noticing that the two books have different titles – *Homo sapiens* for one and *Pan troglodytes* for the other – might express outrage at the unimaginative effrontery of this plagiarism.

No wonder, then, that the apes we see in zoos and on stage, in laboratories or in the wild, provoke that strange shock of recognition, serve as that often unexamined source of fascination and sometimes revulsion, of jokes and insults, of hidden concerns and even considered ethical assessments. The four nonhuman apes, our closest relatives, mirror our faces and bodies, our hands and fingers, our fingernails and fingerprints. They make and use tools, are capable of long-term planning and deliberate deception. They seem to share our perceptual world. They appear to express something very much like the human repertoire of emotions. They look into a mirror and act as if they recognize themselves as individuals, are manifestly capable of learning symbolic language, share with us several recognizable expressions and gestures – and they laugh in situations that might cause us to laugh too.

So people living in the Western tradition have recently come to accept, to a significant degree, a special bridge of kinship between apes and humans (or to understand that from the professional biologist's point of view humans are actually a fifth member of the ape group). Perhaps it is because of this recent cultural perception that Westerners are sometimes particularly surprised to learn that the three African apes – chimpanzees, bonobos, and gorillas – have long been a food source for many people living in Central Africa's Congo Basin (a largely forested region claimed by the nations of Cameroon, Central African Republic, Congo, Democratic Republic of Congo, Equatorial Guinea, and Gabon).

The fact, however, should surprise no one. Around the globe, people living in or on the edges of the world's great forests have traditionally taken the protein offered by wild animals: as true in Asia, Europe, and the Americas as it is in Africa. Moreover, the exploitation of wild forest animals for food is really no different from the widespread reliance on seafood, commonly accepted around the world.

But the African tropical forests are particularly rich in variety and have provided Central Africans with a very diverse wealth of game species – collectively known as *bushmeat* – consumed within a very complex milieu of traditions, tastes, habits, and cultural preferences and prohibitions. Some religious prohibitions (notably, the Muslim prohibition against eating primate meat) and a number of village or tribal traditions have kept apes off the menu in a scattered patchwork across the continent. Local traditions are often rationalized according to familiar myths, and in the case of apes these ancient tales ordinarily evoke the theme of kinship. For example, the Oroko of southwestern Cameroon consider that, since people are occasionally turned into chimps, any hunter discovering and sparing a wild chimp will find the grateful ape has deliberately chased other animals his way. Conversely,

killing the chimp can cast misfortune onto the hunter's family. (Nevertheless, a dead chimp is still edible food for the Oroko.) The Kouyou of north-
ern Congo traditionally forbade the hunting of at least four species – gorillas,
chimpanzees, leopards, and bongo antelopes – and in the case of the two
apes, that prohibition was based upon their closeness to humans. Likewise,
the Mongandu people of north central Democratic Republic of Congo (former
Zaïre) have always, since anyone can remember, eaten everything in their
forests except for leopards, tree hyraxes, and bonobos. While their neighbors
to the south of the Luo River, the Mongo people, will happily hunt and eat
bonobos, the Mongandu say that bonobos are simply too much like people
to eat. They look human, and when actual humans are not watching, these
animals will even stand upright on their hind legs. (Chimpanzees and
gorillas also sometimes walk upright, but bonobos, in fact, are the ape most
distinguished by this surprising tendency. They will even walk considerable
distances on two legs, often when their hands are full, so the Mongandu
prohibition is based upon good observation and a sensible interpretation.)

And yet the very quality – human resemblance – that places apes on
the prohibited list for some traditions actually lands them on the preferred
list in others. Apes look like humans but possess a superhuman strength.
The combination of human resemblance and superhuman strength may
help explain why apes are, in some places, culturally valued as a food for
ambitious men who would like to acquire the strength, and perhaps also the
supposed virility, of an ape. For this reason, possibly, ape meat is strictly a
man's meat for the Zime of Cameroon, so one tribe member told me. Baka
villagers in the southeast of that nation once told me the same thing. For the
Ewondo of Cameroon, according to one informant, women can eat gorilla
meat at any time except during pregnancy, out of concern about the effects
such potent fare might have on the unborn child. This important "mascu-
line" meat also turns out to be a special treat sometimes offered to visiting
dignitaries and other powerful men. The recently elected governor of
Cameroon's Eastern Province was regularly served up gorilla as he toured
his new constituency. Likewise, the Bishhop of Bertoua, according to one
report, is offered gorilla hands and feet (considered the best parts) when he
goes visiting.

These food preferences, based partly upon symbolic value, blend into the
preferential logic expressed by symbolic medicine. Symbolic (or "fetish")
medicine is a thriving business in the big cities of Central Africa; my own
experience suggests that a person can rather easily locate ape parts in the
city fetish markets. In Brazzaville, Congo's capital, I once looked over gorilla

heads and hands. The hands, so the fetish dealer explained, are used especially by athletes who would like to be stronger. They boil pieces of the flesh until the water is all gone. Then they grind the remnants at the bottom of the pot down to a powder and press the powder into a cut in the skin, thus magically absorbing great strength from the great ape. Likewise, according to Mbongo George, an active commercial meat hunter in southeastern Cameroon, rubbing pulverized gorilla flesh into your back will cure a backache, and chimp bones tied to the hips of a pregnant young girl will ease the process of labor when her own hips are narrow.

Yes, there are many domestic alternatives to bushmeat in Central Africa, particularly in the urban areas. City markets offer domestic meat, both imported and home-grown – and indeed at least some of the bushmeat sold in the city markets is more expensive than some domestic meats. I am persuaded this is true for chimpanzee and elephant meat compared to beef and pork, at least, because I once asked an ordinary citizen in Cameroon's capital city of Yaoundé to buy – bargaining as he would in ordinary circumstances – equivalent-by-weight amounts of chimpanzee, elephant, beef, and pork. In that way, I acquired a strange collection of flesh in my hotel room (severed hand of chimp, slice of elephant trunk, cube of cow, etc.), which I weighed and otherwise compared, and concluded that city people were paying approximately twice as much for chimpanzee and elephant as for beef and pork. Why would anyone pay more for chimp and elephant? Taste is clearly an important but not the only factor in people's food preferences. Many Central Africans still prefer the taste of bushmeat, in all its prolific variety, but millions of recent urbanites also value bushmeat as a reminder of their cultural identity and roots in traditional villages.

In the rural areas where people are in many cases still living in a style close to traditional village life, the market cost hierarchy is reversed, with domestic meats more and bushmeat less expensive. For many rural Africans, then, bushmeat is also attractive simply because it's cheaper.

The standard dynamics of supply and demand mean that this pattern of consumption is about to hit a wall. While Africa is by far the most impoverished continent on the planet, it is also (and not coincidentally) the fastest growing. A natural rate of increase of 3.1 percent per year for Middle Africa indicates that human numbers are doubling every twenty-three years in this part of the world. If food consumption habits continue, in short, demand for bushmeat as a source of dietary protein will double in little more than two decades.

While the demand increases so rapidly, the supply is simply collapsing as a result of at least three factors. First, traditional hunting technologies are being replaced by ever more efficient modern ones, including wire snares, shotguns, and military hardware, and as a direct consequence animals across the Basin are being very efficiently *mined*, rather than *harvested*, out of the forests. Wire snares are particularly devastating because they kill indiscriminately; and, since snare lines are only periodically checked, they allow for considerable waste from rot. Wire snares tend to maim rather than kill bigger animals like the apes, but modern shotguns loaded with large-ball *chevrotine* cartridges enable many of today's hunters to target such larger and more dangerous species with impunity. Apes, who would have been unapproachably dangerous quarry for many (though certainly not all) hunters even a few years ago, are now attractive targets offering a very good deal in hunting economics: ratio of meat to cartridge.

Second, a $1 billion per year commercial logging industry, run primarily by European and Asian firms to supply 10 million cubic meters per year of construction, marine, and finish hardwoods primarily for the pleasure and benefit of European and Asian consumers, has during the last two decades cast a vast network of roads and tracks and trails into profoundly ancient and previously remote forests across the Congo Basin. Loggers degrade these forests, haul in large numbers of workers and families, and often hire hunters to supply the bushmeat to feed the workers and their dependents. Most seriously, though, for the first time in history (and the ecological history of these great forests takes us back to the era of the dinosaurs), the loggers' roads and tracks and trails allow hunters in and meat out. Vast areas of forest that even a decade ago were protected by their remoteness are no longer protected at all.

Third, as a result of the new hunting technologies and the new opportunity offered by all those roads and tracks and trails cut by the European and Asian loggers, a small army of African entrepreneurs has found new economic opportunity in the bushmeat trade, which has quite suddenly become efficient and utterly commercialized. Bushmeat is now big business. It is no longer merely feeding the people in small rural villages and other subsistence communities but instead reaching very deeply into the forests and then stretching very broadly out to the towns and big cities throughout Central Africa. In Gabon alone, the trade currently amounts to a $50 million per year exchange. Altogether, this commerce today draws out of Central Africa's Congo Basin forests an estimated and astonishing 5 million metric tons of animal meat per year. That amount is absolutely unsustainable. The depletion of the supply of wild animals and their meat is not even remotely balanced by the replenishment offered via natural reproduction in a stable ecosystem.

A generally accepted estimate holds that around 1 percent of the total bushmeat trade involves the meat of the great apes: chimpanzees, bonobos, and gorillas. A blind and drunk optimist might imagine that 1 percent even of 5 million metric tons is a somewhat tolerable amount. It is not, of course. And even in the best of circumstances, where apes happen to inhabit legally protected forests (that is, national parks and reserves), a recent survey based on responses from professional fieldworkers tells us that chimpanzees are hunted in 50 percent of their protected areas, bonobos in 88 percent, and gorillas in 56 percent.

The impact of the current explosion in market hunting across the Congo Basin is threatening the existence of several wild animal species – but it disproportionately devastates the great apes. Biologists theoretically examining the sustainability of hunting consider, among other things, the ability of a species to replenish itself. A species with a quick rate of replenishment can likely, other factors being equal, withstand a high rate of depletion from hunting. Thinking about the impact hunting has on the survival of any particular species, in other words, requires us to examine that species' reproduction rates; and the great apes are unfortunately very slow reproducers. Perhaps because they are intelligent animals requiring extended periods of immature dependency while the young learn from their elders, apes wean late, reach independence and puberty late, and produce surprisingly few offspring. Altogether, the apes show about one quarter the reproduction rate of most other mammals.

Given such a slow reproduction rate, biologists calculate that chimpanzees and bonobos can theoretically withstand a loss of only about 2 percent of their numbers per year and still maintain a steady population. Gorillas may be able to tolerate losses of 4 percent per year. Monkeys have about the same low tolerance for loss, ranging from 1 to 4 percent, depending on the species. Ungulates, depending on the species, should be able to withstand yearly losses ranging most typically around 25 percent; and rodents can do just fine with losses from 13 percent to 80 percent per year, again depending on the species. In an ideal world, hunters would be equipped with pocket calculators to keep track on how sustainable their hunting is. In the real world, commercial hunters usually shoot whatever happens to wander in front of their guns. As a result, active hunting in a forest tends to deplete the fauna in a predictable progression. Apes and monkeys go first. Ungulates next. Rodents last. Indeed, it ought to be possible to measure the faunal disintegration of a forest by comparing the ratio of monkeys to rats sold in local markets.

The best, most recent estimates tell us that approximately 150,000 to 250,000 chimpanzees survive in the wild, at the most some 50,000 bonobos remain, and roughly 120,000 wild gorillas are still there. To think a little further about those numbers, consider, as a sort of measuring spoon, the Rose Bowl Stadium of Pasadena, California. The Rose Bowl has, I am told, a seating capacity of around 100,000. If you were able to persuade all the wild chimpanzees in the world to take a seat, you would be able to get them all, the entire world population of chimpanzees, to sit down in perhaps somewhere between one and two Rose Bowl Stadiums – two and a half at the very most. If you were able to persuade all the gorillas in the world to take a seat, you could fill up a little more than one Rose Bowl Stadium. And if you could get all the bonobos in the world to sit down – well, at the very best, you might fill up half the Rose Bowl Stadium. Those are actually very small numbers, in other words, especially when one realizes that our own species, *Homo sapiens*, is growing in size by more than two Rose Bowls' worth every day.

Based on the "informed consensus of experts," the commercial hunting of apes for meat is "out of control and unsustainable," and it continues "to spread and accelerate" (Buytinksi 2001: 27). With the current levels and patterns of demand for apes as food, how long can they last?

One measure of how fast commercial hunting can reduce an ape population has been provided by the recent history of eastern Democratic Republic of Congo's Kahuzi-Biega National Park, supposedly protected as a UNESCO World Heritage Site but not protected well enough to keep out the professional hunters. In only three years during the last decade, hunters in Kahuzi-Biega earned a living by transforming into meat ("if our worst fears prove founded," so one investigator writes cautiously – Redmond 2001: 3) some 80 to 90 percent of the 17,000 individuals who until then comprised the subspecies *Gorilla gorilla graueri*.

In sum, conserving biodiversity – saving the apes from extinction – amounts to one argument against using apes as a human food. A second argument has to do with public health. Perhaps all meats amount to a fair bridge for animal-to-human infection. Domestic meats, for example, offer *E. coli* 0157, salmonella, and the hypothetical "prion" causing "mad cow disease" among cattle and the deadly Creutzfeldt–Jakob syndrome among human eaters of cattle. But most domestic meats are regularly inspected and controlled to protect the carnivorous public, while bushmeat is not. Ape meat is particularly suspect if only because it is illegal, often sold covertly, and therefore particularly difficult to monitor or control.

Chimpanzees and gorillas, in any event, appear to be about as vulnerable to the extremely infectious and frequently lethal Ebola virus as people are, and recent events in Central and West Africa have demonstrated that apes can also, like humans, readily transmit that virus not only to each other but also to any humans nearby – hunters handling meat, for instance. Virologists have recently identified a Simian Immunodeficiency Virus (SIV) endemic to chimpanzees as the historical source of HIV (subtypes M, N, and O) in humans, which accounts for the infection of around 99 percent of today's globally distributed AIDS victims. The remaining 1 percent have been infected with HIV 2, a closely related virus that we now know comes from an SIV endemic to the West African monkey popularly known as Sooty Mangabey. A reasonable presumption is that the three historical moments of viral transmission from chimpanzees to humans (producing today's three viable HIV 1 subtypes) – three separate episodes when a chimpanzee SIV successfully leaped into a human host – occurred not during the eating of ape meat, since cooking kills viruses, but during the butchering phase.

Since that event has already happened, it might be imagined that the danger has passed: deed already done. In fact, apes are susceptible to an enormous variety of diseases that will also infect humans, including bacterial meningitis, chicken pox, diphtheria, Epstein–Barr virus, hepatitis A and B, influenza, measles, mumps, pneumonia, rubella, smallpox, whooping cough, and so on. Far more serious, however, is the possible scenario of a person already infected with HIV 1 or HIV 2 coming into intimate contact (through butchering, for instance) with one of several related viruses, the several SIVs endemic among several monkey species, thereby producing a successful cross, a recombinant virus that could become HIV 3. The government of Cameroon recently sponsored an extended study on primate viruses where researchers tested the blood of 788 monkeys kept as pets or sold as meat and discovered that around one-fifth of those samples were infected with numerous varieties of SIV, including five previously unknown types. So the potential for new epidemics based on recombinants should be taken very seriously.

The public health threat is not, of course, limited to Central Africa. Rather, it is a global threat that still tends to be vastly underappreciated by those in the West who are most capable of doing something about it – even as the threat grows with ever-expanding human numbers, international migration, and commerce. In the year 2003, for example, an estimated 11,600 tons of bushmeat (from antelopes, camels, monkeys, snails, snakes, as well as chimpanzees and gorillas) was illegally smuggled into Great Britain.

The final argument against apes as food is perhaps the one many people think of first but often have trouble describing fully or convincingly, and that is the ethical one: the special case against eating the animal who laughs. Many ethical vegetarians refuse to eat animals capable of suffering, thus drawing a distinction between plants and, at least, vertebrate animals, while possibly giving some invertebrates the benefit of the doubt. Indeed, I believe that most thoughtful people maintain an examined or unexamined hierarchy of value in their vision of the natural world that includes distinctions within the vertebrates – recognizing humans, for example, as among the most complex of the vertebrates with the most compelling capacity for suffering, a perception that possibly accounts for our common and particular horror at the idea of nutritional cannibalism. To the degree that we now see humans as surprisingly closely related to apes, or as belonging taxonomically within the larger group of apes, that makes eating the laughing animal also worthy of our special concern.

References

Buytinski, Tom (2001) "Africa's Great Apes," in Benjamin B. Beck, Tara S. Stoinksi, Michael Hutchins, Terry L. Maple, Bryan Norton, Andrew Rowan, Elizabeth F. Stevens, and Arnold Arluke (eds), *Great Apes: The Ethics of Coexistence*, Washington, D.C.: Smithsonian Institution Press, pp. 3–56.

Redmond, Ian (2001) Coltan Boom, Gorilla Bust: The Impact of Coltan Mining on Gorillas and Other Wildlife in Eastern D. R. Congo. Private report sponsored by the Dian Fossey Gorilla Fund and the Born Free Foundation.

Part III

Activists and Their Strategies

11

How Austria Achieved a Historic Breakthrough for Animals

Martin Balluch

The Background

Victories in the animal rights movement are few and far between. Yes, occasionally a company changes its policy, or the law is changed to require that cages are somewhat enlarged. But where have we made real progress? Our experience in Austria suggests that it may be easier to make progress in smaller countries, where people active in social justice movements like animal rights have greater access to politicians.

The first Austrian animal rights conference in Vienna in 2002 unified the movement here in an unprecedented way and laid the ground for a new type of campaign. In November of the same year, just before a national election, the new cooperation among the animal advocacy groups led to the first united press conference in the movement's history. We demanded that the political parties should publicly promise a new nationwide animal protection law. The Conservative Party in government refused even to acknowledge the existence of this demand. Therefore just a few days before the election we occupied their headquarters, simultaneously entering the building not only via the main door, but also from the roof and balcony. After a siege of thirteen hours and much media coverage, we felt we had made our point and left. The result made headline news: "Conservatives promise a new animal law if reelected." And they were reelected.

In March 2003, with this promise very much in mind, we started a concerted campaign to get battery farming banned. At first, we openly rescued seven battery chickens from one of the worst battery farms. A journalist was with us inside the farm and the event was well covered in the media. We reported the farm for a number of breaches of the law: too many chickens per cage, filthy conditions, dead chickens not cleared away, and so on. There was no reaction to our complaint by the authorities. Hence we occupied the office of the provincial governor. Chaining ourselves to the furniture in his office, we laid some of the dead bodies of the chickens from this battery farm on his desk and demanded to be heard. Five hours later he agreed to speak to us and promised an investigation.

As a result of the investigation that followed, the farmer was convicted and received a fine of 200 Euros for having five to six chickens in a cage in which only four chickens were allowed. The trial revealed that the farm had passed an official inspection just before our visit. As correctly counting four chickens per cage is not terribly difficult, this proved that official farm inspections do not prevent breaches of the law.

Hence, within fifteen days in July 2003, we made night visits to the forty-eight largest battery farms across the country, which together account for about 40 percent of Austria's battery chickens. All those farms were filmed and reported to the authorities: more than 90 percent had cages that were illegally overfilled, all were filthy, and many were strewn with dead and dying birds. At the last farm, we liberated nine chickens openly to strengthen the media impact of our findings. And, indeed, the media reaction was gigantic.

In the absence of any agency that can start court procedures on behalf of the battery chickens, we managed to engage the "People's Solicitor," a public institution that exerts pressure on official bodies that fail to meet their responsibilities. The involvement of the People's Solicitor, together with public pressure through the media, led to an unprecedented wave of prosecutions of battery farmers. Their trials revealed that official inspections had been deliberately sloppy and the farmers had taken the leniency of the investigators for granted. They literally said as much in their defense. At least fifteen farms were convicted. Not surprisingly there was also a wave of private prosecutions against me for trespass. I was also charged with the crime of unlawfully removing private property – the chickens.

As the issue of animal rights was so prevalent, the governing Conservative Party felt obliged to appoint a party spokesperson for matters concerning animals, as all the other three parliamentary parties had already done. At the end of 2003, this spokesperson met with us a number of times, but her approach felt more like an exercise to take the heat out of our campaigns than a serious consideration of our demands. In early 2004, the government revealed its proposal for a new animal protection law, which didn't include any apparent improvements. In 2012, the usual battery cages were to be replaced by so-called "enriched cages," but these were required in any case by European Union regulations. Therefore we decided to step up the campaign at the political level and directly confront the major obstacle – the Conservatives.

The 2004 Campaign

We went into factory farms of all kinds and produced an up-to-date video of the situation of farmed animals in Austria, with the chief emphasis on battery farms. In the video, the footage of each type of factory farm was directly related to the Conservatives' suggestions for a new law in each respect, to underline their complete disregard for the wellbeing of the animals. This video was sent around Austria to all animal rights groups, and in all major cities street demos were held, where the video was shown on giant screens with video beamers.

At the same time, we commissioned a representative opinion poll on seven central aspects of the new law. Large majorities supported our demands – for example, 86 percent supported a ban on battery farming and only 7 percent opposed it. This was widely covered in the media. We also started a letter-writing and emailing campaign against the Conservatives. The topic became a major public issue. The largest private nationwide radio station ran a two-hour program with me, discussing animal rights and battery farming, and taking listeners' calls. Conservative politicians had to phone in to get their point across. Later, the Conservatives complained that we had much more media time than they did.

On March 7, 2004, two provinces held their elections. We used the opportunity to make our point: "Conservatives support animal abuse." We confronted the Conservatives at their election rallies and disrupted live televised political debates with our banners. At the largest Conservative rally we were physically attacked, our banner was ripped, and I was punched in the face. But even that turned to our advantage: we took pictures of our attackers and sent them immediately via mobile phone to our head office. The attackers were identified as Conservative candidates and we went public with a press release within an hour of the assault. On election day, all major provincial papers covered the story. The Conservatives lost 50 percent of their votes in the province where this attack took place, and their governor was defeated in the other. Our impact was now undeniable.

On March 11, I was invited to speak with a government advisor. We did not make much headway, and on March 16, the government announced an unacceptable compromise: all battery cages should be enriched by 2009. The media carried the response of the unified animal advocacy movement: "No, thank you." We demanded a complete ban on all cages. On March 30, the Agricultural Minister invited me to speak with him. It became clear that he was not willing to listen. So we started regular demonstrations outside the ministry, as well as daily demos in the capital and weekly demos in other major cities with our video.

On April 9, we stepped up the campaign by openly liberating thirty-seven battery chickens from another farm and then sitting-in on the roof. This action attracted so much media attention that neither the farmer nor the police were willing to intervene. The next day we launched a nationwide campaign with placards illegally posted up all across the country carrying the message that the Conservatives don't care about animals. On April 15, the largest weekly magazine, *NEWS*, invited me to a round table with the Agricultural Minister, the largest battery farmer (who had 450,000 birds), and the animal spokesperson of the opposition Social Democrats. The minister felt that as a vegan I was not in a position to debate animal husbandry, to which I replied that only vegans can truly talk on behalf of animals, as they are the only ones without any personal interest in using animals.

On April 23, a tip-off prompted us to pay a night-time visit to Austria's first battery farm using enriched cages. The Conservatives wanted to promote the farm the next day as the solution to the problem. They had invited a hen expert from Germany, who was quoted in their press release as praising the farm. We released pictures from the very same farm depicting featherless birds in crowded cages, dead birds, and filthy conditions.

The government set up a commission to debate the issue and prepare a compromise. The opposition parties were firmly behind our demands. On each of the three days the commission met, we published, in collaboration with all the major national animal groups, paid advertisements in major daily newspapers asking the Prime Minister to rethink his policy and ban battery cages. The request appeared over the signatures of seventy-eight people prominent in the arts and sciences.

A presidential election was due on April 25. (In Austria, the President is the head of state, but the position is largely a ceremonial one, and the election does not determine the political leadership of the nation.) We again branded the Conservative Party as the obstacle to progress in animal protection. The Conservative candidate originally sided with the government, but was forced to change her position. At her last press conference, on the day before the election, she said that the government would have to rethink its position and that battery farming must be abolished. Too late: she narrowly lost the election.

Over the next two weeks, the public pressure continued to rise. On April 27, just before the commission's second meeting in Parliament, I waited with a TV team in attendance in front of the conference room and handed the Conservative delegation a petition with 10,000 signatures for a battery farm ban, which we had collected since starting the street demos in February. We also showed an enriched cage with life-sized chicken models in it together with photographs from the battery farm with those cages. The Conservatives were outraged and called security, who removed us from Parliament. The TV crew interviewed me in front of Parliament and produced a very favorable report.

On April 28, the Freedom Party, which was the junior member of the governing coalition, invited me to participate in a public panel on the issue in Parliament. A week later, we invited representatives of all Parliamentary parties to visit egg producers who don't use cages. These events were again well covered in the media. Apart from the Farmers' Union, which spent a lot of money on advertisements making wild claims against us, there was virtually no opposition to our views.

The Victory

Suddenly, the government gave in. On May 27, in a historic vote, every single member of Parliament voted in favor of a ban on battery farming coming into effect on January 1, 2009. But in the wake of this ban, riding the wave of public interest in the matter, we were in a position to get a lot more demands accepted on behalf of animals. Under different circumstances, even the opposition would not have endorsed these demands. But now no party could afford to be seen as anti-animal.

Hence, in addition to the battery farm ban, it is now illegal to trade in living cats and dogs in shops, or to display cats and dogs publicly in order to sell them. It is illegal to kill any animal for no good reason, even painlessly. Because inability to find a home for healthy animals is not considered a good reason to kill them, kill-shelters are also now outlawed.

The following statement will be included in the Austrian constitution alongside human rights: "The state protects the life and wellbeing of animals due to the special responsibility of mankind with respect to animals as their fellows." The civil law code already states that animals are not things. The law also requires state and local governments to provide financial support for more animal-friendly husbandry systems, and other projects and activities aimed at animal protection, including furthering a better understanding of animal protection, especially among young people.

Each province must appoint an "Animal Solicitor" for a five-year term. These "Animal Solicitors" have the right to be informed about all animal-related trials, must receive government support, can make independent decisions, and can start court procedures on behalf of animals. If police or state prosecutors have been made aware of breaches of the animal protection law, they are under an obligation to act.

Every two years, the government must write a report on advances in animal protection and a summary of animal court trials and farm inspection results. An animal protection committee has been formed, with nineteen members, one of whom was appointed by animal advocacy organizations. This committee can suggest changes to the law and evaluate the situation with regard to animal abuse. All systems of animal husbandry must be certified before they can go on the market.

A ban on fur farming, which had come into effect in 1998 in six of Austria's nine provinces, is now established on the federal level without any exceptions for free-range farming or the like. In 2002 we had achieved a ban, also at the provincial level, on the use of many species of animals in circuses. According to the new law, as of January 1, 2005, the use of all wild animals – that is, all animals other than domestic or farm animals – in circuses is illegal.

But this general atmosphere led to a different kind of victory. On February 9, 2004, a district court had found me guilty of unlawfully removing someone else's property – the liberated chickens. When a TV film team interviewed people on the streets, showing them the footage of the rescue, everyone said that it was outrageous to find somebody guilty for rescuing animals. On July 12, my appeal against the conviction was heard. We argued that, according to the law, animals are not things and that it was a legally justified emergency rescue which could not have been achieved through informing the authorities or by any other means with less infringement of the farmer's rights.

In a 2:1 split decision, the High Court overturned my conviction. In a historic verdict they argued that although I did break in and remove property from the farmer, the new animal protection law underlines that battery farms are animal abuse, that society at large agrees with my activity, and that, in liberating the hens, I acted rightly and with good intentions. This means that we have a High Court ruling that, basically, breaking in and stealing animals from a factory farm is not a punishable crime – a verdict that sets a promising precedent!

How We Won: Some Tactical Lessons

The new Austrian animal law is one of the most advanced in the world today. A number of ingredients were vital for achieving it. First and foremost we identified our enemy, the Conservative Party, at the right point in time and were able to communicate that to the public. By focusing on them and at the same time having close contact with the other parties, we persuaded the other parties to agree with us, so as not to become our targets too, and thereby made it impossible for the Conservatives to pass the buck if no compromise was reached, which of course they always tried to do. We took the opportunities presented by both the presidential and regional elections to attack the Conservatives, in the media as well as via our poster campaign and in a total of seventy-one separate demonstrations, and we used the usual grassroots tactics like blockades, open rescues, and occupations. Whether because of our campaigns or for other reasons, the Conservatives started losing one election after the other.

Another essential ingredient in winning this battle was to establish very close links with about a dozen journalists who are sympathetic to the animal rights cause. We convinced them that this issue was important, that we were reliable, and that we were able to supply them with up-to-date information and superb photographic and video material. For many of our inspections of battery farms as well as for our three open rescues of battery hens, we had media with us from the start. But to enable these journalists to keep the story in the news over a long period of time, we needed constantly to offer them something new. That is where a wide variety of actions all played their part – occupations, blockades, open rescues, press conferences, petitions, banner drops, opinion polls, visits for politicians to free-range farms, support from prominent people, public events in rural factory farming communities, and presentations of scientific studies. In addition, the trials following our investigations and open rescues all served to highlight the issue.

In the end the media engine ran by itself. Newspapers and TV stations were constantly covering the issue. We managed to create the kind of relentless pressure that had never been seen in Austria before in connection with animal rights. At times it seemed like a miracle, but it was really the result of a lot of hard work by many people.

Since then, all parties have been extremely careful not to do anything that could lead us to target them. They now all have animal spokespeople who stay in contact with us. Animal rights has become a serious political issue that plays a role in election campaigns.

Although different political systems may work in different ways, our experience suggests the following recommendations for anyone attempting a similar campaign:

1 Establish personal contact with influential politicians on this issue. Try to get cooperation from sympathetic politicians across all parties. If one party blocks that cooperation, isolate them and confront them together with the others, if need be, publicly. What scares them the most is the threat of sabotaging their election campaigns. Confront them in permanent demonstrations, disrupt their rallies, and immediately attack any of their press releases. Try to find out which group within the party stands in the way of your goals and try to isolate them or strengthen their opponents within the party.

2 Seek the support of scientists, especially outspoken ones. Persuade them or pay them to write scientific reports, to advise government, and to appear with you at press conferences.

3 Confront politicians, as well as the public, as a unified animal advocacy movement. Give the impression that every single animal advocacy group agrees on this issue. In fact, the message should be that every decent citizen agrees.

4 Use other countries as examples to follow. It may help to facilitate direct contacts between your politicians and politicians from other countries who have had a positive experience with such a ban. In our campaign in Austria, we used mostly Switzerland but also Sweden as shining examples of how backward Austria is, and we also fostered links between Greens from different countries.

5   Talk personally with journalists who are known to support the issue. Get inside knowledge of what might stop them reporting frequently and favorably about it, and talk with the sympathetic journalists themselves about what would be the best strategy to proceed with. Always inform them, regularly, of any new developments. Be very reliable and knowledgeable on the issue, and assure them that they themselves will always be informed first-hand by you of any new developments.

Why Animal Activists Should Work to Change the Law

I have been active in the animal rights movement for many years, and my experience is, generally, that most animal rights advocates do not consider it worthwhile to work to change the law. This view may come from a general, and often well-founded, distrust of politics, the state, and law enforcement. But we have now shown, in Austria, that animal liberation can use state powers, courts, and law enforcement to our advantage.

Imagine that you want to change awareness in people so that more and more people become vegan. Is it ever conceivable that one day vegans will be a majority? I don't think so. In my view, only a limited number of people are willing to change their lives to that extent. In Austria, as noted above, an opinion poll showed that 86 percent of people are against battery farming, but nearly all of those people still eat battery eggs. And even with such a big majority it was almost impossible to change the law and shut down the battery farming industry. In addition, I don't think the number of vegetarians and vegans is increasing much at all, at least at the moment, even though awareness about animal issues is clearly on the rise.

Lasting change begins with a change in awareness. This change in awareness, however, doesn't automatically lead to a change in behavior, at least in the majority of people. But if new laws are achieved bit by bit, the change in awareness is continuously transformed into the normal way of life. And in the next generation, growing up with the new way of life, everyone will accept it as "normal." When wild animals are banned from circuses, for example, the ban actually stops the practice for good. You never have to protest outside animal circuses again and there cannot be a backlash unless somebody revokes the ban. I believe that to be virtually impossible, however, because in my experience only economic arguments stand up against animal rights arguments, and if the practice has been banned for long enough, there will be no economic force behind it. If it has become a normal way of life to have circuses without wild animals, a change of the law back to the old way will become unthinkable.

If you want to compare the success of a campaign to change the law and a campaign to change behavior, or to target certain companies, you have to ask yourself how you can measure success. That is not easy. If a company goes out of business and the abuse moves elsewhere, that is only half a success. Also, when pressuring companies you have to remain ever-vigilant. In Austria in 1998, the clothes company Kleider Bauer gave up selling fur after many protests. Five years later, they started selling it again. Activists were too involved with other companies to have enough resources free to target Kleider Bauer a second time. Hence they are still selling fur today.

No realistic level of guerrilla attacks of the kind carried out by the Animal Liberation Front could have hurt the battery farming industry as much as the new Austrian law does. I hope that the kind of campaigns favored by people in the movement are not determined by what is "cool" and makes you feel better, but, rather, by what is most effective in achieving animal rights. A law banning a whole industry does far more economic damage to the animal abuse industry than anything else the animal movement could do.

The success against battery farming now proves that a ban on a major industry is possible, even if based solely on ethical arguments. Those who claim that capitalism and exploitation always win have been shown to be wrong. We should not lose faith in animal rights activism as a means of achieving lasting change and, eventually, animal liberation.

12

Butchers' Knives into Pruning Hooks

Civil Disobedience for Animals

Pelle Strindlund

They shall beat their swords into plowshares, and their spears into pruning hooks.

Isaiah 2:4

April 1999, World Day for Laboratory Animals

On our way there we were stopped by the police. We were at Gothenburg University, just a few minutes' walk from the lab where they do experiments on animals. A man and a woman got out of the car slowly, with the rocking gait that police often have.

"Where are you going with the ladder?" asked the man.

I didn't want to lie – or, at least, I couldn't come up with anything good on the spur of the moment. On the other hand, I wasn't about to spill the beans.

"Don't intend to say," I said.

"What are you going to do with that ladder?" asked the woman.

"Won't say," said Peter, my student accomplice.

Irritated, the man returned to the patrol car, and sat there with a computer on his lap. In the one hand he held our ID cards; with the other he punched the keys on the computer. After a while he came back, tired but a tad triumphant.

"What is it we usually take you in for, Strindlund?"

"Animal rights activism," I said.

He nodded and asked:

"Why are you wearing protective goggles?"

"Won't say," Peter said.

"What were you planning to do with the ladder?"

"We don't have to answer," said Peter.

No more was said, and they went on their way. The sun was up, but it gave off no warmth as yet.

Helena was waiting at the car when we got there.

"Let's do it, then," she said.

It took some time. After a while an employee passed by – probably a member of the lab staff. She took a good look at us, made a 180, and then sped off. A few more precious minutes went by. In my own mind I had pretty much given up, and started preparing what I would say when the police came. But then the door finally went up. There was no time to lose now.

Peter took the lead up the stairs; I followed behind with a video camera. In my nervousness and excitement I held it upside-down.

A changing-room, a hallway, yet another hallway.

"There!" he pointed.

Peter ran with the beagle pup down the steps – still no guards! still no police! – and disappeared among the trees towards the car.

Helena and I had just climbed up on the entrance roof and taken out a cell-phone in order to call an on-the-spot press conference. At that point the first patrol car arrived. Then more came.

Lunch in jail was served on a tray in my cell. I turned on the television. A program on philosophical questions was being broadcast. Suddenly Peter Singer appeared on the screen, as had James Rachels on another day – the very two moral philosophers who had played such an important role for me when, some years earlier, I had discovered that the way we treat animals is a moral question.

The massive steel door was locked. We were being kept on the top floor of the police station, and I could receive no visitors. But now there were these voices from the television. A salutation? A fatherly blessing?

The interrogator started out by offering, not a cigarette, but a banana. He was a tall man in civilian dress. He had apparently moved to the area from Västerbotten, a province in the north.

"So, who gave you the right to break the law?" he asked.

Usually, in situations of this kind, I become apologetic and defensive; yet I heard myself answering:

"Must one justify one's actions, then, but not one's failure to act? Who has given us the right to let the dog remain there? Who has given us the right to let the vivisectors continue their experiments on her?"

The days went by. On the concrete wall hung a newspaper photo of Tina, as Peter had named the liberated beagle. I lay on the bed, read some thrillers, and chuckled at our amateurism. Twelve days later, they drove us by van to the courthouse. As the vehicle passed the square, I saw people with placards and banners outside the building. We parked in the basement. On the way up in the elevator, the two guards put me in handcuffs. The courtroom was filled to capacity.

The prosecutor, an elegant and restrained man, directed most of his questions at Helena. A good thing too: she was the oldest and most experienced. She sat dignified and straight in her chair.

"I have served," she explained, "on the ethical review board charged with overseeing experiments at the university. And I know it's of no help to the animals."

The plowshares movement is an international peace movement which carries out symbolic disarmament in an open and public manner. The method employed is quite simply to give weapons a pounding – with sledgehammers or ordinary house hammers. The movement takes its name from the prophecy in the Old Testament about a future in which the peoples of the world have beaten their swords into plowshares.

Getting to know a plowshares activist who had taken part in civil disobedience was what put me on the road from dissent to resistance. Hans, a tall and sturdy basketball player, had taken part in a group which had given a fighter jet a hammering. He had served time in prison and been ordered to pay damages, and thus had to contend with a persistent bill collector. Even so, he did not seem to lead a worse life than others. On the contrary. He appeared content with the commitment and lifestyle he had chosen. I too wanted to fight – against the oppression of animals. That so doing would involve risks simply seemed to be possible, normal, and undramatic.

All the same, as I sat in the rental car in summer 2002 and drove in among the buildings at a large egg-producing facility (the purpose being to rescue some more battery hens), I seemed to hear the reproaches of my entire upbringing – my mother's friends, the people in the neighborhood, the postman in his yellow lorry, the coaches on the boys' soccer team. The whole lot of them were saying: "You don't break into other people's property! And with a crowbar – have you gone mad?!! Stop at once!"

Rönnaug sat there in a jumpsuit with a shawl over her head. She looked calm.

It had just become light when we stopped at the first sanctuary and carefully carried out the cardboard boxes to the shed. A woman wearing pajamas and rubber boots emerged; it was she who would be taking care of the hens. A couple of weeks later we got a letter from her. "They have started to walk out on the grass and to scratch the earth," she wrote. "They seem to be doing well."

August 2001

When there were only a few days left before the next action, I told my parents about it. I said nothing about where it would be taking place or when.

My mother was sitting on the kitchen stool; she was upset.

"Don't do it!", she said. "It's good to rescue caged hens, but not to destroy property."

She sighed.

"And prison!"

Dad too was stiff and worried.

"Life is long," he said. "You'll be ordered to pay damages which will always be with you."

It was a fairly big slaughterhouse, yet it had no alarm installed. That was good. Once we had turned on the fluorescent lights, we walked around among the stainless-steel machines, the conveyor belts, and the hooks in the slaughtering hall. It was the first time I had been in a slaughterhouse. Everything was clean, and the ceiling loomed high above us.

"All right, then," someone said.

Ida-Lovisa put on her goggles and set about disabling a circle saw. I took a sledgehammer and started pounding on a steering lever – hesitantly at first, then with greater authority. In an adjoining room, there were butchers' knives hanging on the wall. Fredric set to work in there, hammer in hand; when I finished my first task, I started helping him with his. Soon broken-off knife-tips were scattered over the tile floor.

There were three of us.

We called ourselves: "Farewell, meat industry!"

After about an hour we felt we had finished. There was not much left to disarm. We set out raspberry sodapop and peanut-butter cookies for the employees, together with a letter in which we explained who we were, and assured them we were working *for* the pigs and the cows, and not *against* the employees.

I rang Johan, press spokesman for our support group, and asked him to send out a press release. Ida-Lovisa put in a call to a somewhat bewildered policeman, and asked that the results of our efforts be inspected.

"But do you work there?" he asked.

In a way we did. An important job needed doing, and the three of us had – to the best of our ability – done it.

While we were waiting for the police, we shoved open the door to a small cold-storage room. There the bodies of three slaughtered pigs were hanging low from the ceiling. The vibrations from the door prompted the bodies to twirl slightly on their axes.

Ida-Lovisa and Fredric were sentenced to community service. I had been convicted earlier, and so was given eight months in prison. Together the three of us were ordered to pay $US25,000 in damages – the value of the slaughterhouse equipment which could not be used any longer. We have no intention of paying.

A large part of the animal rights movement, in Sweden and other countries, may be likened to a dissatisfied but obedient child. She complains loudly, with placards and op-ed pieces, about how mom and dad – our responsible politicians – do not do what she wants. Yet she remains obedient, and follows the rules and laws laid down by her parents. Thus she leaves the power and responsibility for important decisions to them, her guardians.

Others confront the eternal Treblinka suffered by animals by throwing Molotov cocktails and spraypainting spiteful messages ("Scum!"). The rage is understandable. But in so doing, they exclude themselves from the civilized forms of intercourse which ordinary people wish to see prevail in society.

What we have seen too little of in our movement is what the scholar-activist Stellan Vinthagen calls "the amicable rebel." The amicable rebel behaves in a civilized manner, even as she takes her civic responsibility seriously and acts resolutely against injustice, rather than delegating this to others. Those who took part in the movement for the independence of India from British rule, and in the movement for civil rights for African Americans in the U.S., were such rebels.

It is not always easy to be creative and to come up with civil disobedience actions which bear on complex and abstract political issues. The question of animal rights, however, appears to be unusually well suited for those wishing to carry out challenging and thought-provoking actions. When animals are set free and slaughterhouse equipment is rendered useless, the iniquitous violence against animals is made visible, while our utopia – a society that takes hens and pigs seriously – is rendered clear and concrete, albeit on a small scale. When we act in this way, our means and our ends coincide.

The primary working methods of the animal rights movement, I believe, will always be leaflets, documentary films, advertising campaigns, and the dissemination of information generally. This is probably as it should be. Yet, if we were to devote just a small proportion of our time and energy – say a tenth – to pursuing the strategy of "the amicable rebel," I believe we could achieve substantial results. If consciousness-raising and the dissemination of information are connected to actions which actually realize and embody the goals described in our leaflets, our message will be more interesting and powerful. At the same time, civil disobedience actions are stronger when they take place not in the radical margins, but under the aegis of large, well-established popular movements.

This does not mean it would be easy to establish such resistance. The small movement to which I myself proudly belong, Räddningstjänsten (The Rescue Service), cannot be said to have succeeded in its purpose: to organize substantial nonviolent resistance for animals in Sweden. It may simply be that we are the wrong people for the task.

Winter 2003

The prison authorities let me sit at my little desk during the days and study. I put my book aside, lie down on the bed to rest, and look up at the postcards covering the wall – Sydney Harbor Bridge, the owl from Patty, Magritte's pipe. Then I turn on the radio and hear – my mother! Apparently she has phoned in to a debate program: what a good thing it is, she says, that we have young people who work for solidarity and justice.

Sunday is visiting day. Annika and I lie down on a mat in the visiting room, and pull a suitable if crumpled blanket over us. We nibble on a chocolate cake she has smuggled in.

The hours pass and the visit is soon over. We lie quiet. It is a late afternoon in January and dusk is falling, for the sun goes down early at this time of year in Sweden. The windowpane is dark. If I try, I can see the three bodies against this background – clearer than ever. How they twist and turn, as if they were still alive. The legs, the Achilles' tendon, and the backbone against the stainless steel and the plastic curtain – all in that strange green fluorescent light.

"How quickly time passes on these Sunday visits," Annika says, turning towards me.

There is no killing on weekends at the Skövde slaughterhouse. But operations resume tomorrow, on Monday.

13

Opening Cages, Opening Eyes

An Investigation and Open Rescue at an Egg Factory Farm

Miyun Park

The nervous chatter stopped abruptly as if a mute button had been pressed. The glow of downtown Washington, D.C., had long since been replaced by the light of an occasional bedroom lamp shining through a farmhouse window. The potholed city roads made way for smooth highways leading to rural Maryland. We were there.

We peered through the dark, hoping the absence of shadows and sound meant no one was inside – except for the 800,000 hens. We weren't even in one of the nine windowless buildings, yet we could smell the stench of thousands of pounds of excrement, disease, and death. As confident as we could be, we ran from our surveillance spot to the nearest shed. When we tried the door, it opened. So far, so good.

The literature on factory farming is extensive. Industry journals detail inhumane – yet standard – practices with cold detachment. Video and photographic evidence of abuse and neglect obtained by animal protectionists provide disturbing visuals. Yet, knowing about the horrors of animal agriculture and of the battery cage system in particular – indisputably one of the most abusive factory farming practices today – could not prepare me for what I would see, smell, and feel once inside a massive egg facility.

In March 2001, I had my first experience inside an egg factory farm. Accompanied by Suzanne McMillan, Lance Morosini, and Paul Shapiro, fellow investigators from Compassion Over Killing (COK) – a nonprofit animal advocacy organization based in Washington, D.C. – I walked into a farm in Cecilton, Maryland, about 100 miles northeast of the nation's capital. COK had received an anonymous tip-off that animal abuse was standard practice at the farm, owned by International Standard of Excellence–America (ISE), and when our written request to visit the facility was ignored, we decided to tour the premises ourselves.

Equipped with video and still photographic equipment, we made our way through a manure pit on the ground level, walking between three-foot-high mounds of excrement extending nearly the length of two football fields. The dim light from our headlamps prevented us from accidentally stepping on the decomposing corpses of hens who had escaped their cages only to fall into the pit and die surrounded by manure. Still-living birds wandered aimlessly around the pit, far from the automated waterers and feeders in the cages above. We slowly climbed stairs to where the hens were kept, trying to stave off the inevitability of witnessing first-hand the horrors of the battery cage system. This method of keeping hens has been banned in Switzerland and Austria and is being phased out across the entire European Union. Germany passed a five-year phase-out of battery cage use which will make them illegal by 2007, and the European Union has a ten-year phase-out to end in 2012. Yet battery cages are still used by U.S. egg factory farmers and there is no legislation in sight that will get rid of them.

Swarms of flies cut through the dust, dirt, and feathers floating in a fine white haze. Our eyes, watery and burning, caught sight of a gas mask hanging on the wall. Workers were offered a reprieve from the toxic ammonia-laced fumes and filth. The hens were not.

Splitting into two teams, we started down an aisle. Four rows of battery cages, wire cages each approximately the size of a filing drawer and typically holding eight birds, were stacked on either side of us, stretching for nearly 200 yards. In just one aisle, there were more than 10,000 egg-laying hens. Comprehending the enormity of the factory farm was impossible. How do you get a sense of 10,000 individual lives confined so intensively in just one aisle in a single building?

Yet such overcrowding is routine in modern animal agriculture, which maximizes profit by minimizing animal welfare. Factory farming seems to be premised on the long-since refuted view that animals are automatons, machines incapable of experiencing pleasure or pain. Accordingly, animal agribusiness treats the more than ten billion land animals raised and killed for food in the United States as nothing more than meat-, dairy-, and egg-production units whose treatment is inconsequential. No federal legislation exists to regulate even minimal animal welfare standards in animal agriculture.

The Humane Methods of Slaughter Act provides some guidelines during the slaughter process, yet excludes birds despite the fact that more than 90 percent of animals killed for human consumption are chickens. The federal Animal Welfare Act specifically states that animals raised for food are offered no protection. In fact, the lack of federal legislation protecting farmed animals allows factory farmers to legally abuse the animals we call food in ways that would warrant cruelty charges if perpetrated against those cats and dogs we call companions.

Consequently, life for egg-laying hens in battery cage facilities is harrowing. Hens stand on wire-mesh flooring so unlike the earth that their nails, which would normally wear down while scratching the ground, curl around the bars. Feather loss is common as hens rub against cages until many appear to have been plucked, their bodies raw with sores. They cannot roost at night, dust-bathe to clean themselves, feel sunlight, breathe fresh air, build a nest, raise their young, or even freely stretch their wings, let alone exercise or roam. The frustration and pressures of battery cage existence elevate levels of aggression. Factory farmers attempt to reduce the impact of stress-induced fighting by searing off the tips of chicks' beaks with a hot blade, mutilations performed without anesthesia and often never healing, making eating and drinking difficult. The animals live in these horrific conditions without rest until their egg production wanes and they are either starved to induce another molt (thereby jarring their damaged bodies through another laying cycle) or they are killed and their bodies rendered, making way for a new shedful of hens.

The dozens of hours of video footage and hundreds of photographs we amassed from ISE's Cecilton factory farm – a typical battery cage facility – document the inevitable costs of raising the most animals with the least time, expense, and effort. We were surrounded by emaciated, featherless hens covered with excrement from those in higher cages. Countless hens were immobilized in the wires of the battery cages, caught by their wings, legs, feet, and necks, some alive, others dead. We helped those we came across, but we know with absolute certainty that hundreds, if not thousands, are struggling to free themselves, and to reach food and water, at this very moment. In some of the cages we saw, hens were left to live with the decomposing bodies of their former cage-mates. We removed the rotting corpses, many of which had been left in cages for so long that they were flattened to an inch.

We filmed hens riddled with cysts, prolapses, infections, and bloody sores – some so weak they could barely lift their heads or drink the water we offered them. Indeed, disease is common on factory farms. Many animals succumb to physiological pressures from living in unsanitary conditions, so overcrowded that movement is severely limited, muscles atrophy, and immune systems are weakened. The compromised bodies of layer hens often fall victim to illness, and as veterinary care costs more than the bird is worth to the producer, they suffer without treatment.

While virtually every aspect of the commercial egg industry is inhumane, the intensive overcrowding of hens in the battery cage system may well be the most abusive. An egg-laying hen requires 290 square inches of space to flap her wings, yet each bird is allotted an average of 52 square inches – smaller than a single sheet of paper – in which she eats, sleeps, lays eggs, drinks, and defecates. Pressure from animal advocates in recent years prompted a handful of food industry giants to institute guidelines or recommendations on cage-space minimums, but the increased space allowance still doesn't allow for freedom of movement. McDonald's, Burger King, and Wendy's voluntary reforms provide hens with 72 to 75 square inches per bird, prohibit forced molting through starvation, and discourage debeaking. On the other hand, the guidelines adopted in 2002 by United Egg Producers, the industry trade association, mandate only 67 square inches per bird with a five-year phase-in period and make no recommendations against forced molting or debeaking.

While landmark in their acknowledgment that the conditions in which egg-laying hens must live are, in fact, worthy of consideration, the food industry reforms still fall short. They do not address the inherent cruelties of intensive confinement that deny animals nearly every habit and instinct natural to them.

At the ISE farm, we witnessed the toll that such severe overcrowding takes on the animals. When just one bird makes a simple movement we perform without forethought – turning around, stretching our arms, taking a single step – nearly every animal in the cage must reposition herself. To reach the single waterer in a cage or the feed trough just outside the bars, hens must maneuver around the others – both alive and dead. The animals commonly stand on each other's backs and wings for lack of space. It's difficult if not impossible to imagine living in these conditions, yet the egg industry confines approximately 300 million hens in battery cage facilities at any given time.

Physically exhausted, mentally taxed, and emotionally drained, we left the ISE farm that first time in the early hours of the morning. The two-hour trip back to D.C. was silent as we each tried to process all we had seen. COK's first investigation had begun.

Our strategy was modeled after the experiences of Australia's Action Animal Rescue Team led by Patty Mark. First we obtained evidence of animal abuse, then we urged Cecil County sheriff's department to investigate violations of Maryland's animal anti-cruelty statute, and asked for prosecution by the state's attorney. After our written requests to the authorities were met with silence or refusals to take action, we provided aid to sick and injured hens, freed as many animals as we could place in safe and caring homes, and accepted full responsibility for the rescue.

The strength of this strategy lies in its openness. Rescues of animals from places of institutionalized cruelty are normally clandestine, with advocates striving to conceal their identity. Patty Mark and her Australian colleagues not only conducted their investigations and rescues unmasked, they began each film sequence by identifying themselves on camera. And after animals were removed, they notified the authorities of the rescues themselves.

Public response had proven positive in Australia, as media attention focused on *why* the activists were forced to act, rather than on the advocates themselves. That is, the news coverage stayed on the animals, the inhumane conditions and misery they must endure, and the reluctance by factory farmers to denounce the indisputable evidence of gross neglect and abuse they inflict. The paper trail to local prosecutors, police, and the factory farm further substantiated that the advocates were left with no options but to rescue the animals, as no one else would. Recognizing the undue influence that animal agribusiness has on U.S. policy, we were unsure how the strategy would be received. Nevertheless, we moved forward, making several night-time visits over two months.

One month into the investigation, we sent footage representative of typical conditions of both the facility and the animals to veterinarians and an animal agribusiness researcher for their expert opinions. Without exception, the reports overwhelmingly disapproved of the intensive confinement system, and vet statements also commented on the poor health of the hens, attributed to battery cage life.

During this time, we met with journalists, offering media outlets the exclusive rights to the findings of our investigation and impending open rescue. After *The Washington Post* agreed to take the story, we prepared for press conferences in Washington and Annapolis, Maryland's capital. In addition, we began reviewing hours of video footage and producing the documentary *Hope for the Hopeless: An Investigation and Rescue at a Battery Egg Facility*, to be released at the Washington news briefing. Anonymous homes were secured for the hens we would free from the factory farm. Everything was in place for our final visit to the ISE farm.

On May 23, 2001, we again made our way to the sheds. But this time, we had eight transport carriers with us. Once inside, we again videotaped ourselves aiding animals. Knowing this would be our last night with the hens at the ISE farm, we dreaded the moment we would have to choose whom we would take with us and whom we would leave behind. How do you choose eight lives out of 800,000? How do you leave behind nearly one million animals to continue living in sheer misery? It was getting late and we were running out of time. We couldn't help but feel we were sentencing to death each hen we didn't take. Taking some comfort in the knowledge that future generations of egg-laying hens may be spared if we could encourage enough consumers to withdraw their financial support from the industry, we selected hens we came to call Jane, Rose, Lynn, Petra, Harriet, Christina, Eve, and Jackie.

We found Lynn and Eve in a manure pit, heads heavy with rock-hard clumps of feces caked on their combs. Rose was immobilized between two cages, her face wedged in a narrow opening in the bars. Petra had such severe feather-loss her body was completely bare except for a few tufts of feathers on her head. Harriet suffered from an infection so inflamed her mucous-filled eye was swollen to ten times its normal size. The cyst on Christina's head flapped over her right eye. Jackie's prolapsed uterus hung outside her body. And Jane was found with a wing pinned in the wires of her cage. She had struggled so violently to free herself that her wing had dislocated, her tendons had torn, and gangrene was eating away at her body.

One by one, we rescued the hens from their cages. While filming our final shot, we heard the metal door – at the end of the very aisle we occupied – beginning to open. Shutting off our headlamps, we fumbled our way through the pitch black as far down the aisle as we could, moving away from whoever was outside. Once the sound of the opening door stopped masking our footsteps, we threw ourselves on the ground. We realized the sheer magnitude of the facility would be our savior: the sweep of the flashlight dissolved into blackness before it could reach us. After what felt like hours but was likely only moments, it was again dark and the door squealed shut. We made our way outside, heavy with our equipment and the eight animals.

The sun had begun to rise by the time we got to my Washington apartment. A veterinarian was scheduled to arrive at 11:00 a.m. to examine the hens. We took them out of their carriers and placed them in a makeshift pen, a space forty times larger than what they had ever experienced. For the first thirty minutes, all eight huddled in a corner, not daring to move. Then, one by one, they began exploring, eating, and drinking. Some basked in the sun shining through the window, their battered bodies stretched on the floor, warming in sunlight they had never felt before. A few ducked under a sheet covering shelves and roosted. And, for the first time in their lives, two of the hens sat with the eggs they had just laid.

After their vet exams, we tried to wash away the months of filth and the misery of their old lives. Once bathed, the hens were visibly more energetic and curious. Finally, it was time to take them to their new homes.

As scheduled, *The Washington Post* exclusive on the investigation and open rescue ran on June 6, 2001, the morning we released our documentary, *Hope for the Hopeless*. National media picked up the story, and the horrors of battery cages could be read over the Associated Press and United Press International wires. ISE stated it wasn't "certain" our footage came from its facility, and the police and state's attorney's office claimed they had never received our letters. We weren't arrested for breaking and entering, trespass, or theft. And the hens were free.

Hope for the Hopeless was shown to thousands, and COK received a deluge of letters and emails from individuals pledging to never again support animal agribusiness. Our first investigation and open rescue were more effective in drawing attention to the plight of egg-laying hens than we had dared hope. In fact, the July 2001 issue of the trade journal *Egg Industry* published an article on COK's investigation, calling it "extremely damaging to the whole industry." And the October 2002 issue wrote about us, too: "A classic example of David trying to bring down Goliath is seen with the efforts of Compassion Over Killing. . . . The organization may be short on staff but has effectively gotten the public's attention through the media."

COK investigations of animal agribusinesses continue, and our investigators have rescued more abused farmed animals. Our third exposé into battery cage facilities in just eighteen months resulted in an exclusive that ran in *The New York Times* on December 4, 2002, and more than seventy media outlets around the world picked up the story. As of this writing, COK has completed its eleventh undercover investigation.

Factory farming and its inherent cruelty must be abolished. Until legislation catches up with consumers, we each have the power to end our complicity in the suffering, mutilations, and deaths of increasing numbers of animals each year. With every bite we take, we can choose compassion over killing by choosing the vegetarian option. And we can take to heart that the animals would thank us if they could.

14

Living and Working in Defense of Animals

Matt Ball

Since the publication of *Animal Liberation* in 1975 and the founding of People for the Ethical Treatment of Animals (PETA) in 1980 – to mention just two seminal events – animal rights and welfare organizations have spent hundreds of millions of dollars, with volunteers working endless hours on many campaigns, trying to improve the treatment of animals in North America and Europe. PETA alone has over 750,000 members and supporters, and an eight-figure annual budget.

By some measures, these efforts have yielded remarkable results. Fast-food chains McDonald's and Burger King have, under pressure from animal advocates, announced steps to improve animal welfare standards. The European Union has gone much further, having passed laws that will eventually limit the use of sow stalls to four weeks, and will phase out battery cages and veal stalls entirely. National media have given animal welfare issues unprecedented coverage. The treatment of animals has become a matter of wide public debate, while animal advocates and the term "animal rights" have become fixtures in Western culture.

The State of Animals Today

And yet despite all this, the number of animals exploited and killed has skyrocketed during the past quarter-century. In the United States alone, the number of mammals and birds slaughtered for food each year has nearly tripled since 1975 – about ten billion. That's over a million every hour

– far more deaths than those from all other forms of animal exploitation combined.

At the same time, the treatment of nearly all farmed animals is worse today than ever before. Hidden away from the public eye, farmed animals endure an excruciating existence. Even Jim Mason and Mary Finelli's gripping description and Miyun Park's harrowing tale in this volume can't convey the true horror of what goes on in factory farms. Photographs and videos come closer – layer hens with open sores, covered with feces, sharing their tiny cage with the decomposing corpses of fellow birds; pigs sodomized with metal poles, beaten with bricks, skinned while still conscious; steers, pigs, and birds desperately struggling on the slaughterhouse floor after their throats are cut. But even videotapes can't communicate the smell, the noise, the desperation, and, most of all, the fact that each of these animals – and billions more unseen by any camera or any caring eye – continues to suffer like this, every minute of every day.

If we are concerned with the suffering of all animals, not just those in labs or fur farms or shelters, these facts demand we reconsider our focus. As *The Economist* pointed out in its cover story on August 19, 1995, animal advocates in the United States have focused on fur and medical research, while advocates in Britain and much of Europe have focused on animals killed for food. As a result, not only is vegetarianism more widespread in some countries in Europe, farmed animals there are also afforded much greater protection.

The Choice for Activists

Given the unfathomable horrors of factory farms, the overwhelming numbers of animals involved, and the fact that every individual in society makes choices every day that can perpetuate the suffering or help end it, it is hard to imagine a compelling argument as to why the animal liberation movement should focus on anything else. When viewed in this light, the truism "When you choose to do one thing, you are choosing not to do another" is more poignant than ever. Of course, it would be nice if we could address all areas of exploitation and suffering at once. But as individuals and as a movement, our time and resources are extremely limited, especially in comparison to the industries we seek to change or abolish.

Having participated in a variety of animal advocacy measures – from protests, public fasts, and civil disobedience to presentations, tables, and letter writing – I have seen no more effective way of working in defense of animals than promoting vegetarianism through positive outreach. Exposing people to the hidden atrocities of factory farms and providing them with details of the vegetarian alternative not only removes support from inherently cruel industries, but also helps change society's fundamental view of animals. Even without including the abstract idea of "societal change," the numbers are compelling. On average, each person in the United States eats dozens of factory-farmed mammals and birds a year – thousands over the course of a lifetime! Convincing just one person to change his or her diet can spare more animals than have been saved by most of the high-profile campaigns against animal research, fur, and circuses.

Purity vs Progress

It is clear that, if we want to maximize the good we accomplish for the animals, expanding the boycott of factory farms through the promotion of vegetarianism is the best use of our limited time and resources. How, then, should we proceed?

First, we must truly commit to the difficult process of outreach. For a caring individual who is aware of what goes on in factory farms and industrial slaughterhouses, outrage and anger are common – almost inevitable. The difficulty is in finding a constructive outlet for this anger. With meat-eating firmly entrenched in our culture, factory farms hidden, and people's inconsistent attitudes towards animals (those we love, those we consume) tolerated, promoting vegetarianism can be taxing on activists. Frustrated by an inability to make large changes in society – to organize armies to storm the factory farms or pass laws abolishing them – and feeling that incremental, one-person-at-a-time change is too slow, it is tempting to give up on outreach-based advocacy altogether. It is easier to simply turn to what we can control: ourselves – seeking out and avoiding everything with a connection to animal exploitation (whey, honey, sugar, film, pesticides, manure, medicine, etc.).

The desire to avoid complicity with any aspect of animal exploitation is understandable, but this inward turn can actually hinder efforts to prevent animal suffering. In a society where the cruelty inherent in eating a chicken's leg is not recognized, few people will be able to identify with an activist who shuns a veggie burger because it is cooked on the same grill as beef burgers. Unnecessary suffering and cruelty-free options are no longer the issue if we equate eating oysters and shrimp with consuming veal calves and pigs. Most

people are going to have a hard time giving vegetarianism serious consideration when they perceive us to be concerned about insects' rights, sugar
processed with bone char, microingredients such as diglycerides, and so
forth.

If we are to work effectively on behalf of animals, we must encourage
everyone to boycott cruelty. We can't do this by fostering the impression
that "It's too hard to be a strict vegetarian – animal products are in everything." We can't act as if we're following a religion, with adherence to a
certain dogma the sole issue. We can't preach that harvesting honey is a
holocaust. We can't imply that every farm – from the largest megafactory to
the smallest free-range organic farm – is equally cruel.

Cleveland Amory, founder of the Fund for Animals and author of numerous books, once observed that people have an infinite capacity to rationalize
– especially when it comes to something they want to eat. In today's society,
the vast majority of people are actively trying to ignore the implications of
eating animals. So they are happy to change the subject away from their
complicity in cruelty, and instead bicker over the number of field mice killed
during crop harvests, whether milk is a "deadly poison," the plight of third
world farmers, Eskimos needing to fish, and so on. Anything that keeps the
focus off factory farms is more than welcome to people who are resistant
to separating themselves from friends and associating with a judgmental,
self-righteous vegan crowd.

Our example and actions should be clearly and directly motivated by a
reasoned, practical opposition to cruelty. Rather than simply avoiding something because it isn't "vegan," we should always have a straightforward
explanation for the consequences of our actions. It is better to allow for
uncertainty – for example, telling people that we have decided to give shrimp
the benefit of the doubt even though we don't know whether they are
capable of the subjective experience of suffering – than to simply recite
"shrimp isn't vegan."

Beyond Sound Bites, Beyond Veganism

This is the goal Jack Norris and I had when we founded Vegan Outreach
(originally Animal Liberation Action) in 1993: to help animals by providing
as many people as possible with thorough and honest information on the
suffering behind the standard American diet, as well as on the vegan alternative. We have found that the most effective way of getting past people's

barriers is to avoid making ourselves or our particular diet the issue. Rather, we work to keep the focus on undeniable yet avoidable cruelty. Most individuals have a cursory awareness of vegetarianism and animal rights, so to bring about real change in people's attitudes and actions, it is necessary to move beyond sound bites to distributing compelling and accurate information. Providing others with printed information – such as our publications *Why Vegan?* and *Try Vegetarian!* – allows them to digest the ideas and implications in their own time, without becoming defensive and feeling the need to justify themselves and their past actions.

Convincing others to change is not easy, regardless of the tactics employed. The public is constantly bombarded with "documented facts" from all sides (the benefits of the meat-heavy Atkins diet, the advantages of modern farms, etc.). People won't be swayed by what we say simply because we are personally convinced our arguments are correct. We need to be appropriately wary of blindly accepting and repeating claims that seem to support our position, while not simply dismissing those that don't.

Yet having truth on our side is of no use if nothing changes. Not only must we stick to materials that our target audience will find convincing, we also need to reach out to them in such a way that they will consider the ideas. Depending on the audience, this might mean avoiding the words "vegan" or "animal rights," handing out a Christian vegetarian booklet such as *Honoring God's Creation*, or displaying happy animal images instead of graphic pictures of cruelty. We should do whatever it takes to increase the likelihood that our audience will reflect on the information.

Positive, constructive outreach requires that we check our egos at the door. Everyone is unique; to maximize the amount of good accomplished, we need to understand people's motivations and goals. A good way of doing this is to read Dale Carnegie's *How To Win Friends and Influence People*, as well as Robert B. Cialdini's *Influence: Science and Practice*.

We also need to be realistic in our goals. Given that U.S. per capita animal consumption reached an all-time high in the last millennium (*ERS Agricultural Outlook*, January–February 2002), it is counterproductive to expect everyone to convert to veganism. Rather, we need people to recognize the cruelties of modern agriculture and take steps – however tentative or gradual – to end their support of factory farms. If they buy meat from an organic farmer down the road, or continue to eat fish, or don't avoid all dairy, we should neither vilify them nor spend our limited time and resources trying to "fully convert" them. Instead, we need to support and encourage everyone in the steps they take, while continuing to reach out to others.

We don't have a duty to *speak* for the animals; we have an obligation to be *heard* for the animals. Millions more need to be reached.

A History of Success

Our experience at Vegan Outreach shows it is possible to be honest while still being efficient and effective. With a budget that is a tiny fraction of the major animal groups, the members of Vegan Outreach distributed over half a million copies of our literature in 2003 – over three million in the past decade. It only takes a moment to stock a display rack, or an hour to leaflet at a local school, yet this can have a profound and lasting impact. Each day we receive feedback from individuals who have stopped eating animals and become advocates after receiving a copy of one of our publications. Convincing people to change their diets by providing them with a *Why Vegan?* or *Try Vegetarian!* is very cost-effective – it only costs a fraction of a penny to spare an animal a torturous life and horrible death.

Being vegan is a powerful response to the tragedy of industrial animal agriculture, but it is only the first step. At its core, the compelling concept behind being a vegan is working to end suffering. We must always remember that the bottom line is suffering, not veganism. Compared to one's effect as a pure – but isolated and impotent – vegan, supporting and participating in positive, constructive outreach will have an impact that is orders of magnitude greater.

Further References

veganoutreach.org.
"Tips for Promoting Veganism," *veganoutreach.org/advocacy/*.
"Meet Your Meat," videotape available from Vegan Outreach, *veganoutreach.org/catalog/*.

15

Effective Advocacy

Stealing from the Corporate Playbook

Bruce Friedrich

I've been active in human rights and animals rights struggles since 1982. Something I've noticed is that those of us who are trying to make the world kinder often become so overwhelmed by the enormity of suffering we're trying to prevent that we act without stopping to ponder our effectiveness. All of us owe it to the animals to force ourselves to pause for a moment to think strategically about the most effective ways to lessen animal suffering and to bring about animal liberation – not to agonize endlessly, of course, but to make a concerted effort to stop, step back and really think once in a while about how to be as effective as possible. As hard and as smart as people on Wall Street work to sell stocks, and advertisers work to sell the latest SUV, we need to be working that hard in our cause.

First, we must make activism a priority in our lives. Many of us are so encumbered by personal needs and commitments that it can be hard to carve out time to be the animals' voice. But, if we going to apply the "Golden Rule" to suffering animals, it is essential that we do find that time. It isn't that hard to pass out leaflets for a few hours a week at some busy area in our town, to keep our church or temple literature area stocked with vegetarian information, and/or to monitor our local newspaper and take the time to send in a few lines about animal issues.

Similar to making our activism a priority is making our activism more effective. One of the most common ways in which we go wrong is that, even if we are working extremely hard, few of us are working to become more effective.

And that's what this essay will focus on – some tips for making our activism more effective – first by discussing some basic "human nature" tips for advocating for animals, and then by discussing a few specific things that we often do wrong. I want to stress that all of my observations are based on my many years of doing things in what I now believe to be the wrong way. My goal with this essay is to help others learn from my mistakes.

Selling Animal Rights: Creating a Movement Others Want to Join

Dale Carnegie's *How to Win Friends and Influence People* (1990), which could easily be retitled *The Basics of Human Nature*, offers some very useful tips for effective advocacy. Some of the information is a bit outdated, but mostly it's a book about having integrity in our interactions with others.

Carnegie Principle 1: Be Respectful

The first principle essential to our advocacy is to always be respectful, even if the other person seems not to warrant it. When someone says to you, "But don't plants feel pain?" or "But animals eat other animals" or whatever else, you may have a strong urge to reply in a way that shows the other person (and those around you) just how absurd the question is. But as hard as it may be to believe, they didn't say that in order to be stupid, and if you respond as though they are stupid, that will not help you to convince them that you're right; they'll feel too defensive to listen to you.

Of course, some people do say things just to be stupid and offensive, but I've found that, even if many of these people are not instantly reachable, if we refuse to lower ourselves to their level and come up with a response that allows them to save a bit of face, we can create a conversation. If someone is clearly antagonistic, you can even say, "I'm not sure if you really feel that way, but I really do feel strongly about these things and I have to tell you that your demeanor and the things you're saying strike me as kind of disrespectful." That gives them a moment to embrace their better nature. I'm consistently amazed at how someone can behave so nastily at the beginning of a conversation, and yet come around by the end. But they won't come around if we act defensively, condescendingly, or in some other untoward manner in return. Everyone wants to be liked. Everyone thinks of themselves as a decent person. If we grant people the opportunity to be heard, even if they seem not to deserve it, we can be far more effective in our interactions with them, and certainly everyone witnessing the conversation will come away with a good impression of us, and thus animal rights activists in general, in a way that they won't if we allow ourselves to sink to the level of the antagonist.

Carnegie Principle 2: Be a People Person

The second Carnegie principle I want to focus on is almost cliché. Likeable people, people who listen to other people, are more effective advocates, and self-absorbed misanthropes are very unlikely to convince anyone to consider something new, let alone change their behavior. It is crucially important in our interactions with people that we strive to be likeable human beings. Fortunately, it's an easy thing to do, if we're aware of our limitations and really make the effort. All you have to do is take a real interest in others. Malcolm Gladwell in *The Tipping Point* (2002) analyzes the people who turn fads into trends, and the thing that is true of all of them is that they are friendly, optimistic, and interested in others and the world around them. They express a genuine interest in others, and that is returned by the people they're talking with. Dale Carnegie courses are focused almost completely on this aspect of the Carnegie principles. It is a simple fact that how you say something is generally even more important than what you say. The most effective advocates are the ones who make their case with a smile and genuine interest in others.

Carnegie Principle 3: Dress for Success

The third principle I take from Carnegie is that we should look presentable, so that our appearance is not the issue. The question we have to be continually asking ourselves is what would we want if we were the chicken on the factory farm, drugged and bred so that we can't even stand, or the pig in the slaughterhouse, drowning in scalding hot water. Is our desire to reject society's norms really as important as advocating effectively for the animals?

For years in the early nineties, I had a full beard and shoulder-length hair, wore only clothes I figured no one else would want, and refused to bathe more than once per week. I guarantee that since I began sporting a conservative appearance, I've changed many more people to veganism.

Right or wrong, it is a reality in our society that some people will write us off by the way we look. Few, if any, will write you off because you look conservative, but many, many people will write you off if you don't. If our goal is to be as effective as we possibly can be on behalf of the animals, it is absolutely essential that we put our fashion desire second to the animal's desire to have us be effective advocates.

Carnegie Principle 4: Be Optimistic

The last Carnegie principle I want to address here is that we be optimistic, upbeat, and positive. In the face of so much suffering, optimism is not reasonable, I know. It's reasonable to think of the horrific suffering of animals and to be constantly down about it. But again, we have to ask what will be most effective in helping animals, and depression or anger, however reasonable, will not be as effective as a more good-natured attitude. Everyone wants to be a part of the winning team. Think of the people whom you find most appealing. They are the ones who are smiling, who are upbeat, laughing out loud, and having a good time. We have to strive to be like that.

And in fact, there is a lot to be optimistic about; for just one thing, each person you convince to go vegetarian will save 3,000 animals from the miseries of factory farms and thousands more fish from the horrors of trawling ships. That really is worth celebrating. That you are trying to make the world better for animals, and that so many people are, is also something to celebrate.

So those are a few of the things that we should try to do as activists. I would now like to briefly address four things that I think many of us do as activists that we should reconsider.

Four Things We Do Wrong: Four Strategies for Animal Liberation

1. Personal Purity v. Effective Advocacy

The number one thing that we do wrong – and I am speaking from many years of doing exactly these sorts of things – is that we place personal purity ahead of being as effective as possible in advocacy for the animals. We lose sight of the fact that veganism is about minimizing our support for suffering, not eliminating it.

Everything we consume involves use of resources that displace and harm animals. Every non-organic thing we eat involves pesticide use that kills birds. Organic foods use animal fertilizer and that supports factory farming. Bike tires and the rubber on even vegan shoes include some small amount of animal ingredient. No matter what, you're somewhat complicit in the abuse of animals. It is simply not true to think that vegans are pure, or that if you root out every obvious animal ingredient, you are not causing any suffering. Veganism is about trying to reduce our support for suffering, but it also has to be about advocating for veganism as effectively as possible, because that will save far more animals than even being vegan yourself. It's basic math. Your adopting a vegan diet will save about 100 animals every single year from horrible suffering. Your converting one more person will save another 100 animals. And so on. But the reverse is also true: If you do something that prevents another person from adopting a vegan diet, you will hurt animals by putting up a barrier where you might have built a bridge.

We all know that the number one reason why people don't go vegan is because they don't think it's convenient enough, and we all know people whose reason for not going vegan is that they can't give up cheese or ice cream. Instead of making it easier for them, we often make it more difficult. Instead of encouraging them to stop eating everything except cheese or ice cream, we preach to them about dairy cow oppression, all but guaranteeing that they're not going to make any progress at all.

Similarly, some of us focus on veganism as an ingredient list, rather than on decreasing suffering. But veganism isn't a dogma. Veganism is about reducing suffering. So if you're at a holiday party with meat-eaters, and you're talking about how you can't eat the bread because you don't know if it has some tiny amount of whey in it, or you're at a restaurant and there's a veggie burger on the menu and you give the server the third degree about the ingredients, I would suggest that you've just made veganism seem difficult, placing barriers to the others at the table who might have otherwise adopted the diet. And that does significantly more harm to animals than you would have by consuming that tiny bit of whatever.

In the same vein, some vegans talk about whether sugar or beer bottle labels or whatever else is "really vegan." If we start telling people that we can't order a bottle of beer because of the glue on the label or we can't eat bread because of some tiny amount of natural butter flavor, we're both wrong – we're pretending that what we're eating didn't cause any suffering – and we're making it look to non-vegans like vegans can't eat or consume *anything!*

If you're worried about what you're going to eat in a restaurant, call ahead and figure out what meets your standards, and then order it with gusto. If you're worried about what you're going to eat at the office party or family gathering, get on the catering committee, bring along some great vegan food to eat or share, and make sure that grandma knows what you do and don't eat. But please never say that being vegetarian or vegan is this big chore, and never make it seem like a chore when you're eating out or at other public functions.

In the same vein, I went years refusing to eat with meat-eaters. I can certainly understand that if you have one of those personalities where if you sit down at a table and there are corpses in front of you, you know you're just going to become the most unpleasant person on the face of the planet, then removing yourself from that situation may be doing what's best for the animals. But please be aware that many meat-eaters read your non-attendance as self-righteousness, and that is not what we want people thinking about vegetarians. Also, it makes vegetarianism seem difficult – you can't even go to parties, can't go out to eat, whatever. Who wants to adopt a diet like that? Finally, if you're at an event with a bunch of meat-eaters and you're not eating any, people are likely to ask you about it, especially if they know you're a vegetarian. This is your perfect chance to get a bit of information into their heads. You need to do it in an upbeat way, and you need to gauge the situation so that you don't alienate everyone, but you should be able to present the basic moral argument, and you'll have been asked for it. If you're going to a function where bringing food is appropriate, please be sure to bring some good vegan food along.

2. We Apologize or Minimalize

Another thing we do wrong is that we apologize or minimalize. We represent our vegetarianism as, for example, a personal decision. I have heard it said that it's acceptable if someone asks why you are a vegetarian to say that it's a "personal decision and I don't want to talk about it." Well, how does that help animals? And why would anyone, hearing that answer, ever come to realize that this is a moral concern? They won't; they'll think it's just your own personal quirk. In fact, vegetarianism is not a personal decision any more than beating a child is a personal decision. In both cases there's another being with feelings and interests who is being harmed.

Now, tactically speaking, there are going to be situations where having an in-depth discussion of slaughterhouse and factory farm practices will hurt animals more than it helps them. Especially at a table full of meat-eaters, in most instances people aren't going to want to listen to a conversation about chicken abuse no matter how well you can articulate it. Most likely, the eight meat-eaters at the table are going to leave thinking: "What a killjoy. I want no part of that . . ." So at a dinner table, when it seems like not the time to have the discussion and somebody asks, "Why are you a vegetarian?," or whatever, do not say "It's a personal decision" or "I don't want to talk about it," but also don't launch into a thirty-minute explanation. Instead, you can say something that takes thirty seconds. You can say something like, "I just really hate to support the awful cruelty that happens on factory farms and I feel so much better as a vegetarian, but I've found that having this discussion with a table full of meat-eaters is often unpleasant for everyone and I don't want to dominate the entire conversation. But I do have some literature and I have some videos and I'd love to talk with you about this privately later." Boom. You've raised the moral issue *and* you come across as the hero of the table. Everyone who, when that person asked, "Why are you a vegetarian?," hunkered down to listen to your long moral screed will be delighted that all you did was raise the ethical issue but not dwell on it. And you will have raised it, which is crucially important.

Never ever say that vegetarianism is a personal decision; never say it's just about your health; and never say it's just about the environment. You can raise those issues, in addition, of course. But if you have only one issue to talk about, make it about the animals. We're not going to get to animal liberation if everybody's adopting a vegetarian diet for self-interested reasons, however important and useful those arguments may be.

3. We Don't Prepare or Practice

Another thing we do wrong is that we often don't prepare and we don't practice what it is that we want to say. We've all heard arguments like "What about abortion?" and "Don't plants feel pain?" a million times, so there is no excuse for any of us to "wing it" in responding to these questions. The animals require that we study the frequently asked questions and come up with good responses. We should know what we consider to be the most powerful responses and we should be ready to answer in a friendly and engaging manner.

4. We Neglect the Little Things

Finally, we have to remember the little things like wearing buttons and T-shirts and putting bumper stickers on our cars. And when we go out, we should always have a button or a T-shirt on and we should be carrying some literature. I can't stress enough how important it is that we do these little things, in addition to the bigger things.

These are just a few hugely effective but simple things for you that can make a massive difference for animals; you convert one person to veganism and you've saved thousands of animals. People see the bumper sticker or they ask you about your "Ask me why I'm vegan" T-shirt and, boom, you've got a leaflet and you can hand it to them and talk to them about that issue. Every time a new person thinks about animal rights or thinks, "Hey, that guy or that woman in the car, they look pretty normal and they advocate animal rights," that's a victory for animals.

Closing: We Are Winning

Animal activism in the developed world has never been stronger or more effective. We have more and more people going into the streets showing what happens on factory farms and in slaughterhouses, taking seriously the need not just to be active, but to be as effective and focused as possible. The internet, of course, is making our advocacy efforts more and more effective. People for the Ethical Treatment of Animals (PETA) now gives out its vegetarian starter kit (which includes a free DVD titled *Meet Your Meat*) to more than 200,000 individuals each year via online orders.

Up until five years ago, there wasn't anyone studying cognitive function in chickens or fish, and now we're learning that chickens do better on some cognitive tests than dogs and cats and that fish have memories and use tools, which, up until very recently, anthropologists were telling us was what distinguished human beings from any other animals. And we know that, according to Donald Broom, Ph.D., a Professor of Animal Welfare at Cambridge University's Veterinary School, pigs have cognitive functioning abilities similar to that of a three-year-old human child (*Cambridge Daily News*, March 29, 2002). Many wonderful things are happening in animal advocacy that we'd not have thought possible just a few years ago.

Let me close by saying that although some of what I'm suggesting is counterintuitive (for example, if someone is nasty to you, it makes sense to be nasty back) these suggestions represent what I believe is necessary to have the most positive effect for animal rights. Thus, they are what animals would ask of us if they could.

In the U.S., given the quantity of other animals' suffering, the extent to which they are suffering, and the stupid and gluttonous reasons they are intentionally made to suffer so horribly, I am convinced that animal liberation is the moral imperative of our time and that our focus should be on ending the suffering as quickly and effectively as possible.

The eighteenth century saw the beginnings of our democratic system. The nineteenth century abolished slavery in the developed world. The twentieth century abolished child labor, criminalized child abuse, and gave women the vote and blacks wider rights. If we all do as much as we can, the twenty-first century will be the century of animal rights.

References

Carnegie, Dale (1990) *How to Win Friends and Influence People*, New York: Pocket Books.

Gladwell, Malcolm (2002) *The Tipping Point: How Little Things Can Make a Big Difference*, New York: Back Bay Books.

16

Moving the Media

From Foes, or Indifferent Strangers, to Friends

Karen Dawn

There are few homes without television sets, and many people spend more time listening to the voices on those sets than they do listening to friends or family members. The media shape the way our society views all issues – including the appropriate treatment of members of other species. They are incomparably powerful, and the animals need powerful friends. By letting the media know that animal stories please viewers and readers, we encourage more of those stories and make the media our friends.

Feedback as Force

I decided to create an organized effort to encourage media feedback after seeing the impact of feedback on a TV station's presentation of a visiting circus.

There is a weekly show airing on the New York 24-hour news station NY1 on which a representative from *Parenting* magazine recommends fun things to do with the kids on the weekend.

One Saturday morning I watched with dismay as *Parenting*'s Shelley Goldberg announced that Ringling Brothers was in town; she recommended we take our children to the circus. Those of us in the animal rights movement are familiar with the cruelty of the circus. We have seen the footage of trainers beating screaming baby elephants with bullhooks. We know that if the animals were really trained with positive reinforcement, trainers would be in the circus rings waving bags of treats rather than sharp metal sticks.

On the weekend, NY1 plays about three hours of programming in a continuous loop – the same shows air over and over. So as I watched the segment I realized that it would replay many times over the weekend for hundreds of thousands more New Yorkers. At first I felt angry and helpless. Then I remembered that a friend of mine who hosted a show on NY1 had told me that the station manager read every single email that came in. So, for a start, I sent an email to the station praising the station's overall work but expressing surprise that it was giving the circus a free promotion rather than covering it as a controversial news story.

Then I sent a note to activist Susan Roghair, who had an extensive email alert list (which I had never seen focus on media). I gave her the station's contact information and asked if she might let her New York subscribers know that the segment had aired and would do so many more times. Within minutes, as one of her New York subscribers, I received an email telling me about the circus story and asking me to politely complain to the station.

Quite a few people must have written or called, because I watched NY1 for the rest of the weekend and for the first time in my memory of that station, the *Parenting* segment was taken out of the weekend loop.

That alone would have been inspiring, but it got better.

Pat Kiernan, the anchor who hosts *Parenting* on the weekend, has a segment on weekday mornings called *In the Papers*. He looks through the four New York dailies, reads the headlines, and then chooses one or two stories from within the paper on which to focus. The Wednesday following the *Parenting* circus promotion, Kiernan chose a story from deep within one of the tabloids. He held up the paper and showed us an article revealing that Ringling Brothers had been charged with violations of the Animal Welfare Act. The very anchor who no doubt had been privy to the feedback on the circus promotion made sure, four days later, that NY1 morning viewers were aware of a somewhat buried story on circus cruelty.

The following Saturday, on the *Parenting* segment, Shelley Goldberg recommended we take our kids to the puppet show. She looked at the camera and said, "We want all of our viewers to know that no animals were harmed during the making of the puppet show."

It was clear that feedback on a segment had not only caused a change in the programming over the weekend it appeared, but had also made two on-air personalities keenly aware that the circus is not a light topic but rather a controversial issue that their viewers care about.

And so I was inspired to launch DawnWatch. Its aim is to generate responses to as many stories as possible, but, just as importantly, to teach activists about the power they have, as readers and viewers, to affect the output of their local media outlets. Though the example above shows the impact of negative feedback (or constructive criticism), DawnWatch concentrates largely on positive feedback; it can be just as effective. When I send out DawnWatch alerts I prefer to focus on animal-friendly stories in order to decrease the likelihood that the media will receive any vicious email, unlikely to aid in our effort to make friends.

The following is an example of the wonderful effect of positive feedback.

Slaughterhouse Five TV

There is a saying in television news, "If it bleeds, it leads." If only that were true for the animals. Sadly, however, most news stations refuse to air any graphic footage of animal suffering. They say people find it too disturbing and will just change the channel and watch the station's competitors.

In May 2000, a brave reporter named Duane Pohlman managed to persuade the NBC affiliate in Seattle, Channel Five, to air horrifying slaughterhouse footage. He put together a shocking report using undercover footage taken by an employee at the IBP plant. The Humane Farming Association had provided the hidden camera.

Pohlman told viewers: "By law, cows are supposed to be unconscious when they're slaughtered. But workers say some of these animals are very much aware of what's happening as they're butchered. . . . Every day, animals pass down the belt alive." The segment included interviews with workers who described cows blinking, mooing, and kicking as they are cut up. Viewers saw the footage.

The story was available online on the station's website, so those in Seattle who missed it, as well as activists all over the country, could see it. Media-sensitive activists urged people to thank the station for airing the story. A follow-up was aired, with the anchors noting that the station had received hundreds of emails after the first story. And the follow-up received more positive feedback. In total, the station aired over a dozen stories on the IBP slaughterhouse violations, all showing some of that graphic footage. Paul McCartney has said, "If slaughterhouses had glass walls, everyone would be vegetarian." I suspect a lot of people became vegetarian in Seattle that month.

Recently, I spoke with Pohlman, now an Emmy-winning reporter, about the effect of the audience feedback on the coverage. He told me that the station had been reluctant to air even the first segment. With regard to the follow-ups, he said, "Without the overwhelming email response it would have been highly unlikely that the station would have committed to the number of follow-ups it did. It gave the station footing, and me coverage, to continue. I could say 'look at this – people are moved about this, even people across the country. It is incumbent on us to follow up.' "

ABC producer Judy Muller has given us similar information on the power of feedback. In her acceptance speech, upon receiving a Genesis Award in 2002 for a series of animal friendly stories on ABC *World News Tonight*, she said, "The good news is that the audience response to these stories is wonderful, and that means that these stories will keep coming. In the hard-hearted world of network news that's the bottom line." I asked Pohlman for his take on that quote – I asked if advertising dollars, and the ratings that bring them in, are not really the bottom line. He reminded me that feedback lets the station know which stories are affecting the ratings by affecting the viewers. So feedback is very much part of that bottom line.

Love–Hate Relationships

Is any press good press? People for the Ethical Treatment of Animals (PETA – the largest American animal rights organization) says yes – or at least yes for now, at this stage of our movement, as its campaigns that lack shock value are largely ignored. Other groups say no. Compassion Over Killing has managed, by going into intensive farms, rescuing animals, and then sharing their photographs and footage with the media, to get some great coverage. That coverage has included large sympathetic stories in *The New York Times* and *Baltimore Sun* and one on the cover of the *Washington Post* style section. The stories mentioned the suffering of the animals being rescued and portrayed the activists sympathetically. Similarly, attorney Steve Wise, who campaigns for legal rights for great apes, has received serious coverage of his work. His no-nonsense approach has inspired prom-inent stories in *The New York Times*, the Sunday *Boston Globe*, on the cover of the *Washington Post* style section and on the front page of *The Wall Street Journal*.

But that sprinkling of coverage does not compare with the flood that follows each one of PETA's most "offensive" campaigns. PETA's tactic is to put out something outrageous that excites the press. Journalists attack PETA, then their papers will generally publish PETA's letters of response in which animal suffering is detailed. PETA spokespersons are asked onto talk shows to defend the campaign. The hosts of the shows attack the campaign, and PETA representatives talk about animal suffering in grue-some detail. They plug the relevant website, usually resulting in thousands of hits to a site where people can view graphic photos or video of the abuse in question. Some viewers may be left, after the coverage, with the impression that animal rights activists are wacky or misanthropic, but they also learn that animals suffer egregious abuse in our society to an extent they had not known. Thus PETA relies on the notion that the press can be kind to animals without being kind to representatives of the animal rights movement.

Got MADD Mothers?

One of PETA's most notorious campaigns is "Got Beer?" – a take-off of the national "Got Milk" campaign (launched by the California Milk Processor Board). Aimed at college students, it suggests that drinking beer would be better for their health than drinking milk. The group's *milksucks.com* website details the possible health risks of dairy consumption and the suffering of cows in the dairy industry.

When PETA launched the campaign, the U.S. media responded with full force. PETA spokespersons appeared on many talk shows. Most major newspapers picked up the story. "PETA says drink beer, not milk, to pre-vent cruelty to cows" was the lead story on the front page of the March 13, 2000, *Washington Times*. The article said little about animal suffering – it focused largely on the ire of Mothers Against Drink Driving (MADD). But in response to the front-page story, the paper published a full page of reader responses to the front-page story, heading the section "a six-pack of letters." All but one discussed either animal suffering or the health risks of cows' milk consumption by humans. So thanks to the back-up response from animal advocates, PETA's campaign resulted in a full page in the *Washington Times* devoted to the downside of milk.

Here we see a common PETA strategy. Since newspapers rarely publish letters on topics not currently in the news, PETA uses outrageous methods to get animal cruelty issues into the news so that they can be discussed on the editorial pages and in the letters to the editor section. A 1994 study of 296 newspapers, conducted by the National Conference of Editorial Writers, reported, "Large- and medium-sized papers that have conducted surveys

consider the letters to the editor column to be 'one of the best-read items.'"
No newspaper reported that the letters column was below average in
readership. Animal advocates must learn to take advantage of that well-
read section by whatever means possible.

Taboo Topics on the Editorial Page

Another potentially offensive PETA campaign is "Holocaust on Your Plate."
At the website *masskilling.com*, and in a photo display that travels from city
to city across the world, PETA has juxtaposed pictures from the Holocaust
with pictures of nonhumans in similar circumstances. We see men stacked
in wooden beds, and chickens stacked in battery cages. We see humans in
cattle cars and cattle in cattle cars. The campaign caused an outcry from the
Anti-Defamation League. It has engendered angry articles about PETA's
misanthropy in many papers. But it also inspired an op-ed by Stephen R.
Dujack, grandson of the Nobel Prize-winning Jewish vegetarian author Isaac
Bashevis Singer, in which he wrote, "Like the victims of the holocaust,
animals are rounded up, trucked hundreds of miles to the kill floor and
slaughtered. Comparisons to the Holocaust are not only appropriate but
inescapable." Bringing to major newspapers an argument readers of J. M.
Coetzee might know from *The Lives of Animals* (1999) (since published in
Elizabeth Costello, 2003) he continued:

> To those who defend the modern-day holocaust on animals by saying that
> animals are slaughtered for food and give us sustenance, I ask: If the victims
> of the Holocaust had been eaten, would that have justified the abuse and
> murder? Did the fact that lampshades, soaps and other "useful" products were
> made from their bodies excuse the Holocaust? No. Pain is pain.

That commentary piece, first published under the heading "Animals
Suffer a Perpetual 'Holocaust'" in the *Los Angeles Times* (April 21, 2003),
went on to be published in many major papers throughout the United States.
Passionate debates about the piece followed on the letters to the editor
pages. *The Los Angeles Times*, for example, printed seven letters on the issue,
some supportive and some critical. Who would have predicted that some
of the largest papers in the country would be hosting discussions on whether
or not our society's treatment of nonhumans can justly be compared to
the Holocaust? Though many have been offended by the campaign, it has

succeeded, with the help of reader feedback, in one of its aims: It has made those who read the editorial pages think, in the context of another mass killing based on prejudice, about the way we treat animals.

"Direct Action" – Shifting the Media Focus

Some campaigns, or actions, even more controversial than PETA's, get much press. With acts of violence against property, and even threats against humans, the militant fringe of the animal rights movement has been making front-page news. Such press would not traditionally be called "good." Generally, it is not sympathetic to our movement and it does not detail animal suffering. But the focus of the press can be shifted, and feedback can play a part in that shift.

In August 2003, the *San Francisco Chronicle* ran a front-page story headed, "Animal-rights vandals hit chef's home, shop; Activists call French-style foie gras cruel to birds." We read that the "animal rights vandals" had done about $50,000 worth of damage to a restaurant soon to be opened that would specialize in foie gras. Also, they had splashed acid on the owner's car, spray-painted his house, and sent him threatening letters along with a videotape they had taken of his family at home. The focus of the story was on the suffering of the human victim rather than on that of the animals. But readers did learn that foie gras has become controversial because of the way it is produced. They learned that "ducks or geese are force-fed grain through tubes that are put down the birds' throats" and that PETA considers it to be "one of the most egregiously cruel food products out there."

Such information in a front-page story was a boon, and the flurry of letters on the issue kept the topic hot. The paper printed nine letters about foie gras over the next ten days, five taking the animal rights position. One spelled out the way controversial campaigns can work: "The animal-rights groups are wrong to vandalize or threaten chefs but, unfortunately, it seems to have worked – front page of *The Chronicle*. It is too bad that the simple truth about factory farms isn't enough to get a front-page story. . . ."

Fortunately that statement isn't quite accurate. In that year, 2003, the simple truth about factory farming did make the front page of some American newspapers. In April the *Los Angeles Times* ran a front page story covering factory farming and slaughterhouse issues headed, "Killing Them Softly." In June, Cleveland's *The Plain Dealer* did a front-page series on egg farms. And New Jersey's *Bergen Record* ran a front-page story in July about humane farming standards. But indeed, while stories featuring violent actions, or sabotage, generally make the front page, articles that focus on industrial cruelty to animals rarely do. The important point is that no matter how the front-page story is achieved, we can keep it alive, and often give it an animal-friendly slant, with letters to the editor.

The *Chronicle* ran a follow-up story announcing that some chefs in the city were rethinking their menus due to the violence over foie gras. Then the ABC affiliate in San Francisco covered the story on the nightly news, making no attempt to hide that the attacks inspired the story. Reporter Dan Noyes said, "Few people have seen how foie gras is made, and that's the motive behind this recent spree of vandalism." Viewers were warned that they would see disturbing images. They saw ducks with metal tubing forced deep into their guts, kicking their legs in struggle as food was pumped into their stomachs. They saw ducks looking near death, unable to even hold up their heads let alone stand, after the feeding. Again, viewer feedback was important. When I asked Noyes about audience response to the story, he told me that the station received over 300 emails, and that "The contact from the public reinforces that we are reporting stories our audience finds important." The station aired five follow-up pieces, all including graphic footage.

In September 2004, Governor Arnold Schwarzenegger signed a bill into law that prohibits force-feeding birds for the purpose of enlarging their livers, and bans the sale of all food produced that way. It will take effect throughout California, the fifth largest economy in the world, in 2012. Senate President pro-tem John Burton, from the San Francisco area, introduced the bill just a few months after the "animal rights vandals" story made the front page of his city's main paper, and the graphic foie gras footage aired on San Francisco television. Burton, who, years ago, had shown some interest in a foie gras ban, was given an excuse to pursue that goal when the issue became hot on the San Francisco editorial pages, and his constituents were exposed to the horrifying footage on their evening news. The massive reader and viewer response to the initial coverage helped make the issue into a big recurring story, paving the way for a groundbreaking law.

More Explosive Topics

Most animal rights activists oppose actions that endanger any animal life, human or nonhuman. But bombs always make the front page. What should we do when those fighting for our cause set them? In August and September 2003, animal rights activists detonated bombs in the middle of the night at two companies in the San Francisco area that have ties to the notorious animal testing laboratory Huntingdon Life Sciences. The ensuing front-page articles inadvertently reminded people that animal testing is an issue serious enough to be violently opposed by some. But, as one would expect, the articles did not describe the suffering of animals used at the lab. I had hoped that letters to the editor might, and was disappointed to see a letter sent to the *San Francisco Chronicle*, from a leading animal rights activist, that condemned the bombings but did not take the opportunity to condemn vivisection.

The press is powerful, vital, and elusive. Though we may wish to distance ourselves from violent acts, we cannot waste the opportunity to tell the public what motivates those who carry out such acts. Some may feel that trading on the event compromises their moral objection to the use of violence, but the animals, being slaughtered by the billions, cannot afford our moral piety or posturing. We can argue against the use of violence, but as their self-designated representatives, we must argue for the animals whenever we are given the opportunity.

Influencing the Coverage, Not the Campaigns

Groups working to give our movement a respectable mainstream image often criticize those who get publicity by engaging in outrageous stunts or violent acts. Discussing tactics can never hurt, but attacking other groups can. Before we attack each other's work, it is always good to ask, "What if I am wrong?" We can never know all of the repercussions of a campaign – some might be far more positive than we would expect. If we are convinced that somebody else's campaign is hurtful to the cause and we do what we can to undermine it, we might be hurting the animals. Would it not be better to use the publicity generated in order to help the animals?

Though we see some positive shifts, overall, the animals, still viewed as things to be used or eaten, could not be doing all that much worse than they are. Their suffering is not the result of our movement being disliked – they suffer just as much from the media's benign neglect, which assures the continuation of the status quo. The media are incomparably influential, but not so hard to influence; the animals need their attention. For their sake, we must take every opportunity, born of sympathy or antagonism to our movement, to gently and persuasively exert our influence. We must work to change the focus and slant of initially negative stories, and, with feedback, keep animal-friendly stories alive.

References

Coetzee, J. M. (1999) *The Lives of Animals*, Princeton: Princeton University Press.
—— (2003) *Elizabeth Costello*, New York: Viking Penguin.

17

The CEO as Animal Activist: John Mackey and Whole Foods

John Mackey, Karen Dawn, and Lauren Ornelas

John Mackey founded Whole Foods Market in 1980, when he was 27, beginning with a single store in Austin, Texas. In 1985, when the company had grown to the point at which it had 600 employees, Mackey took some of them on a series of weekend retreats. Together, they worked out a "Declaration of Interdependence" that made all the employees stakeholders in the company, and set the company's guiding principles – sell quality food, please customers, satisfy employees, create wealth, respect the environment, and conduct a responsible business. In line with those principles, Whole Foods gives a minimum of 5 percent of its annual profits to nonprofit organizations, puts solar panels on the roofs of some of its stores, and pays employees wages while they do community service.

Whole Foods now has nearly 33,000 employees, 163 stores, an annual turnover of $4 billion, and is poised to enter *Fortune* magazine's list of America's 500 biggest businesses. Mackey is currently Chief Executive Officer and Chairman of the Board of Whole Foods. Clearly, he has shown that running an ethical business is no barrier to making good profits. Some say that by getting big he has "sold out." In response, he asks why it is supposed to be bad to take the idea of an ethically responsible way of doing business into the mainstream.

The CEO as Animal Activist

On May 3, 2004, John Mackey was interviewed by Karen Dawn, host of *Watchdog*, a radio program on animal issues that airs on KPFK-FM, the Los Angeles affiliate of the nonprofit Pacifica Radio Foundation. Also on this segment of the program was Lauren Ornelas, of Viva! USA. The following transcript includes only the part of the discussion that centered on John Mackey and Whole Foods.

Karen Dawn: John Mackey, I have heard a little about your story, and want to find out more. I heard you went vegetarian some years ago and more recently vegan. Will you tell us something about your personal journey – what inspired both of those changes?

John Mackey: I've been a vegetarian for about thirty years, since I was around 21, when I moved into a vegetarian co-op here in Austin. I wasn't vegetarian at the time I moved into the co-op, I think to meet women who I thought would be interesting. But living in the co-op, I started eating vegetarian. I drifted into that direction, not out of any real ethical commitment, but just because I thought it would be a healthier diet and trendy, cool, neat.

Then I read Peter Singer's book *Animal Liberation* a few years ago and that really was kind of a wake-up call for me. But I didn't fully wake up until early last summer when I re-read it, and a dozen other books such as *Dominion* by Matthew Scully and other books about veganism, animal welfare, and animal rights. I realized I just couldn't continue to eat animal products – I just wanted to be a vegan. I felt it aligned with my ethical beliefs and so I made the decision and it's been a really good decision for me personally.

KD: So before that, you had been vegetarian. You'd done it because it was healthy and kind of cool?

JM: And I would've said, out of compassion for animals, but I didn't have much conviction about it. And when it came to dairy products and eggs, I just looked the other way. I think I didn't want to be fully conscious of it, even though as CEO of Whole Foods I was much more aware than the ordinary person about farms and the conditions animals lived under. It's tempting to think: "I'm doing enough and this is good enough" – a bit of denial, I think. But this summer I just moved out of the denial space and aligned my values with my actions a hundred percent.

KD: Now, I think our other guest, Lauren Ornelas of Viva! USA had something to do with that. I'm always amused when McDonald's or some other corporation, after months or years of pressure, decides to make some little animal welfare change, and they deny that those horrible animal rights activists had anything to do with it. But I know you're open to giving animal rights activists some credit for some of the changes happening at Whole Foods.

JM: Absolutely, Lauren was a catalyst for my own "conversion" because in our annual meeting in Santa Monica in 2003 in March, Lauren and PETA [People for the Ethical Treatment of Animals] were there and they were picketing us about our duck standards. After the meeting was over Lauren came up and we continued our dialogue and exchanged business cards. We struck up an email correspondence and Lauren challenged a lot of my beliefs. And she didn't quite say it in these words but it boiled down to "Well, gee, Mr Mackey, you're well intentioned but I don't think you're very well informed about the actual conditions of the animals." She challenged me to learn more. And I took that challenge on, and I did learn more, and the information persuaded me to change my mind.

KD: Lauren, I'm going to ask you a little bit about that campaign. I know John Mackey isn't your average corporate guy but still I think we can learn something about tactics from what happened here so I'd like to get, from your perspective, how the campaign against Whole Foods began and what it led to.

Lauren Ornelas: When we at Viva! USA started our campaign in regard to duck meat, we did an investigation of factory farms across the country and found that the conditions in which these animals lived were appalling. They lived in filthy crowded sheds, they had the tips of their bills cut off, and they were denied access to water in which to immerse themselves – which ducks need in order to maintain their health. We contacted grocery stores across the country, sending them video footage and our full report as well as our other campaign materials about how these ducks are treated. Whole Foods was actually selling duck meat from two of the factory farms we had investigated. At one of their shareholders' meetings, in March 2001, they stated they were going to stop buying from Maple Leaf Farms, a corporation that kills Peking ducks for meat. But Whole Foods continued to sell duck meat from the other factory farm we had investigated, Granada

Farms. So we continued our campaign efforts with activists around the country, calling, emailing, and leafleting outside Whole Foods stores. We faxed Whole Foods petitions, letting them know that their customers did care about the treatment of animals. Trader Joe's stopped carrying all duck meat because of our efforts, but while Whole Foods made some changes as well, we really felt it wasn't enough. I'm from Texas. I grew up with Whole Foods, always loved Whole Foods, and really felt that they knew better. I knew that they would not approve of these kinds of practices.

KD: That's interesting. You're giving them the benefit of the doubt rather than assuming that they are the enemy. Of course, that's easier to do with Whole Foods than with other stores. Still, I like the idea that you're assuming that if they knew the facts, they wouldn't do it.

LO: That's what everybody believed of Whole Foods. People hold Whole Foods to a higher standard. When people go to Whole Foods, they expect a lot; we expected a lot as well. We expected that they wouldn't sell animals who were raised in such horrible conditions. And in the end we were right. We were right in the sense that they were willing to take a look at things and listen to us seriously. Now they are re-vamping how all of the animals whose products are sold at Whole Foods are going to be raised and killed.

KD: So you had this meeting, and then you entered into email exchanges with John Mackey. Did you send him books? Is that how he ended up reading those books?

LO: No, John really did it on his own in a sense. He and I had a dialogue regarding the farm they were buying from. (As well as the idea some people had that we were really striving to get Whole Foods to become an all-vegan grocery store. But we were just trying to talk about the farm.) Then John emailed me out of the blue after several months and told me that he had done all this reading on his own, and that he had made a decision to go vegan. I basically fell out of my chair but was very happy to hear it!

KD: I want to hear about the wonderful new animal-compassionate standards. John, can you tell us a little bit about them?

JM: Well, we started with ducks. So far we've had three meetings. We had our final meeting on ducks a few weeks ago. We had several animal rights and animal welfare groups participating with us: Viva!, PETA, Animal Welfare Institute, Animal Rights International – those four organizations have been to all three of the meetings. Our final duck standards have now been determined. The next phase is to develop a contract with our producers and get them to agree to produce to those standards. If they don't, we'll probably stop doing business with them. But we also need to learn more about more humane methods of animal farming. That knowledge has been lost. Factory farms have taken over. There are not that many small producers any longer who really remember how to produce by non-factory farm methods. There is some humane production going on in other countries, such as in Europe, and we want to gather that knowledge together and pass it on to farmers in America.

KD: You say you've got the duck standards in place. What are those standards?

JM: They've got to be able to get out – not in cages. They've got to be able to get outside, to get in the sunlight and fresh air. They need to have water that they can swim in. They cannot be mutilated. They can't have their bills trimmed. We don't want them to have their toes cut off. Those are some of the common mutilations that happen to poultry animals.

KD: I'm glad you mentioned that they are common mutilations –

JM: They're very common. We want to make sure that they can forage. They need to be able to hunt for food, even though you might make the food easily accessible to them. Part of their natural duck behavior is to want to search for food so you don't want them to be just in the dirt. You want them to be able to have ground cover so that they can explore and hunt for food. In the case of the breeding ducks, you want to let them establish nests that are comfortable and safe and –

KD: I'm getting the feeling that these standards are probably going to be similar for the other animals too. You're talking about basic animal needs here – freedom, searching for food –

JM: Yes. There are two types of goals in animal production in the United States. Goal A is to minimize the pain and suffering of the animals and to maximize their health and wellbeing while they're alive. Goal B is to maximize productivity and efficiency. What's happened in America is that Goal A is completely irrelevant. Now, all that matters is Goal B – maximizing productivity, lowering costs, and producing the animal as cheaply as possible. So animal welfare has become irrelevant except insofar as it impacts on productivity. And really what we aim to do at Whole Foods with ducks and all the other animals is to put Goal A first. Minimize the pain and suffering. Maximize health, wellness, and wellbeing. Animal welfare. Animal happiness. Put *that* as the most important goal and make productivity – well, you can't dismiss that as irrelevant, but it needs to be subordinate to Goal A. That's what our standards are all going to be about. The duck standards are the first standards we've upgraded to that level. Lauren, what are some of the other things I've left out that you think are relevant to the standards I've described?

LO: I think you've got the basic ones. The standards are created to make sure each duck is getting what he or she needs. When we were creating the standards we were discussing specifying the depth of water that the ducks needed. But instead of specifying the depth of water, the standard is about making sure all the birds are going to be able to swim.

It's amazing. It's incredible to sit in one of these meetings and hear John talk about these animal welfare issues, and about making sure that the ducks are not mutilated and that they have access to the outdoors. Then there is the nest box, which I think some people might have overlooked, and how Muscovy ducks need some form of privacy when they lay. We're looking at all these animals, the breeders and the meat ducks, and each have different needs. Each species has different needs too. So some of the things Muscovy ducks need might be different from what the Peking ducks need.

KD: It's funny because you're talking about the particular needs of particular species, but I think that everybody knows that ducks need to swim. I wonder if people realize that for ducks raised for food, to be able to swim is unusual.

JM: Unusual? It's nonexistent.

KD: And I guess you're not going to be selling any foie gras at Whole Foods?

JM: We already don't sell foie gras at Whole Foods. We haven't sold foie gras for many years.

KD: So we have an interesting situation here today. We're talking about improving standards for the humane care of animals used for food, whereas none of my guests actually eat animal products. I've received an email about a campaign aimed at persuading Whole Foods to stop selling animal products altogether, asking me to write and ask them to do that. Talking with you, John Mackey, I'm fairly sure that you'd be delighted if there wasn't any demand at all for animal products. That would fit your personal vision. So I thought I'd ask you to comment on the Whole Foods choice to go more humane rather than, say, to go vegan.

JM: Whole Foods exists to meet the needs and desires of its customers, and not to pursue the personal philosophies of the founder/CEO, whatever those personal philosophies might be. Those cannot be what business is based upon. We have to center our business around our customers. Our research has indicated that approximately 10 percent of our customers are vegetarians and 3 percent of our customers are vegans. If our customers didn't want to purchase animal products, then we wouldn't sell them, but the fact of the matter is that if we tried to do that, we would very quickly go out of business. Well, actually, that's not quite true, because before that happened I'd be fired as CEO and replaced with somebody who was willing to put the customers' needs first. And if Whole Foods continued to pursue that direction, then it would fail as a business, because, if anything, the world is kind of moving the other direction right now. If you look at the whole low-carb movement and the Atkins diet, we're selling more animal products right now as a percentage of sales than we've sold in many years. There are more animal products being consumed because we have an obesity epidemic in America. Ironically, I don't know too many vegans who are fat. I'm certainly not, I know Lauren is not, but in America right now, people believe that eating animals is the way to get slim.

KD: Isn't that a shame.

John, you say, "Well, we have to look after our customers, and if they didn't want animal products, we wouldn't sell them." The fur industry could say the same thing, so I wonder about that reasoning.

But I also wonder if, tactically, getting people who are compassionate into your store where they are exposed to other products besides the meat that they might be planning to buy might be, well, a tactic. And I also was wondering what Lauren thinks about the idea of stores that have humane food, that don't necessarily sell only vegan food.

LO: We can't underestimate the fact when we go grocery shopping with people who consume animals, they may see a veggie burger and may see a meat burger, and choose maybe one day to try the veggie burger. And so it's a way of conversion, and to provide the options. Our job is to show people how great-tasting vegan food can be, and to inform them about the suffering of the animals. Hopefully when they go into places like Whole Foods, they may seek humane choices.

Since this interview, Whole Foods Market has launched the Animal Compassion Foundation, intended to "help meat producers create environments and conditions to support every animal's natural physical needs, natural behaviors, and well-being." To get the foundation started, Whole Foods made January 25, 2005 "Global 5% day" and donated 5 percent of all sales in all stores on that day – a total of $550,000 – to the Animal Compassion Foundation.

18

Ten Points for Activists

Henry Spira and Peter Singer

Introductory Note by Peter Singer

Henry Spira was probably the most effective American animal activist during the crucial years, in the last quarter of the twentieth century, when the modern animal movement began. His remarkable 1976 campaign against experiments that involved mutilating cats at New York's American Museum of Natural History was the first ever to succeed in stopping a series of experiments on animals. That led to him tackling cosmetic testing, with a full-page advertisement in *The New York Times* that asked a single question: "How many rabbits does Revlon blind for beauty's sake?" In the middle of the page was a picture of a white rabbit, with sticking plaster over both eyes. Within a year, Revlon agreed to donate $750,000 to Rockefeller University for a three-year research project aimed at finding non-animal alternatives to testing cosmetics on the eyes of rabbits. That led to other leading cosmetic companies doing the same, and eventually, to the virtual elimination of the testing of cosmetics on animals.

Spira was born in Belgium in 1927 and came to the United States in 1940 with his family, who were refugees from the Nazis. His first career, as a merchant seaman, came to an abrupt halt when, as a result of his involvement in political activities on the left, he was thrown off the ships as a "security risk" during the McCarthy era. Ironically, however, he was then drafted into the U.S. Army, where he served in Berlin in 1953–4. In the same decade he marched for civil rights for African Americans in the South, and visited Cuba soon after Castro came to power, to report on the revolution for *The Militant*, a left-wing newspaper. Later, when he was allowed to return to his career as a seaman, he

This chapter draws on Peter Singer, *Ethics into Action: Henry Spira and the Animal Rights Movement*, Lanham, MD: Rowman and Littlefield, 1998. Some quotations from Spira are taken from "Singer Speaks with Spira," *Animal Liberation* (Australia), January–March 1989.

became a member of a group that sought to reform the National Maritime Union, an organization that lined the pockets of its leaders while selling out its members. The group's leader was severely beaten by thugs armed with iron pipes, and suffered brain injuries. The attack was widely believed to have been instigated by the union leadership. Eventually the corrupt union boss was forced to quit. But by then, Spira, who gained a degree by studying part-time at Brooklyn College, had become a teacher in a New York high school, teaching English literature to kids from the ghetto.

Until he was 45 years old, Spira didn't think much about animals. Then he read my essay "Animal Liberation," published in *The New York Review of Books* in April 1973. That led him to think that, if he was on the side of the weak and exploited, animals were at the bottom of the heap. He began to study the issue, drawing on his political experience to think how he could campaign effectively for animals.

Spira contributed an essay called "Fighting to Win" to the first edition of this book. Sadly, he died in 1998, and so was unable to revise it for this new edition. But before he died, he wrote up some notes entitled "Ten Points for Activists." Around this time, I recorded several interviews with him about his campaigns, and the lessons he had learned from them, for a book that was to become *Ethics into Action: Henry Spira and the Animal Rights Movement*. What follows is Spira's "Ten Points for Activists," amplified and elaborated upon by my own notes from the interviews.

Ten Points for Activists

1. *Try to understand the public's current thinking and where it could be encouraged to go tomorrow. Above all, keep in touch with reality.*

Too many activists mix only with other activists and imagine that everyone else thinks as they do. They then start to believe in their own propaganda and lose their feel for what the average person in the street might think. Then they no longer know what is achievable and what is a fantasy that has grown out of their own intense conviction of the need for change. It's a lesson Spira learned from his time with the Socialist Workers Party, where members were so used to the Marxist-Trotskyist framework they all accepted that they lost contact with the real world in which they were trying to make a revolution. As Spira put it: "You need to have a crap-detector rotating all the time."

Spira seized every opportunity to talk to people outside the animal movement. He would start up a conversation with the person sitting next to him on a bus or train, mention an issue he was concerned about, and listen carefully to their responses. How did they react? Could they feel themselves in the place of the victim? Were they outraged? What in particular did they focus on?

2. *Select a target on the basis of vulnerabilities to public opinion, the intensity of suffering, and the opportunities for change.*

Target selection was essential to the success of Spira's campaigns. Spira knew that he could run an effective campaign when he felt sure that, as he said about a New York state law allowing laboratories to take dogs and cats from shelters: "It just defies common sense that the average guy in the street would say, 'Hey, that's a real neat thing to do.'"

Another way of knowing that you have a good target is that, by merely stating the issue, you put your adversary on the defensive. In the case of the American Museum of Natural History campaign, Spira could ask the public: "Do you want your tax monies spent to mutilate cats in order to observe the sexual performance of crippled felines?" The Museum was then immediately in a very awkward position. Cosmetic testing made another good target, because you only had to ask: "Is another shampoo worth blinding rabbits?" to put Revlon officials on the defensive.

Keeping in touch with reality is a prerequisite for selecting the right target: if you don't know what the public currently think, you won't know what they will find acceptable and what will revolt them.

The other elements of point 2 suggest a balance between the good that the campaign can do, and its likelihood of success. When Spira selected the cat experiments at the American Museum of Natural History as his first target, he knew that he would directly affect, at best, about sixty cats a year – a tiny number compared to many other possible targets. But the opportunity for change was great because of the nature of the experiments themselves, and the location and vulnerability of the institution carrying them out. In 1976 it was vital for the animal movement to have a victory, no matter how small, to encourage its own supporters to believe in the possibility of change, and to gain some credibility with the wider world. With that victory gained, Spira began to give more weight, in choosing his targets, to the amount of suffering involved. Even so, that was never the dominant consideration. When you multiply x and y, no matter how large x may be, if y is zero the product will also be zero. Similarly, no target should be chosen without considering both the amount of suffering and the opportunities for change.

3. Set goals that are achievable. Bring about meaningful change
     one step at a time. Raising awareness is not enough.

When Spira first took an interest in opposing animal experimentation, the anti-vivisection movement had no goal other than the abolition of vivisection, and no strategy for achieving this goal other than "raising awareness" – that is, mailing out literature filled with pictures and descriptions of the horrors of vivisection. This was the strategy of a movement that talked mainly to itself. It had no idea how to get hold of the levers of change, or even where those levers might be located. It seemed unaware of its own image as a bunch of ineffective cranks, and did not know how to make vivisection an issue that would be picked up by the media. Spira's background in the civil rights movement told him that this was not the way to succeed:

> One of the first things that I learned in earlier movements was that nothing is ever an all-or-nothing issue. It's not a one-day process, it's a long process. You need to see the world – including individuals and institutions – as not being static but in constant change, with change occurring one step at a time. It's incremental. It's almost like organic development. You might say, for instance, that a couple of blacks going into a lunch counter and demanding to be seated really doesn't make a hell of a lot of difference because most of them don't even have the money to buy anything at a lunch counter. But it did make a difference, it was a first step. Once you take that first step and you have that same first step in a number of places, you integrate a number of lunch counters, you set a whole pattern, and it's one of the steps that would generate the least amount of resistance. It's something that's winnable, but it encourages the black struggle and it clearly leads to the next step and the next step. I think that no movement has ever won on the basis of all or none.

Spira was not opposed to raising awareness. When other issues were quiet, he ran advertising campaigns against eating meat. But raising awareness was never his main weapon in a campaign. Awareness follows a successful campaign, and a successful campaign will have achievable goals. While some activists think that accepting less than, say, the total abolition of vivisection is a form of compromise that reduces their chances of a more complete victory, Spira's view was: "I want to abolish the use of animals as much as anybody else, but I say, let's do what we can do today and then do more tomorrow." That is why he was willing to support moves to replace the

LD50 – then a standard measure of toxicity, which required researchers to find the lethal dose of the substance being tested for 50 percent of a sample of animals. To find that quantity, all of the animals had to be severely poisoned, until half of them had died. The replacement acceptable to scientists and regulators was the approximate lethal dose test, which still used animals, but far fewer of them.

Spira looked for targets that were not only winnable in themselves, but would also have expanding ripple effects. Will success in one campaign be a stepping stone towards still bigger targets and more significant victories? His campaign against Revlon was an example: because it made research into alternatives respectable, its most important effects have been felt beyond Revlon and even beyond the cosmetics industry as a whole.

> 4. *Establish credible sources of information and documentation.*
> *Never assume anything. Never deceive the media or the public.*
> *Maintain credibility, don't exaggerate or hype the issue.*

Before starting any new campaign, Spira spent several months gathering information. Information obtained under Freedom of Information legislation was an important source, but a lot of information is already out there, in the public domain. Experimenters report their experiments in scientific journals that are available in major libraries, and valuable information about corporations may also be a matter of public record. Spira was never content simply to quote from the leaflets of animal rights groups, or other opponents of the institution or corporation that he was targeting. He always went to the source, preferably a publication of the target itself, or else a government document. That is why newspapers like the *New York Times* were prepared to run advertisements that make very specific allegations of wrong-doing against people like the chicken producer Frank Perdue. When Spira took the advertisement to the newspaper, every allegation had been carefully checked.

Once he had accurate information, Spira was careful not to go beyond it. Some organizations describing experiments, for example, will conveniently neglect to tell their readers that the animals were anesthetized at the time. But those who do this eventually lose credibility. Spira's credibility was extraordinarily high, both within the animal movement and with its opponents, because he regarded it as his most important asset. He never sacrificed it for a short-term gain, no matter how tempting that may have been at the time.

5. *Don't divide the world into saints and sinners. This can lead to time-wasting and unproductive speculation about adversaries' motives, when the real issue is moving forward.*

When Spira wanted to get someone – a scientist, a corporate executive, a legislator, or a government official – to do something differently, he would put himself in the position of that person:

> [The question to ask yourself is:] If I were that person, what would make me want to change my behavior? If you accuse them of being a bunch of sadistic bastards, these people are not going to figure: "Hey, what is it I could do that's going to be different and make those people happy?" That's not the way the real world works.

Being personally hostile to an opponent may be a good way of letting off steam, but it doesn't win people over. When Spira wanted to persuade scientists working for corporations like Procter & Gamble to develop non-animal alternatives, he saw their situation as similar to that of people who eat animals:

> How do you change these people's behavior best? By saying you've never made a conscious decision to harm those animals. Basically you've been pro-grammed from being a kid: "Be nice to cat and doggy, and eat meat." And I think some of these researchers, that's how they were taught, that's how they were programmed. And you want to reprogram them, and you're not going to reprogram them by saying we're saints and you're sinners and we're going to clobber you with a two-by-four in order to educate you.

In the words of Susan Fowler, editor of the trade magazine *Lab Animal* at the time of the Revlon campaign:

> There is no sense in Spira's campaign of: "Well, this is Revlon, and no one in Revlon is going to be interested in what we are doing, they're all the enemy." Rather . . . he looks for – and kind of waits for, I think – someone to step out of the group and say: "Well, I understand what you're saying."

Although it took a *New York Times* advertisement to persuade people at Revlon that it was worth talking seriously to Spira at all, if his attitude had been more hostile, the opportunity to change the company's approach to the use of animals could easily have been missed.

Not dividing the world into saints and sinners isn't just sound tactics; it was also the way Spira himself thought. "People can change," he would say. "I used to eat animals and I never considered myself a cannibal."

6. *Seek dialogue and attempt to work together to solve problems. Position issues as problems with solutions. This is best done by presenting realistic alternatives.*

Because he didn't think of his opponents as evil, Spira had no preconceptions about whether they would or would not work with him to reduce animal suffering. So he opened every campaign with a polite letter to the target organization – the American Museum of Natural History, Revlon, Frank Perdue, or whoever the target was – inviting them to discuss the concerns he had with something they were doing. Sometimes Spira's invitations were ignored, sometimes they received an equally polite response from a person skilled in public relations who had no intention of doing anything, and once or twice they led directly to productive dialogue that brought results without any public campaigning at all. But the fact that he sought dialogue showed that he wasn't just stirring up trouble for the fun of it. He would always try to go as far as he could within the system.

Spira put considerable thought into how the people or organizations he was approaching could achieve their goals while eliminating or substantially reducing the suffering now being caused. The classic example of an imaginative solution was Spira's proposal to Revlon and other cosmetics manufacturers that they should fund research into alternatives to the Draize eye test. For more than a year before his campaign went public, Spira had been seeking a collaborative rather than confrontational approach with Revlon. In the end, after the campaign finally did go public, Revlon accepted his proposal and, together with other companies, found that for a very small expenditure, relative to their income, they could develop an alternative that enabled them to have a more precise, cheaper form of product safety testing that did not involve animals at all.

Having a realistic solution to offer means that it is possible to accentuate the positive, instead of running a purely negative campaign. In interviews and leaflets about the Draize test, for example, Spira always emphasized that *in vitro* testing methods offered the prospect of quicker, cheaper, more reliable, and more elegant ways of testing the safety of new products.

It is always possible to find a positive aspect if you look hard enough, though not one that will appeal to everyone involved on the other side.

There was nothing Spira could propose that would appeal to Lester Aronson, the cat researcher at the American Museum of Natural History, who had spent decades mutilating animals and was too near the end of his career to try something different. But Aronson could not continue to experiment without the support of the American Museum of Natural History, and the National Institutes of Health. The interests of the museum and of NIH were not the same as Aronson's. Spira sought to split his adversaries by arguing that the pointless cruelty of the cat research was actually turning sensitive young people away from the life sciences. Closing Aronson's lab would be an opportunity to put the museum's research funds into something creative and respectful of life that would inspire people to choose a career in biology.

The problem was to convince the museum and the National Institutes of Health that this really was a better outcome. To do so, Spira had to generate problems for them. For the museum, that turned out to be the prospect of continuing bad publicity, and threats to its public funding. For the NIH, it was pressure from Congress that could have had an impact on its overall budget. With such negatives in the offing, the previously spurned positive solution of closing the lab and funding different kinds of research started to look more attractive.

In terms of offering a positive outcome, the difference between the campaigns against the cat experiments and against the Draize test was one of degree, not of kind. Whether the toothpaste is going to come out of a blocked tube will depend on how badly blocked the tube is, and how much pressure is exerted on it. So too, whether an institution or corporation will adopt an alternative will depend on how negatively it views the alternative and how much pressure it is under. Even Revlon needed to be convinced that it had a serious public relations problem before it could be induced to grasp the alternative that Spira held out to it. But in general, the more realistic the alternative is, the less pressure will be needed to see it adopted.

7. *Be ready for confrontation if your target remains unresponsive.*
   If accepted channels don't work, prepare an escalating public
   awareness campaign to place your adversary on the defensive.

If point 6 is about making it easy for the toothpaste to come out of the tube, point 7 is about increasing the pressure if it still won't come. The public awareness campaign may take various forms. At the American Museum of Natural History, it started with an article in a local newspaper, then it was kept up by pickets and demonstrations every weekend, and finally it spread through the national media and specialist journals like *Science*. The Revlon campaign went public with a dramatic full-page advertisement in the *New York Times*, which itself generated more publicity, and was continued with demonstrations outside Revlon's offices. Other campaigns relied much more heavily on advertising and the use of the media. Unfortunately, advertising takes money (on which, see below).

8. *Avoid bureaucracy.*

Anyone who has been frustrated by lengthy committee meetings absorbing time and energy will share Spira's desire to get things done rather than spend time on organizational tangles. Worse still, bureaucratic structures all too often divert energy into making the organization grow, rather than getting results for the cause. Then when the organization grows, it needs staff and an office. So you get a situation in which people who want to make a difference for animals (or for street kids, or to save the forests, or whatever the cause may be) end up spending 80 percent of their time raising money just to keep the organization going. More time usually has to be spent in ensuring that everyone in the organization gets along with each other, feels appreciated, and is not upset because he or she expected to be promoted to a more responsible position, or given an office with more windows.

Spira was able to avoid these hassles by working, essentially, on his own. He started working for animals without any organization at all, just meeting with some people in his apartment, and it was only after his success at the American Museum of Natural History that he founded Animal Rights International, basically to give himself a more impressive letterhead. ARI had – and still has – no members. Instead of impressing people with claims of a large membership, ARI had a long list of advisors, including many well-known names and others with impressive credentials. The board consisted of trusted close friends on whom Spira could rely for support without hassles.

To make this work, of course, Spira had to be able to raise some money when he needed it. He didn't need a lot. He took $15,000 a year to live on, and $5,000 a year for expenses. For example, in a year in the mid-1990s, the total income of Animal Rights International might have been $140,000, and of this by far the largest proportion, perhaps as much as $100,000, would have gone on advertising, information services, and education. At first, when Spira wanted to place an advertisement, he sketched out a mock-up and then looked for someone to put their name on it and pay for it. Through her organization, the Millennium Guild, Pegeen Fitzgerald paid for the first full-page *New York Times* advertisement Spira placed, on the cat sex experiments. Fitzgerald also paid for the two full-page *New York Times* advertisements that were crucial to the success of the Revlon campaign. Subsequently, Spira found other donors – people who wanted to see their money making a difference, and not just be used to pay for more direct mail fundraising. Spira's track record ensured that these donors continued to give enough to meet the needs of his campaigns.

You don't have to be big to make a difference. A small group, in touch with a larger public concern, can find openings in the structure of the largest and most powerful corporations or government institutions. But when Spira needed more clout, he would put a coalition together – as he did when fighting against the Draize and LD50 tests. Since his early success at the American Museum of Natural History, other organizations became eager to join his coalitions and share in his success. At their height, these coalitions included hundreds of organizations, with memberships in the millions. Here too, though, Spira kept hassles to a minimum. Organizations were welcome to participate at whatever level they wished. Some got their supporters out to demonstrate or march, while others didn't. Some paid for full-page advertisements, and others asked their supporters to write letters to newspapers, where they were able to reach millions without spending a cent. What no organization could do is dictate policy to Spira. He consulted widely, but in the end made his own decisions, thus avoiding the time-consuming and sometimes divisive process of elections and committee meetings. Clearly, in the case of major disagreements, organizations had the option of leaving, but Spira was unable to recall this ever happening.

9. *Don't rely on legislation or legal action to solve the problem.*

Spira occasionally used elected representatives in his campaigns to put pressure on government agencies and to gain publicity. But the only campaign in which he achieved his aim through legislation was the repeal of the New York State law allowing laboratories to take dogs and cats from shelters. Here, since bad legislation was the target of the campaign, he had no choice. Otherwise Spira stayed out of conventional political processes and kept away from the courts. "No congressional bill, no legal gimmickry, by itself, will save the animals," he said. He saw laws as basically maintaining the status quo. The danger of getting deeply involved in the political process is that it often deflects struggles into what Spira called "political gabbery" – a lot of talk with no result. Political lobbying or legal maneuvering can become a substitute for action. (Spira was, of course, thinking of the U.S.; he would not have wished to discourage campaigns seeking to change legislation in other countries where it may be easier to make a change by this method. See, for an example, Martin Balluch's essay in this volume on the Austrian campaign against the battery cage.)

10.   Ask yourself: *"Will it work?"*

For Spira, all of the preceding points were directed towards this last one. Before you launch a campaign, or continue with a campaign already begun, ask yourself if it will work. If you can't give a realistic account of how what you plan to do will achieve your objectives, you need to change your plans. Keeping in touch with what the public is thinking, selecting a target, setting an achievable goal, getting accurate information, maintaining credibility, suggesting alternative solutions, being ready to talk to adversaries, or to confront them if they will not talk – all of these are directed towards creating a campaign that is a practical means of making a difference. The overriding question is always: *"Will it work?"*

A Final Word

Peter Singer

In the Introduction I mentioned the review essay of *Animals, Men and Morals*, edited by Stanley and Roslind Godlovitch and John Harris, that I wrote for the *New York Review of Books* in 1973. I entitled the essay "Animal Liberation," and it was my first publication on that topic. It ended with a paragraph that saw the challenge of the animal movement as a test of human nature:

> Can a purely moral demand of this kind succeed? The odds are certainly against it. The book holds out no inducements. It does not tell us that we will become healthier, or enjoy life more, if we cease exploiting animals. Animal Liberation will require greater altruism on the part of mankind than any other liberation movement, since animals are incapable of demanding it for themselves, or of protesting against their exploitation by votes, demonstrations, or bombs. Is man capable of such genuine altruism? Who knows? If this book does have a significant effect, however, it will be a vindication of all those who have believed that man has within himself the potential for more than cruelty and selfishness.

So how have we done? Both the optimists and the cynics about human nature could see the results as confirming their views. Significant changes have occurred, in animal testing and other areas of animal abuse. In Europe, whole industries are being transformed because of the concern of the public for the welfare of farm animals. Perhaps most encouraging for the optimists is the fact that millions of activists have freely given up their time and money to support the animal movement, many of them changing their diet and lifestyle to avoid supporting the abuse of animals. Vegetarianism and even veganism are far more widespread in North America and Europe than they were thirty years ago. It is difficult to know how much of this relates to concern for animals, but undoubtedly some of it does.

On the other hand, although many philosophers have come to favor the view that speciesism is indefensible, popular views on that topic are still very far from the basic idea of equal consideration for the interests of beings irrespective of their species. Most people still eat meat, and buy what is cheapest, oblivious to the suffering of the animal from which the meat comes. The number of animals being consumed is much greater today than it was thirty years ago, and increasing prosperity in East Asia is creating a demand for meat that threatens to boost that number far higher still. Meanwhile the rules of the World Trade Organization threaten advances in animal welfare by making it doubtful if Europe will be able to keep out imports from countries with lower standards. In short, the outcome so far indicates that as a species we are capable of altruistic concern for other beings; but imperfect information, powerful interests, and a desire not to know disturbing facts have limited the gains made by the animal movement.

W. E. H. Lecky, an immensely learned scholar and the author of a fascinating nineteenth-century multi-volume *History of European Morals*, wrote: "At one time the benevolent affections embrace merely the family, soon the circle expanding includes first a class, then a nation, then a coalition of nations, then all humanity, and finally, its influence is felt in the dealings of man with the animal world" (1955 [1869]: 100–1). Some may think that this is too optimistic a view of history. It is true that we still have a long way to go in expanding the circle of moral concern even to human beings of different cultural and ethnic groups, especially when they live far from us. But bad as our attitudes may be, they have progressed a long way from the days when Africans could be captured, shipped to America and sold, much as nonhuman animals can be today. Just as we have progressed beyond the blatantly racist ethic of the era of slavery, so we are now starting to move beyond the even more firmly entrenched speciesist ethic of our own era. Moral revolutions of this scope do not happen quickly. We should not ask "When will we get there?" because, without the ability to see into the future, we cannot tell. We should instead ask the more modest question: "Are we moving in the right direction?" The essays in this book strongly suggest that we are.

References

Lecky, W. E. H. (1955 [1869]) *The History of European Morals from Augustus to Charlemagne*, Vol. 1, New York: George Braziller.

Singer, Peter (1973) "Animal Liberation," *The New York Review of Books*, April 5. Available at: *www.nybooks.com/articles/article-preview?article_id=9900.*

Further Reading: Books and Organization Websites

Books

General

Armstrong, Susan J., and Botzler, Richard G. (eds), *The Animal Rights Reader*, London: Routledge, 2003. A collection of articles and extracts on various topics.

Bekoff, Marc, and Meaney, Carron A. (eds), *Encyclopedia of Animal Rights and Animal Welfare*, Westport, CT: Greenwood, 1998. A valuable one-volume work of reference.

Braun, Nathan, and Kaufman, Steve, *Good News for All Creation*, New York: Lantern Books, 2004. Addresses the health, environmental, and animal welfare reasons for vegetarianism, from a Christian perspective.

Cavalieri, Paola, *The Animal Question: Why Nonhuman Animals Deserve Human Rights*, New York: Oxford University Press, 2001. A concise but very tightly argued statement of the case of attributing basic rights to animals.

Cavalieri, Paola, and Singer, Peter (eds), *The Great Ape Project: Equality Beyond Humanity*, New York, St Martin's Press, 1994. A manifesto for rights for great apes.

Cohen, Carl, and Regan, Tom, *The Animal Rights Debate*, Lanham, MD: Rowman & Littlefield, 2001. For and against animal rights.

Davis, Karen, *Prisoned Chickens, Poisoned Eggs: An Inside Look at the Modern Poultry Industry*, Summertown, TN: The Book Publishing Company, 1996. The American poultry industry is closely examined in this book, and it is not a pretty picture.

Dawkins, Marian Stamp, *Animal Suffering: The Science of Animal Welfare*, London: Chapman & Hall. How animal welfare can be scientifically assessed.

DeGrazia, David, *Taking Animals Seriously: Mental Life and Moral Status*, Cambridge: Cambridge University Press, 1996. One of the most thorough and careful studies of the ethics of how we should treat animals.

——, *Animal Rights: A Very Short Introduction*, Oxford: Oxford University Press, 2002. Exactly what the title says, clear, well argued, and very short.

Godlovitch, Stanley, Godlovitch, Roslind, and Harris, John (eds), *Animals, Men and Morals*, London: Gollancz, 1972. When this volume appeared, it broke new ground in taking the treatment of animals as a serious moral issue.

Linzey, Andrew, *Animal Theology*, Urbana and Chicago: University of Illinois Press, 1995. A radical Christian view of how we should treat animals.

Mason, Jim, *An Unnatural Order: How We Broke Our Primal Bonds with Animals and Nature*, New York: Lantern Books, 2004. An exploration of the roots of our domination of nature and of animals.

Peterson, Dale, *Eating Apes*, Berkeley: University of California Press, 2003. A gripping account of the threat to great apes caused by the demand for their flesh.

Regan, Tom, *The Case for Animal Rights*, Berkeley: University of California Press, 1984. A detailed philosophical argument for animal rights.

——, *Empty Cages: Facing the Challenge of Animal Rights*, Lanham, MD: Rowman & Littlefield, 2004. A more accessible introduction to the topic than *The Case for Animal Rights*.

Regan, Tom, and Singer, Peter (eds), *Animal Rights and Human Obligations*, 2nd edn, Englewood Cliffs, N.J.: Prentice Hall, 1989. An anthology of both old and recent writings on the ethics of our treatment of animals.

Rowlands, Mark, *Animals Like Us*, London: Verso, 2002. An argument based on justice and a reworking of the social contract tradition in ethics.

Ryder, Richard, *Animal Revolution: Changing Attitudes Towards Speciesism*, Oxford: Blackwell, 1989; 2nd edn, Oxford: Berg, 2000. A historical account of our attitudes to animals.

Salt, Henry, *Animals' Rights*, Fontwell, Sussex: Centaur Press, 1980 (first published 1892). An early classic.

Scully, Matt, *Dominion: The Power of Man, The Suffering of Animals, and the Call to Mercy*, New York: St Martin's Press, 2003. Strong arguments against animal abuse written from a conservative Christian perspective.

Singer, Peter, *Animal Liberation*, New York: HarperCollins, 2001. First published in 1975, this book argues an ethical case against our treatment of animals.

Sunstein, Cass, and Nussbaum, Martha (eds), *Animal Rights: Current Debates and New Directions*, New York: Oxford University Press, 2004. A collection of recent articles, blending philosophical and legal issues.

Waldau, Paul, *The Specter of Speciesism: Buddhist and Christian Views of Animals*, New York: Oxford University Press, 2002. A scholarly investigation of how two major religions view animals.

Wise, Stephen, *Rattling the Cage: Toward Legal Rights for Animals*, Cambridge, MA: Perseus, 2001.

——, *Drawing the Line: Science and the Case for Animal Rights*, Cambridge, MA: Perseus, 2003.

Animals in Research

Baird, Robert, and Rosenbaum, Stuart (eds), *Animal Experimentation: The Moral Issues*, Buffalo, N.Y.: Prometheus, 1991. This collection offers a variety of perspectives for and against the use of animals in research.

Blum, Deborah, *The Monkey Wars*, New York: Oxford University Press, 1994. A distinguished science journalist takes a look at the debate about the use of animals in laboratories.

Rudacille, Deborah, *The Scalpel and the Butterfly: The Conflict between Animal Research and Animal Protection*, Berkeley: University of California Press, 2001. An account of the conflict by an author who is not committed to either side.

Ryder, Richard, *Victims of Science: The Use of Animals in Research*, 2nd edn, Fontwell, Sussex: Centaur Press, 1980. First published in 1975, this is still a valuable account of the use of animals in research.

Farmed Animals and the Meat Industry

Eisnitz, Gail, *Slaughterhouse: The Shocking Story of Greed, Neglect, and Inhumane Treatment Inside the U.S. Meat Industry*, Amherst, N.Y.: Prometheus, 1997. If every American would read this book, it is hard to imagine that many of them would continue to eat meat.

Harrison, Ruth, *Animal Machines*, London: Vincent Stuart, 1964. The book that started the campaign against factory farming.

Marcus, Erik, *Meat Market: Animals, Ethics, and Money*, Boston: Brio Press, 2005. A succinct recent critique of factory farming coupled with a thoughtful discussion of effective activism.

Mason, Jim, and Singer, Peter, *Animal Factories*, New York: Crown, 1980. The health, ecological, and animal welfare implications of factory farming, with many photographs.

Schlosser, Eric, *Fast Food Nation*, New York: HarperCollins, 2002. Not specifically about animals, but a stunning exposé of the fast-food industry and the food it sells.

Veganism and Vegetarianism

Marcus, Erik, *Vegan: The New Ethics of Eating*, revised edn, Ithaca, N.Y.: McBooks, 2001. Offers a wide range of arguments for a vegan lifestyle.

Melina, Vesanto, and Davis, Brenda, *Becoming Vegetarian: The Complete Guide to Adopting a Healthy Vegetarian Diet*, revised edn, New York: Wiley, 2003. This book tells you all you need to know about being a vegetarian.

——, *Becoming Vegan: The Complete Guide to Adopting a Healthy Plant-Based Diet*, Summertown, TN: The Book Publishing Company, 2000. Similar to the previous book listed, but focused on being vegan.

Robbins, John, *The Food Revolution*, Berkeley: Conari Press, 2001. Written by the heir to the Baskin Robbins fortune, who renounced his fortune and became a vegan advocate, this book is a favorite of many American vegetarians.

Sapontzis, Steve (ed.), *Food For Thought: The Debate over Eating Meat*, Amherst, N.Y.: Prometheus, 2004. A collection of essays on the philosophical, nutritional, environmental, and cultural aspects of eating meat.

Stepaniak, Joan, *Being Vegan*, New York: McGraw-Hill, 2000. Another guide to being a vegan.

Organization Websites

www.AnimalConcerns.org. An information clearinghouse on animal rights and animal welfare.

www.animalaid.org.uk. Animal Aid is the largest animal rights organization in the UK. It campaigns against all forms of animal abuse.

www.ari-online.org. Animal Rights International was founded by Henry Spira. Peter Singer is now its president.

www.cahiers-antispecistes.org. For information about, and articles from, the French journal *Les Cahiers antispéciste*, which discusses animals and ethics.

www.christianveg.com. The Christian Vegetarian Association was founded to challenge Christians to treat animals better.

www.ciwf.org.uk. Compassion in World Farming, based in Britain, is a leading campaigner against factory farming. The website includes links to CIWF's affiliates in Ireland, France, and the Netherlands.

www.cok.net. Compassion Over Killing, the organization described in Miyun Park's essay, opposes cruelty to animals in agriculture and carries out open rescues of farm animals.

www.dawnwatch.com. Karen Dawn operates this site to keep watch on news stories about animal issues.

www.farmedanimal.net. The website of "Farmed Animal Watch" (a free electronic digest of critical news and research for people interested in the treatment of animals raised for food).

www.farmsanctuary.org. Farm Sanctuary, an organization focusing on improving the situation of farm animals.

www.FishingHurts.com. Information on fish, their capacity to suffer, and what happens to them.

www.GoVeg.com. Advocacy and everything you need to know about being a vegetarian.

www.greatapeproject.org. Originally founded by Paola Cavalieri and Peter Singer, the Great Ape Project seeks basic rights for our closest relatives: chimpanzees, bonobos, gorillas, and orangutans.

www.happycow.net and *www.vegdining.com*. Both these websites provide information on vegetarian restaurants around the world.

www.hsus.org. The Humane Society of the United States operates an informative website on a variety of animal issues.

www.islamicconcern.com. A website about concern for animals and vegetarianism in Islam.

www.jewishveg.com. Information about Judaism and vegetarianism.

www.oltrelaspecie.org. An Italian-language website that covers issues about animal rights, and the use of animals in agriculture, research, zoos, etc. Links to many other Italian websites can be found here too.

online.sfsu.edu/~rone/Religion/religionanimals.html. Resources about animals for Buddhists, Hindus, Jews, Christians, and Muslims.

www.openrescue.org. This website provides information on open rescues of animals.

www.peta.org. People for the Ethical Treatment of Animals, America's largest radical pro-animal organization.

www.raddningstjansten.org. The Swedish organization with which Pelle Strindlund is associated. (Currently Swedish only.)

www.rspca.org.uk. The Royal Society for the Prevention of Cruelty to Animals, founded in 1824, is the mother of all anti-cruelty organizations, and the most significant in Britain.

www.tufts.edu/vet/cfa. The Center for Animals and Public Policy at Tufts University, directed by Paul Waldau.

www.upc-online.org. The website of United Poultry Concerns, an advocate of chickens and turkeys, who are among the most abused of all animals.

www.vegan.com. A source of useful information on being vegan.

www.veganhealth.org. Covers all the health issues in being vegan.

www.veganoutreach.org. Matt Ball works for this organization, which provides literature and resources on being vegan, in several languages.

www.vegcooking.com. Recipes, vegan shopping guide, cookbook recommendations, and more.

www.vegsource.com. Vegetarian community on the Web – resources, experts, articles, discussion boards, and more.

www.vgt.at. The website of the organization with which Martin Balluch is associated, with links to many other European websites. (German only.)

www.viva.org.uk and *www.vivausa.org* are the British and U.S. websites of Viva!, an organization that campaigns against the use of animals for food, and for vegetarianism.

worldanimal.net. The world's largest network of animal protection societies, its world Animal Net Directory is a database with more than 15,000 listings and more than 8,000 links to websites.

Index

Index